Supply Chain Resilience, Sustainability, and Digital Innovation

Anupama Sethi
Monash University, Australia

Sivakumar V.
https://orcid.org/0000-0002-0139-5249
Alagappa University, India

Iyappan A.
https://orcid.org/0000-0003-0789-4011
International Institute of Business Studies, India

IGI Global
Scientific Publishing
Publishing Tomorrow's Research Today

Vice President of Editorial	Melissa Wagner
Director of Acquisitions	Mikaela Felty
Director of Book Development	Jocelynn Hessler
Production Manager	Mike Brehm
Cover Design	Jose Rosado

Published in the United States of America by
IGI Global Scientific Publishing
701 East Chocolate Avenue
Hershey, PA, 17033, USA
Tel: 717-533-8845 | Fax: 717-533-7115
Website: https://www.igi-global.com E-mail: cust@igi-global.com

Library of Congress Cataloging-in-Publication Data

(CIP Data Pending)
ISBN13: 979-8-2600-1855-2
Isbn13Softcover: 979-8-2600-1856-9
EISBN13: 979-8-2600-1857-6
British Cataloguing in Publication Data
A Cataloguing in Publication record for this book is available from the British Library.

Table of Contents

Detailed Table of Contents

and smallholder farmers alike. The study emphasizes that adapting supply chain values to meet evolving consumer expectations is critical for achieving long-term nutritional and health sustainability.

It can be argued that the development in logistics services has developed into one of the most vital determinants of customer satisfaction while purchasing from online stores: it relates mainly to the development of e-commerce and changing trends of shopping. The present study intends to assess the attributes of importance affecting the satisfaction of online young e-commerce users while shopping online. Timely update of delivery information, delivery options, and the return policy made a significant contribution to building satisfaction among users, based on the analysis of the data. A correlational analysis showed that the ease of delivery was related positively and significantly to satisfaction, thus indicating that e-commerce platforms need to improve their logistics.

The study explores the potential of artificial intelligence and supply chain integration in optimizing aspects of Microinsurance, such as transparency, operational efficiency, and inclusivity. It uses Knowledge spill over theory, Network theory, and Resilience theory to address the impact of AI and supply chain integration in the sector. The research is based on 1240 research papers from 2014 to 2024, focusing on authorship networks, citation dynamics, keyword co-occurrences, and theme grouping. The study predicts an increase in interest in this area in the past decade, focusing on predictive analytics of AI and addressing practical issues like data privacy and regulatory implications. The study aims to address research gaps in practical applications and long-term socioeconomic effects of insurance, providing

Preface

INTRODUCTION

The modern global economy is deeply interwoven with supply chains that span continents, industries, and technologies. In recent years, these supply chains have faced unprecedented disruptions from pandemics and geopolitical tensions to climate change and rapid technological shifts. These challenges have underscored the urgent need for supply chains that are not only efficient, but also resilient, sustainable, and digitally empowered.

Supply Chain Resilience, Sustainability, and Digital Innovation brings together scholarly insights and practical perspectives to explore how organizations can navigate this evolving landscape. The volume highlights the convergence of sustainability imperatives with digital transformation, emphasizing that resilience is no longer optional but a strategic necessity.

A key theme throughout this book is the role of emerging technologies such as artificial intelligence, blockchain, the Internet of Things, and big data analytics in reshaping supply chain operations. Equally important is the integration of environmental and social considerations, ensuring that economic growth aligns with responsible and ethical practices.

The contributors examine diverse contexts, with a particular emphasis on emerging economies, where resource constraints coexist with immense opportunities for innovation. Through empirical studies, theoretical frameworks, and policy analyses, the chapters collectively provide a roadmap for academics, practitioners, and policymakers seeking to build adaptive and future-ready supply chains.

This book ultimately aims to inspire a shift from reactive supply chain management toward proactive, intelligent, and sustainable systems that can withstand uncertainty while creating long-term value. Below is a chapter by chapter summary of the book to supplement the reading.

CHAPTER OVERVIEWS

Chapter 1: Advancing Sustainable Supply Chain Practices in Emerging Economies

This chapter explores how sustainable supply chain management (SSCM) can drive economic and environmental progress in emerging markets. It highlights key challenges such as limited resources and socio-economic disparities, while emphasizing opportunities arising from green technologies and increased consumer awareness. The chapter underscores the importance of digitalization, circular economy practices, and social responsibility. It also stresses leadership, collaboration, and government support as critical enablers of sustainable transformation.

Chapter 2: Crisis Preparation Strategies and Developing Resilient Supply Chains

Focusing on global disruptions, this chapter examines how supply chains are adapting to climate change, political instability, and evolving consumer demands. It identifies predictive analytics, artificial intelligence, and machine learning as essential tools for anticipating risks. The chapter also discusses regulatory pressures and sustainability initiatives, highlighting the role of governments and international organizations in shaping resilient and eco-friendly supply chains.

Chapter 3: The Role of Artificial Intelligence in Transforming Global Supply Chains

This chapter provides a comprehensive overview of how artificial intelligence is revolutionizing supply chain management. It explains applications such as demand forecasting, inventory optimization, and predictive maintenance. By integrating AI with big data and IoT, organizations can achieve real-time visibility and improved decision-making. The chapter also discusses challenges, including data privacy and implementation costs, and offers strategic recommendations for adoption.

Chapter 4: Revolutionizing Supply Chains in Indian Industries with Emerging Technologies

This chapter examines the combined impact of AI, IoT, blockchain, and big data on supply chains in India. It highlights how these technologies enhance transparency, agility, and efficiency. While the potential benefits are significant, the chapter also addresses barriers such as high costs, skill shortages, and data security concerns. It emphasizes the need for technological integration to remain competitive in a globalized economy.

Chapter 5: Harnessing Emerging Technologies for Enhancing Supply Chain Resilience

This chapter introduces a new perspective on resilience by focusing on proactive and technology-driven strategies. It discusses advanced tools like AI and Bayesian networks for risk management. The chapter highlights the shift from lean to "just-in-case" supply chain models to recent global crises. Despite the promise of digital tools, challenges such as cybersecurity and limited digital maturity remain key constraints.

Chapter 6: Sustainable Supply Chain Practices in Emerging Agricultural Entrepreneurship

This chapter investigates sustainability in agricultural supply chains, with a focus on Tamil Nadu. It identifies key drivers such as resource efficiency and green logistics, along with barriers like financial limitations and infrastructure gaps. The study demonstrates how digital solutions and fintech can enhance sustainability, while policy support and capacity-building are essential for long-term development and food security.

Chapter 7: Revamping Nutri-Cereal Supply Chains for Digital Natives

This chapter explores how digital technologies can transform nutri-cereal supply chains to meet the expectations of modern consumers. It emphasizes traceability, transparency, and personalized nutrition through blockchain, IoT, and AI. The chapter highlights the importance of ethical sourcing and regenerative agriculture, showing how digital engagement can build trust and promote healthier consumption patterns.

Chapter 8: The Essential Role of Logistics in Driving Customer Satisfaction in E-Commerce

This chapter focuses on logistics as a critical determinant of customer satisfaction in e-commerce. It identifies factors such as delivery speed, tracking transparency, and return policies as key drivers. The findings reveal a strong positive relationship between efficient logistics and customer satisfaction, suggesting that e-commerce platforms must continuously improve their delivery systems.

Chapter 9: Mapping the Convergence of AI and Supply Chain Optimization in Microinsurance

This chapter presents a bibliometric analysis of research on AI and supply chain integration in microinsurance. It explores how these technologies improve transparency, efficiency, and inclusivity. The study identifies growing research interest and highlights challenges such as data privacy and regulatory issues. It also provides recommendations for advancing innovation and addressing socioeconomic impacts.

Chapter 1
Advancing Sustainable Supply Chain Practices in Emerging Economies

Seema Vinod
http://orcid.org/0009-0003-4558-7757
Gandhigram Rural Institute, India

B. Pathinettampadiyan
http://orcid.org/0009-0007-1753-0373
Gandhigram Rural Institute, India

H. Samuel Thavaraj
http://orcid.org/0009-0005-7541-4608
Gandhigram Rural Institute, India

Rincy James
http://orcid.org/0009-0006-4047-9468
Mother Theresa Women University, India

T. Mary Josephine Isabella
Sakthi College of Arts and Science for Women, India

ABSTRACT

The study observes the critical part of sustainable supply chain management in developing financial prudence, highlighting the unique challenges and opportunities in adopting eco-friendly and socially responsible practices. While rapid sector, resource constraints, and socio-economic disparities pose significant barriers, emerging economies are increasingly leveraging rising consumer awareness and green technologies to advance sustainability. The study explores how digitalization

DOI: 10.4018/979-8-2600-1855-2.ch001

and circular economy principles are transforming supply chain practices, improving efficiency, and minimizing waste. It also underscores the importance of addressing social dimensions, including employee rights, workplace safety, and diversity, to foster a comprehensive approach to sustainability. Strategies such as dynamic capabilities and horizontal collaboration are particularly valuable for micro and medium enterprises determined to develop resilience and sustainability. This research highlights the necessity of leadership, teamwork, and supportive government policies in driving SSCM.

1 INTRODUCTION

1.1 Sustainable Management Practices

Sustainability is a global priority, influencing entire supply chains. It extends beyond individual organizations, integrating eco-friendly, social, and economic factors. They move to improve the integrated organic of production, distribution, and consumption. Businesses now adopt sustainable practices to decrease environmental problems. the public benefit from responsible resource management and ethical sourcing. A holistic approach ensures long-term growth while preserving the planet. (Seuring & Müller, 2008; Zhu et al., 2018). Sustainable Supply Chain Management integrates eco-friendly practices, ethical labour standards, and efficient resource utilization. It promotes economic growth while ensuring social equity and environmental responsibility. By reducing waste and enhancing efficiency, SSCM supports long-term sustainability. This approach benefits businesses, communities, and the planet alike (Carter & Rogers, 2008; Sarkis et al., 2011). Developed economies have large driven sustainability efforts, setting global standards. However, emerging economies are now key players in this transition. Their growing commitment to eco-friendly policies strengthens global sustainability. Collaborative efforts ensure a more balanced and inclusive green future (Dubey et al., 2017; Sarkis et al., 2011).

1.2 Global Perspective

Sustainability has become a global priority, influencing entire supply chains and extending beyond individual organizations to integrate eco-friendly, social, and economic factors. This shift highlights the interconnected nature of production, distribution, and consumption, emphasizing the need for businesses to adopt sustainable practices that reduce environmental impact while ensuring economic growth and social responsibility. Communities benefit from responsible resource management and ethical sourcing, ensuring that sustainability efforts extend beyond corporations to impact society at large. A holistic approach to sustainable supply chain management ensures long-term growth while preserving the planet, as emphasized by (Seuring & Müller, 2008; Zhu et al., 2018)

Sustainable Supply Chain Management integrates eco-friendly practices, ethical labor standards, and efficient resource usage to promote economic growth while ensuring social equality and environmental sustainability. By decreasing waste, improve efficiency, and implementing responsible sourcing strategies, SSCM supports long-term sustainability, benefiting businesses, communities, and the planet alike (Carter & Rogers, 2008; Sarkis et al., 2011). Developed economies have long driven sustainability efforts, setting global standards for responsible business practices. However, emerging economies are now key players in this transition, with their growing commitment to eco-friendly policies strengthening global sustainability. Collaborative efforts between governments, industries, and consumers ensure a more balanced and inclusive green future, reinforcing the importance of collective action in addressing sustainability challenges (Dubey et al., 2017; Sarkis et al., 2011).

Developing economies meeting distinct challenges in implementing Sustainable Supply Chain Management, as rapid industrialization often leads to environmental strain and resource depletion. Limited infrastructure restricts efficient logistics and the adoption of sustainable practices, while socio-economic disparities further complicate ethical labor standards and fair trade. Overcoming these barriers requires strategic policies, investment, and global collaboration, underscoring the necessity of systemic reform and regulatory support (Geng et al., 2017; Govindan et al., 2015)Despite these challenges, emerging economies hold immense potential for sustainable growth, as rising consumer awareness drives demand for ethical and eco-friendly products. Global markets increasingly favor sustainable exports, creating new economic opportunities for businesses that prioritize sustainability. Additionally, advancements in green technologies enable these economies to adopt innovative solutions, helping them transition toward sustainable business models and environmental responsibility (Diabat et al., 2012; Thomas et al., 2019).

Emerging economies can leverage digitalization to improve supply chain improvement and enhance resource management. Modern technologies such as blockchain, and the Internet of Things, artificial intelligence, enable real-time monitoring, decrease waste and increase logistics. Digital transformation helps streamline supply chain operations, increase transparency, and mitigate inefficiencies that often hinder sustainability efforts. The integration of circular economy principles further supports this transition by promoting recycling, reuse, and sustainable production, ensuring that businesses minimize their environmental footprint while maintaining profitability. These strategies help mitigate resource constraints while minimizing environmental impact, positioning emerging economies for long-term sustainability and global competitiveness (Agyabeng-Mensah et al., 2023; Rajeev et al., 2017).

By embracing digital transformation and adopting circular economy practices, businesses can reduce reliance on finite resources and enhance supply chain resilience, strengthening their sustainability performance while meeting regulatory requirements and consumer expectations.

1.3 Role of Sustainable Supply Chain Management

The chapter examines the crucial role of Sustainable Supply Chain Management in emerging economies, especially the balance between economic growth, environmental conditions, and social responsibility. Key challenges, including infrastructure limitations and regulatory constraints, are explored in detail, emphasizing the need for targeted interventions to support sustainable business practices. Additionally, this research identifies significant opportunities, such as the adoption of green technologies and increasing market demand for sustainable products. Analyzing strategies like collaborative innovation and dynamic capabilities it provides a comprehensive framework for the effective implementation of SSCM in developing markets. The role of supportive policy frameworks is also discussed, as regulatory measures play a critical role in ensuring that businesses comply with sustainability standards and prioritize environmental responsibility. Leadership plays a fundamental thing is driving to sustainable supply chain practices, as strong authority structures and corporate responsibility initiatives facilitate the adoption of ethical business models. Cross-sector partnerships are crucial for fostering innovation and shared responsibility, as collaboration between government and non-government sectors strengthens the effectiveness of sustainability initiatives. Capacity-building initiatives further support the development of skills and infrastructure necessary for long-term sustainability, equipping businesses and supply chain partners with the knowledge and resources needed to navigate complex regulatory landscapes. By integrating leadership, cross-sector partnerships, and capacity-building efforts, emerging economies can accelerate the adoption of SSCM and strengthen their position in the global sustainability movement (Dubey et al., 2017; Mishra et al., 2018).

Emerging economies more potential to become global leaders in sustainability efforts, as their integration of economic, environmental, and social priorities strengthens sustainable development. By aligning business strategies with sustainability goals, companies can enhance their market competitiveness while contributing to global sustainability objectives. This study highlights the need for policies that neutralize economic improvement with ecological responses, low s coring the importance of rules interventions, sector large collaboration, and consumer involvement in driving sustainable supply chain practices. Addressing these factors enables emerging economies to shape a more inclusive and resilient future, ensuring that sustainability becomes a central tenet of global economic development.

Sustainability-driven business models require organizations to embed responsible sourcing, waste reduction, and energy efficiency at every stage of the chain. The shift improves a fundamental transformation in supply chain management, necessitating proactive engagement from public sector, private sector and customers.

1.4 Green Initiatives

Green procurement is one of the pillars of Supply chain, as it selecting suppliers on the environmental performance, commitment to sustainability. Businesses that adopt green procurement practices reduce their carbon footprint, promote ethical labor practices, and encourage responsible resource consumption. Companies that prioritize sustainability in procurement benefit from reduced regulatory risks, enhanced operational efficiency, and improved relationships with stakeholders. However, implementing green procurement strategies presents challenges, including supply chain complexities, cost considerations, and the absence of standardized sustainability criteria. Overcoming these barriers requires businesses to establish clear sustainability goals, engage with suppliers, and leverage technology to track and measure sustainability performance.

Energy-efficient production processes further contribute to SSCM by optimizing resource use and reducing greenhouse gas emissions. Corporate management, energy-control systems and production optimization techniques enhance their sustainability performance while improving their bottom line. However, transitioning to energy-efficient production requires significant capital investment, technological expertise, and policy incentives. Governments and industry stakeholders must collaborate to create supportive regulatory frameworks, provide financial incentives, and facilitate knowledge-sharing initiatives to accelerate the adoption of energy-efficient practices.

Closed-loop supply chains represent another critical aspect of SSCM, as they emphasize the design of products with end-of-life considerations, enabling recycling, remanufacturing, and reuse. Businesses that implement closed-loop supply chains benefit from reduced waste generation, lower dependence on virgin resources, and cost savings. However, establishing closed-loop systems requires robust infrastructure for material collection, processing, and reintegration into the supply chain. Overcoming these barriers necessitates investment in recycling technologies, collaboration with industry partners, and consumer awareness programs to promote responsible consumption and waste reduction.

Digital technologies have revolutionized SSCM by improving supply chain model, empowering data-driven strategy decision-making capability, and developing operational efficiency. Blockchain technology provides secure and immutable records of transactions, allowing companies to verify product authenticity, track sourcing practices, and ensure compliance with sustainability standards. Artificial intelligence and machine learning facilitate predictive analytics, demand prediction, and risk control for businesses to improve supply chain operations and mitigate disruptions. The Internet of Thoughts enables real-time monitoring of supply chain maintenance, enhancing efficiency and reducing waste. Despite these benefits, the widespread adoption of digital technologies in SSCM faces challenges such as high adoption costs, cybersecurity risks, and interoperability problems. Addressing these challenges requires strategic investments, regulatory frameworks, and cross-industry collaboration to develop scalable and secure digital solutions.

1.5 Future of Supply Chian Management

The future of SSCM lies in continuous innovation, collaboration, and a firm commitment to sustainability principles. As world challenges such as environment change, resource problem, and social inequalities continue, businesses must adopt forward-thinking strategies to enhance supply chain resilience and sustainability. Investing in research and development, embracing circular economy principles, and leveraging emerging technologies will drive the next phase of SSCM evolution. Collaboration among governments, industry leaders, academia, and non-governmental organizations is unique to address informative struggles and analysing a sustainable global supply chain ecosystem. By fostering cooperation, regulatory support, and technological innovation, SSCM can serve as a powerful tool for achieving long-term sustainability, resilience, and economic growth while driving positive environmental and social outcomes.

Emerging economies encounter distinct struggles in implementing Sustainable Supply Chain Management. High growth industrialization often leads to environmental strain and resource depletion. Limited infrastructure restricts efficient logistics and sustainable practices. Socio-economic disparities further complicate ethical labour standards and fair trade. Overcoming these barriers requires strategic policies, investment, and global collaboration (Geng et al., 2017; Govindan et al., 2015). Despite challenges, emerging economies hold immense potential for sustainable growth. Rising consumer awareness drives demand for ethical and eco-friendly products. Global markets increasingly favour sustainable exports, opening new economic opportunities. Advancements in green technologies enable these economies to adopt innovative solutions. By leveraging these factors, they can leapfrog traditional models toward sustainability (Diabat et al., 2012; Thomas et al., 2019). Emerging economies can utilize digitalization to enhance supply chain efficiency and resource management. Advanced technologies enable real-time monitoring, reducing waste and optimizing logistics. Embracing circular economy principles promotes recycling, reuse, and sustainable production. These strategies help mitigate resource constraints while minimizing environmental impact. By integrating innovation, economies can achieve both economic growth and ecological balance. Such efforts drive long-term sustainability and global competitiveness (Agyabeng-Mensah et al., 2023; Rajeev et al., 2017).

The paper shows the unique role of Sustainable Supply Chain Management in emerging economies. It focusses the balance between economic growth, environmental problem, and responsibility. The study explores key challenges, including infrastructure limitations and regulatory constraints. Additionally, it identifies opportunities such as green technologies and sustainable market demand. Strategies like collaborative innovation and dynamic capabilities are analysed for effective implementation. The role of supportive policy frameworks in driving sustainability is also discussed. By addressing these factors, emerging economies can transition toward more resilient and ethical supply chains. This research provides insights for policymakers, businesses, and stakeholders in fostering sustainable development (Chardine-Baumann & Botta-Genoulaz, 2014; Walker & Jones, 2012). The research the role of leadership in driving sustainable supply chain methods. Cross-sector partnerships are crucial for fostering innovation and shared responsibility. Capacity-building initiatives help develop skills and infrastructure for long-term economy. Emerging economies have the potential to become leaders in global sustainability efforts. Their integration of economic, environmental, and social priorities strengthens sustainable development. This research highlights the need for policies that balance growth with ecological responsibility. By addressing these factors, emerging economies can shape a more inclusive and resilient future. The study contributes to the discourse on aligning monetary progress with environmental and social imperatives (Dubey et al., 2017; Mishra et al., 2018).

Sustainable Supply Chain Management plays a crucial role in balancing ecological, fiscal, and social priorities, especially in emerging economies. These economies face distinct challenges, such as rapid industrialization, limited infrastructure, and socioeconomic disparities. However, they also present significant opportunities for sustainable growth through rising consumer awareness and technological advancements. These strategies promote resilience, inclusive development, and collaboration across industries. By adopting these approaches, emerging economies can enhance their competitiveness while supporting global sustainability goals. Ultimately, the study offers valuable insights into creating supply chains that align economic, environmental, and social imperatives for sustainable progress. Sustainable Supply Chain Management (SSCM) plays a crucial role in balancing ecological, fiscal, and social priorities, particularly in emerging economies where rapid industrialization and socio-economic disparities present both challenges and opportunities. These economies are undergoing transformative shifts, and the need for sustainability in supply chain operations has never been more pronounced. By integrating environmental considerations, ethical labor practices, and economic efficiency, SSCM helps organizations navigate complex global markets while ensuring long-term viability. The adoption of sustainable practices in supply chains is not merely a compliance requirement but a strategic necessity that contributes to resilience, innovation, and competitiveness. Emerging economies often struggle with limited infrastructure, regulatory inconsistencies, and financial constraints that hinder the implementation of sustainable supply chain practices.

However, these same economies possess immense potential for sustainable growth, driven by increasing consumer awareness, technological advancements, and governmental initiatives aimed at fostering sustainability. Businesses in these regions must adopt innovative strategies that optimize resource utilization, reduce waste, and enhance overall efficiency. One of the key drivers of SSCM is digitalization, which enables real-time monitoring, predictive analytics, and improved decision-making. Through artificial intelligence, blockchain, and the Internet of Things, supply chains can become more transparent, responsive, and accountable. These technologies help businesses track sustainability metrics, ensure compliance with environmental regulations, and mitigate risks associated with supply chain disruptions. Circular economy principles play a pivotal role in enhancing SSCM by promoting resource efficiency, waste reduction, and product lifecycle extension. Instead of the traditional linear model of production and consumption, circular supply chains focus on reusing, recycling, and remanufacturing materials to minimize environmental impact. This approach not only reduces dependency on finite resources but also generates economic benefits by creating new business opportunities and cost-saving mechanisms. Companies adopting circular economy principles gain a competitive edge by meeting the growing consumer demand for sustainable products while reducing operational costs associated with resource depletion and waste management. Leadership and cross-sector partnerships are essential for advancing SSCM initiatives.

Effective leadership fosters a culture of sustainability within organizations, ensuring that sustainability goals are embedded in corporate strategies. Leaders who prioritize sustainability encourage innovation, enhance stakeholder engagement, and drive organizational change. Cross-sector collaborations between businesses, governments, non-governmental organizations, and academia facilitate knowledge exchange, capacity-building initiatives, and the development of industry-wide sustainability standards. These partnerships play a crucial role in addressing systemic challenges, such as supply chain fragmentation, resource scarcity, and policy enforcement. Capacity-building initiatives enhance the ability of businesses and supply chain partners to adopt sustainable practices. Training programs, workshops, and skill development initiatives equip stakeholders with the knowledge and tools necessary to implement SSCM effectively. Education and awareness campaigns help suppliers, manufacturers, and consumers understand the benefits of sustainable supply chains and encourage proactive participation. Governments and industry associations must work together to create incentive structures that reward businesses for adopting sustainable practices, thereby fostering a business environment that prioritizes long-term sustainability over short-term gains. Resilience is a critical component of SSCM, especially in the face of economic uncertainties, climate change, and geopolitical tensions. Businesses that integrate sustainability into their supply chains build resilience by diversifying supplier networks, reducing dependency on volatile resources, and investing in adaptive technologies. Flexible supply chain models that incorporate digitalization, automation, and local sourcing enable organizations to respond effectively to disruptions while maintaining sustainability commitments. By fostering resilience, companies can navigate challenges more effectively and sustain growth even in dynamic market conditions. Inclusive development is another important aspect of SSCM, ensuring that supply chain benefits are equitably distributed across stakeholders, including small and medium enterprises (SMEs), workers, and local communities. Ethical sourcing, fair trade practices, and social responsibility initiatives contribute to social sustainability by improving labor conditions, promoting gender equality, and supporting economic empowerment. Businesses that prioritize inclusivity in their supply chains enhance their reputations, build stronger stakeholder relationships, and contribute to broader societal well-being. Collaboration across industries is essential for scaling SSCM initiatives and achieving collective sustainability goals.

1.6 Industrial Collaborations

Industry-wide collaborations foster innovation, enable resource-sharing, and drive the development of standardized sustainability metrics. Collaborative efforts between competitors, suppliers, and regulatory bodies create a unified approach to sustainability, ensuring that best practices are widely adopted and continuously improved. These collaborations facilitate the pooling of resources for large-scale sustainability projects, such as renewable energy adoption, sustainable packaging solutions, and carbon footprint reduction initiatives. By adopting a holistic approach to SSCM, emerging economies can enhance their competitiveness while contributing to global sustainability efforts. Sustainable supply chains create value not only for businesses but also for society and the environment. Companies that integrate sustainability into their supply chain strategies experience improved brand reputation, increased consumer trust, and enhanced investor confidence. Consumers are increasingly making purchasing decisions based on sustainability considerations, and businesses that fail to adapt risk losing market relevance. Government policies and regulations play a fundamental role in driving SSCM adoption. Regulatory frameworks that enforce environmental standards, promote corporate social responsibility, and incentivize sustainable practices encourage businesses to integrate sustainability into their supply chain operations. Governments must work collaboratively with industry stakeholders to develop policies that strike a balance between sustainability objectives and economic growth. Public-private partnerships can accelerate the implementation of sustainable supply chain initiatives by leveraging resources, expertise, and technology. The transition towards SSCM requires a paradigm shift in business operations, moving from short-term profit maximization to long-term value creation. Companies that embrace sustainability as a core business principle achieve operational efficiencies, reduce costs associated with environmental fines and resource wastage, and enhance innovation capabilities. Sustainable supply chains not only mitigate risks but also create opportunities for differentiation and market leadership. Investment in research and development (R&D) is crucial for advancing SSCM. Businesses that allocate resources to sustainability-focused R&D drive innovation in eco-friendly materials, energy-efficient technologies, and waste reduction solutions. Collaboration between academic institutions and industry players fosters knowledge-sharing and the development of cutting-edge sustainability solutions. Companies that invest in sustainability-oriented R&D position themselves as pioneers in their respective industries, gaining a competitive advantage in an increasingly sustainability-conscious market. Financial incentives and funding mechanisms are essential for supporting businesses in their sustainability transitions. Access to green financing, sustainability-linked loans, and impact investment opportunities enable businesses to implement SSCM initiatives without compromising financial stability.

Governments and financial institutions should collaborate to create funding programs that incentivize businesses to adopt sustainable practices while ensuring economic feasibility. Financial support mechanisms can accelerate the adoption of renewable energy, sustainable logistics, and carbon-neutral manufacturing processes. Stakeholder engagement is fundamental to the success of SSCM. Transparent communication with stakeholders, including investors, employees, consumers, and suppliers, builds trust and fosters accountability. Businesses that actively engage stakeholders in sustainability initiatives create a culture of shared responsibility and collective action. Sustainability reporting, third-party certifications, and corporate sustainability disclosures enhance transparency and demonstrate a company's commitment to sustainable practices. Consumer behavior plays a pivotal role in shaping the demand for sustainable products and services. Companies that educate consumers on the environmental and social impacts of their purchasing decisions contribute to a more sustainable marketplace. Marketing strategies that highlight sustainability attributes, eco-labeling, and green certifications influence consumer preferences and drive demand for responsibly sourced products. Businesses that align their supply chain strategies with consumer sustainability expectations gain a competitive edge and strengthen brand loyalty.

Global supply chains are interconnected, and sustainability challenges require collaborative solutions. International cooperation, knowledge-sharing platforms, and cross-border partnerships facilitate the exchange of best practices and the development of harmonized sustainability standards. Organizations such as the United Nations, World Trade Organization, and sustainability-focused industry consortia play a vital role in fostering global sustainability efforts. Businesses that actively participate in international sustainability initiatives contribute to a collective movement towards a more sustainable and equitable global economy. The future of SSCM lies in continuous innovation, commitment, and collective action. As environmental and social challenges intensify, businesses must proactively integrate sustainability into their supply chain operations. The adoption of emerging technologies, adherence to sustainability principles, and engagement in industry collaborations will drive the evolution of sustainable supply chains. Companies that prioritize SSCM will be better positioned to navigate regulatory changes, consumer expectations, and market dynamics. By embedding sustainability into supply chain strategies, businesses can create long-term value, enhance resilience, and contribute to global sustainability goals. The transformation towards sustainable supply chains requires a multi-stakeholder approach, involving governments, businesses, consumers, and civil society. As the global economy continues to evolve, SSCM will remain a fundamental driver of responsible business practices, economic stability, and environmental preservation. By embracing sustainable supply chain management, businesses can shape a future where economic growth and sustainability go hand in hand, fostering a more resilient and equitable world.

2 OBJECTIVES

1. This study identifies actionable strategies to address resource constraints, reduce waste, and enhance efficiency.
2. It explores the potential of digitalization and circular economy principles to drive innovation and foster long-term sustainability.
3. It emphasizes the importance of leadership, cross-sector partnerships, and capacity-building initiatives.

3 REVIEW OF LITERATURE

Sustainable Supply Chain Management (SSCM) has emerged as a key element in global efforts to tackle urgent ecological, social, and economic issues. As industries face increasing pressure to balance profitability with sustainability, SSCM offers a holistic framework. It integrates eco-friendly practices, ethical labour standards, and efficient resource utilization into supply chain processes. By prioritizing sustainability, SSCM promotes responsible sourcing, reduces environmental impact, and fosters fair working conditions. This approach not only enhances operational efficiency but also strengthens corporate social responsibility. Furthermore, SSCM supports long-term profitability by aligning business strategies with global sustainability goals. As industries continue to evolve, SSCM provides a critical pathway for achieving sustainable development. The adoption of these practices helps businesses mitigate risks and build resilience in an increasingly interconnected world.

Ultimately, SSCM enables companies to contribute positively to society while maintaining competitive advantage (Esfahbodi & Zhang, 2020). The concept of Sustainable Supply Chain Management (SSCM) has gained substantial momentum over the past two decades. Research has increasingly focused on key themes such as innovation and disruption management within supply chains. Circular economy principles have become integral, emphasizing waste reduction and resource efficiency. Environmental sustainability remains a central concern, with a growing emphasis on reducing carbon footprints and conserving resources. This body of research reflects the evolving need for businesses to adapt to environmental challenges. As industries face greater scrutiny, adopting SSCM practices becomes crucial for long-term success. The expanding research highlights the strategic importance of sustainability in supply chain operations (Aladaileh et al., 2024; Bhawna et al., 2024). The adoption and implementation of Sustainable Supply Chain Management (SSCM) in emerging economies face significant challenges. Socio-economic disparities often hinder access to resources and sustainable technologies, limiting the ability to implement eco-friendly practices. Institutional voids, such as weak regulatory frameworks and lack of infrastructure, further complicate the process. Resource constraints, both financial and technical, restrict the capacity of businesses to transition to sustainable supply chains. These economies also face difficulties in aligning local practices with global sustainability standards. Despite these hurdles, emerging economies hold immense potential for innovation and sustainable growth. Overcoming these challenges requires targeted policies, investment in infrastructure, and capacity-building initiatives. By addressing these obstacles, emerging economies can unlock opportunities for more resilient and sustainable supply chains (Geng et al., 2017; Silvestre, 2015), 2017).

Sustainable Supply Chain Management (SSCM) is increasingly recognized as a critical strategy for tackling today's environmental, social, and economic challenges. As organizations work to align their operations with sustainability goals, SSCM provides a comprehensive framework to guide their efforts. It integrates eco-friendly practices, such as reducing carbon emissions and minimizing waste, into supply chain processes. Ethical labor standards are also a key component, ensuring fair treatment and safe conditions for workers. Efficient resource utilization helps companies reduce costs while conserving natural resources. By adopting SSCM, organizations can enhance their competitive advantage while contributing positively to global sustainability. This approach not only improves operational efficiency but also strengthens a company's reputation. Ultimately, SSCM supports long-term profitability and resilience by aligning business practices with sustainability imperatives.

Researchers like (Esfahbodi & Zhang, 2020; Sarkis et al., 2011) emphasize the transformative potential of Sustainable Supply Chain Management (SSCM). They highlight how SSCM enables businesses to achieve a balance between profitability and sustainability. By integrating eco-friendly practices and ethical standards, companies can thrive financially while minimizing their environmental impact. This approach drives long-term success and resilience in a competitive global market. Over the past two decades, the field of Sustainable Supply Chain Management (SSCM) has experienced significant growth. Research has increasingly concentrated on critical themes such as innovation and disruption management within supply chains. Circular economy principles, focusing on recycling, reusing, and reducing waste, have gained prominence. Ecological sustainability remains a central focus, with an emphasis on minimizing environmental impact and conserving resources. The growing body of research reflects the need for businesses to adapt to evolving environmental challenges. It also underscores the strategic importance of aligning supply chains with sustainability goals. As industries continue to face global pressures, these themes are crucial for building resilient, future-ready supply chains (Aladaileh et al., 2024; Bhawna et al., 2024). The adoption of Sustainable Supply Chain Management (SSCM) in emerging economies faces significant challenges. Socio-economic disparities limit access to sustainable technologies and practices. Resource constraints, both financial and technical, hinder the ability to invest in sustainable initiatives. Institutional gaps, including weak regulations and poor enforcement, make it difficult to align operations with sustainability goals. These factors create barriers to the widespread implementation of SSCM in these regions (Silvestre, 2015).

Sustainable Supply Chain Management (SSCM) has proven effective in enhancing environmental performance. By implementing practices like reducing emissions, minimizing waste, and optimizing resource use, businesses can significantly lower their ecological footprint. These strategies help mitigate environmental damage, particularly in emerging economies where rapid industrialization leads to increased pollution and resource depletion. Adopting SSCM practices can foster more responsible production and consumption, helping to protect natural ecosystems. For emerging economies, this approach supports long-term sustainability while enabling economic growth. The integration of eco-friendly practices not only reduces environmental impact but also enhances business competitiveness. Ultimately, SSCM provides a pathway for both environmental preservation and economic development (Mani et al., 2018; Mugoni et al., 2024). Green procurement policies, energy-efficient production methods, and closed-loop supply chains have shown effectiveness in tackling environmental challenges.

These practices promote the use of sustainable materials and reduce waste throughout the supply chain. Energy-efficient production methods lower carbon emissions and operational costs. Closed-loop supply chains minimize resource depletion by recycling and reusing materials. Together, these strategies help businesses enhance their environmental performance while contributing to sustainability goals (Esfahbodi et al., 2016; Theeraworawit et al., 2022) highlight how circular economy principles centred on recycling and resource efficiency can drastically reduce environmental footprints. Despite the advancements in Sustainable Supply Chain Management (SSCM), several barriers persist in its implementation. Limited access to green technologies in emerging economies hinders the adoption of eco-friendly practices. Weak regulatory frameworks and poor enforcement make it challenging for businesses to comply with sustainability standards. Additionally, insufficient financial incentives reduce the motivation for companies to invest in sustainable initiatives. Without strong policy support and accessible technologies, businesses struggle to integrate SSCM into their operations. These obstacles highlight the need for stronger governance and financial mechanisms to promote sustainability. Overcoming these barriers is crucial for enabling widespread adoption of SSCM practices (Ahmed et al., 2024; Sánchez-Flores et al., 2020).

Policymakers and industry leaders must play a pivotal role in overcoming barriers to Sustainable Supply Chain Management (SSCM). Offering subsidies and financial incentives can help businesses invest in green technologies and sustainable practices. Enforcing stringent environmental regulations will ensure compliance and drive accountability within supply chains. Additionally, fostering public-private partnerships can encourage collaboration and resource-sharing, facilitating the adoption of SSCM. These partnerships can also help address infrastructure limitations and build capacity in emerging economies. A supportive policy environment is essential for creating the conditions necessary for SSCM to thrive. Ultimately, collective action is required to drive long-term sustainability across industries (Karmaker et al., 2023; Luthra & Mangla, 2018). Despite the advancements in Sustainable Supply Chain Management (SSCM), several barriers persist in its implementation. Limited access to green technologies in emerging economies hinders the adoption of eco-friendly practices. Weak regulatory frameworks and poor enforcement make it challenging for businesses to comply with sustainability standards. Additionally, insufficient financial incentives reduce the motivation for companies to invest in sustainable initiatives. Without strong policy support and accessible technologies, businesses struggle to integrate SSCM into their operations.

These obstacles highlight the need for stronger governance and financial mechanisms to promote sustainability. Overcoming these barriers is crucial for enabling widespread adoption of SSCM practices (Mani et al., 2018; Palazzo & Vollero, 2022). Despite the advancements in Sustainable Supply Chain Management (SSCM), several barriers persist in its implementation. Limited access to green technologies in emerging economies hinders the adoption of eco-friendly practices. Weak regulatory frameworks and poor enforcement make it challenging for businesses to comply with sustainability standards. Additionally, insufficient financial incentives reduce the motivation for companies to invest in sustainable initiatives. Without strong policy support and accessible technologies, businesses struggle to integrate SSCM into their operations. These obstacles highlight the need for stronger governance and financial mechanisms to promote sustainability. Overcoming these barriers is crucial for enabling widespread adoption of SSCM practices. Studies by (Alzate et al., 2022; Bhawna et al., 2024) highlight the positive impact of socially sustainable practices on both organizational performance and community well-being. These practices, which focus on fair labor standards, workplace safety, and equitable benefit sharing, lead to increased employee satisfaction and improved morale. When employees feel valued and secure, their productivity and commitment to the organization grow, enhancing overall supply chain performance.

Furthermore, socially sustainable practices foster stronger community engagement, building trust and positive relationships with local stakeholders. This, in turn, contributes to a more resilient and adaptive supply chain. By addressing social issues, companies can reduce the risk of labor disputes and supply chain disruptions. The integration of social sustainability into business operations not only strengthens employee loyalty but also enhances a company's reputation, making it more competitive. Ultimately, these practices create a mutually beneficial environment for businesses, workers, and communities, leading to improved long-term performance. Collaborative networks and strong leadership are essential for advancing social sustainability, especially in regions with deep-rooted socio-economic inequalities. In such areas, collaboration between businesses, government agencies, non-governmental organizations (NGOs), and local communities is key to addressing complex social issues. These networks can pool resources, share knowledge, and implement effective strategies that benefit all stakeholders. Strong leadership is equally important in driving change, setting clear sustainability goals, and ensuring accountability within the supply chain. Leaders must champion social responsibility and empower teams to adopt ethical practices that prioritize workers' rights, safety, and fair wages. By fostering an inclusive and transparent approach, leaders can encourage a culture of responsibility that extends beyond the organization to the entire supply chain. Moreover, leadership that prioritizes social sustainability can help bridge gaps in access to education, healthcare, and economic opportunities. The combined force of collaborative efforts and visionary leadership creates a foundation for positive social transformation. Ultimately, these efforts lead to stronger, more resilient communities and sustainable business practices (Nambela, 2020; Pakdeechoho & Sukhotu, 2018). Achieving social sustainability necessitates the development of robust policy frameworks that promote fair labour practices, equitable distribution of resources, and social protections. These frameworks must include clear regulations and enforcement mechanisms to ensure compliance and accountability across industries. In addition to policy, cultural shifts within organizations and societies are crucial for fostering an environment that values workers' rights, diversity, and social equity. Organizations must embrace inclusive practices and challenge traditional norms that perpetuate inequality. Continuous stakeholder engagement is equally important, as it ensures that all voices, particularly marginalized groups, are heard and their needs are addressed. Ongoing dialogue between businesses, governments, and communities helps identify emerging social issues and craft appropriate solutions. This engagement also builds trust, strengthens relationships, and fosters a collective responsibility towards social sustainability. Over time, these efforts will contribute to long-lasting changes that promote equality, opportunity, and fairness. Ultimately, achieving social sustainability requires a concerted, multi-faceted approach that integrates policies, cultural change, and active collaboration (Esfahbodi & Zhang, 2020).

The combination of innovative technologies like blockchain, artificial intelligence (AI), and the Internet of Things (IoT) has significantly revolutionized Sustainable Supply Chain Management (SSCM). These technologies enhance supply chain visibility, enabling businesses to track and monitor every stage of the supply chain in real-time. Blockchain, for instance, ensures transparency by securely recording transactions and verifying the origin of products, making it easier to uphold ethical standards and trace sustainability efforts. AI-driven analytics allow businesses to optimize resource use and predict potential disruptions, contributing to more efficient and sustainable operations. IoT devices enable continuous monitoring of goods and resources, providing valuable data that can help reduce waste and improve decision-making. This integration of advanced technologies not only streamlines operational processes but also enhances the accuracy and reliability of sustainability efforts. It allows companies to identify inefficiencies, improve resource allocation, and reduce their environmental footprint. As a result, these innovations lead to more resilient, sustainable, and transparent supply chains.

Ultimately, the adoption of these technologies is critical for businesses aiming to align their operations with global sustainability goals (Wangsa et al., 2022; Zamani et al., 2023). Blockchain technology plays a crucial role in ensuring transparency and accountability in procurement processes by providing a decentralized, immutable ledger that tracks every transaction. This transparency helps organizations verify the authenticity of products and uphold ethical sourcing standards throughout the supply chain. AI-driven analytics further enhance SSCM by enabling predictive maintenance, allowing businesses to anticipate equipment failures before they occur, thereby minimizing downtime and maintenance costs. AI also improves risk management by identifying potential disruptions and enabling proactive responses. Meanwhile, IoT applications, such as sensor-based monitoring, optimize resource allocation by providing real-time data on inventory levels, production processes, and energy consumption. This data allows businesses to identify inefficiencies and implement corrective actions to minimize waste and reduce environmental impact. Together, these technologies foster smarter, more sustainable supply chains by enhancing decision-making, improving operational efficiency, and ensuring greater accountability. Ultimately, they help companies align with sustainability goals while maintaining high levels of performance and resilience (Shoomal et al., 2024).

Despite the significant benefits of technologies like blockchain, AI, and IoT for Sustainable Supply Chain Management (SSCM), their widespread adoption remains hindered by several constraints. High implementation costs are a major barrier, particularly for small and medium-sized enterprises (SMEs) in developing markets that often lack the financial resources to invest in advanced technologies. Additionally, data privacy concerns arise as the use of these technologies involves the collection and sharing of sensitive information across various stakeholders in the supply chain, making companies wary of potential breaches. Interoperability challenges also present a hurdle, as different systems and technologies may not seamlessly integrate, complicating the implementation and management of these solutions. SMEs in developing markets, in particular, may face difficulties in adapting to these complex technological ecosystems due to limited technical expertise and infrastructure. To overcome these barriers, businesses and policymakers must collaborate to create affordable, scalable solutions and regulatory frameworks that address data privacy and promote interoperability. As the cost of technology decreases and solutions become more user-friendly, the adoption of these technologies is expected to grow, enabling SMEs to fully leverage the potential of SSCM (Ahmed et al., 2024; Bhawna et al., 2024).

Collaborative efforts involving governments, technology providers, and industry leaders are critical to overcoming the barriers that hinder the adoption of advanced technologies in Sustainable Supply Chain Management (SSCM). Governments can play a pivotal role by providing financial incentives, subsidies, and regulatory frameworks that encourage businesses, especially SMEs, to invest in sustainable technologies. Technology providers can work to reduce implementation costs by offering scalable, affordable solutions that are tailored to the specific needs of smaller businesses. Industry leaders can collaborate to create shared platforms and frameworks that promote interoperability and ensure seamless integration of different technologies across supply chains. Additionally, knowledge sharing and capacity-building initiatives can help improve technical expertise within SMEs, enabling them to adopt these innovations effectively. Such collaboration will not only make advanced technologies more accessible but also help scale their application across industries, contributing to more sustainable and resilient supply chains. Together, these stakeholders can foster an environment where technology-driven sustainability solutions become widely adopted and beneficial to all players in the supply chain. Ultimately, the collective action will pave the way for long-term sustainability in global supply chains (Sánchez-Flores et al., 2020; Silvestre, 2015).

The COVID-19 pandemic exposed vulnerabilities in global supply chains, highlighting the urgent need for greater resilience and sustainability. The widespread disruptions underscored the fragility of traditional supply chain models and accelerated the shift towards more sustainable and flexible systems. As businesses faced unprecedented challenges, the crisis acted as a catalyst for adopting Sustainable Supply Chain Management (SSCM) practices. This shift emphasized the need for digitalization, with companies increasingly relying on technology to improve visibility, streamline operations, and enhance decision-making. Green technologies also gained prominence, as organizations sought to minimize their environmental impact while ensuring business continuity. Additionally, the pandemic fostered collaborative strategies, with companies, governments, and suppliers coming together to mitigate disruptions and build more resilient supply chains. The integration of these practices has reshaped the approach to supply chain management, encouraging businesses to prioritize sustainability, innovation, and adaptability in their operations. In the post-pandemic era, SSCM is now seen as a critical component of long-term supply chain success, driving not only recovery but also future-proofing businesses against potential shocks (Ahmed et al., 2024; Jaiswal et al., 2024).

Circular economy principles gained significant prominence as businesses sought to reduce waste, optimize resource use, and minimize environmental impact. By shifting from traditional linear models of "take, make, dispose" to more sustainable practices, companies began to embrace strategies like recycling, reusing, and refurbishing materials and products. This approach helps extend the lifecycle of resources, reducing the need for new raw materials and decreasing waste sent to landfills. In the context of supply chain management, circular economy principles encourage businesses to rethink their processes, focusing on sustainability and resource efficiency at every stage. The adoption of these principles has led to innovations in product design, manufacturing, and distribution, promoting a more sustainable and responsible approach to business operations. Ultimately, the circular economy not only benefits the environment but also creates new opportunities for cost savings, increased efficiency, and competitive advantage. As more companies prioritize sustainability, the circular economy is expected to play a pivotal role in shaping the future of global supply chains (Bhawna et al., 2024; Pakdeechoho & Sukhotu, 2018).

The pandemic not only exposed the vulnerabilities in global supply chains but also highlighted pre-existing challenges, particularly in emerging economies, such as digital immaturity and resource constraints. Many businesses in these regions struggled to adapt to the rapid digitalization required to navigate disruptions, and limited financial resources made it difficult to invest in necessary technologies. To enhance resilience, businesses must prioritize capacity building, equipping employees with the skills and knowledge to leverage new technologies effectively. Adopting flexible supply chain models that can quickly adapt to changing circumstances and disruptions is also essential for ensuring continuity in uncertain times. Strengthening stakeholder partnerships, including collaborations with suppliers, governments, and technology providers, is another critical strategy. These partnerships enable shared resources, knowledge exchange, and collective problem-solving, helping businesses build more resilient and sustainable supply chains. By addressing these challenges head-on, businesses can better prepare for future disruptions and strengthen their position in an increasingly unpredictable global marketplace (Alzate et al., 2022; Esfahbodi & Zhang, 2020). Integrated frameworks are essential for addressing the complex and multifaceted challenges of Sustainable Supply Chain Management (SSCM). These frameworks help organizations navigate the various environmental, social, and economic dimensions of sustainability by providing structured approaches to decision-making and problem-solving.

Research emphasizes the use of methodologies such as multi-criteria decision-making (MCDM) models and interpretive structural modelling (ISM) as effective tools for identifying and prioritizing the key drivers of SSCM adoption. MCDM models enable businesses to evaluate multiple sustainability criteria simultaneously, balancing trade-offs between environmental performance, economic viability, and social impact. ISM, on the other hand, helps map out the relationships and interdependencies between different factors affecting SSCM, providing a clear visualization of the pathways to successful implementation. Key drivers identified through these frameworks include management commitment, which ensures that sustainability initiatives are prioritized and adequately resourced, as well as policy support, which creates a regulatory environment conducive to sustainable practices. Stakeholder collaboration also plays a pivotal role, as it enables shared responsibility and collective action across the supply chain. By using these integrated frameworks, organizations can better understand the complexities of SSCM and develop targeted strategies to drive its successful adoption and implementation (Ahmed et al., 2024; Luthra & Mangla, 2018). Circular supply chain models, which emphasize closed-loop systems and resource efficiency, have emerged as a key strategy for accelerating sustainability efforts. Unlike traditional linear supply chains that follow a "take, make, dispose" approach, circular models focus on maximizing resource utilization by promoting recycling, remanufacturing, and reusing materials.

These models reduce dependence on virgin resources, minimize waste generation, and lower environmental impact. By integrating closed-loop systems, businesses can recover valuable materials, extend product lifecycles, and create sustainable production-consumption cycles. Circular supply chains also enhance cost efficiency by reducing raw material procurement expenses and mitigating risks associated with resource scarcity. Additionally, they align with evolving regulatory requirements and consumer preferences for sustainable products. Companies adopting circular supply chain practices are better positioned to achieve long-term sustainability goals while maintaining competitiveness in the global market. As industries increasingly recognize the benefits of circularity, these models are expected to play a critical role in shaping the future of sustainable supply chain management (Bhalaji et al., 2024; Theeraworawit et al., 2022). However, the economic benefits of these models are not always immediate, requiring a long-term perspective and sustained commitment from stakeholders (Ahmed et al., 2024; Esfahbodi et al., 2016). Despite the progress made, significant challenges persist in SSCM implementation. Institutional voids, socio-economic disparities, and inadequate regulatory frameworks delay the widespread acceptance of viable practices in developing economies (Sánchez-Flores et al., 2020; Silvestre, 2015). Upcoming investigation should effort on empirical educations to evaluate the effectiveness of SSCM initiatives across diverse industrial and regional contexts. Collaboration among governments, businesses, and academia is essential to foster innovation, share knowledge, and create a supportive ecosystem for SSCM adoption (Aladaileh et al., 2024; Karmaker et al., 2023). Addressing these challenges and leveraging emerging opportunities can position SSCM as a transformative tool for achieving global sustainability goals, particularly in regions striving to balance development with ecological and communal imperatives.

4 METHODOLOGY

The research has incorporated literature reviews, surveys, and Discussions to investigate the Advancing Sustainable Supply Chain Practices in Emerging Economies in India. The chapter observes the crucial areas of sustainable supply chain management in developing financial prudence, highlighting the unique challenges and opportunities in adopting eco-friendly and socially responsible practices. While rapid sector, resource constraints, and socio-economic disparities pose significant barriers, emerging economies are increasingly leveraging rising consumer awareness and green technologies to advance sustainability. The study explores how digitalization and circular economy principles are transforming supply chain practices, improving efficiency, and minimizing waste.

Figure 1. Research methodology

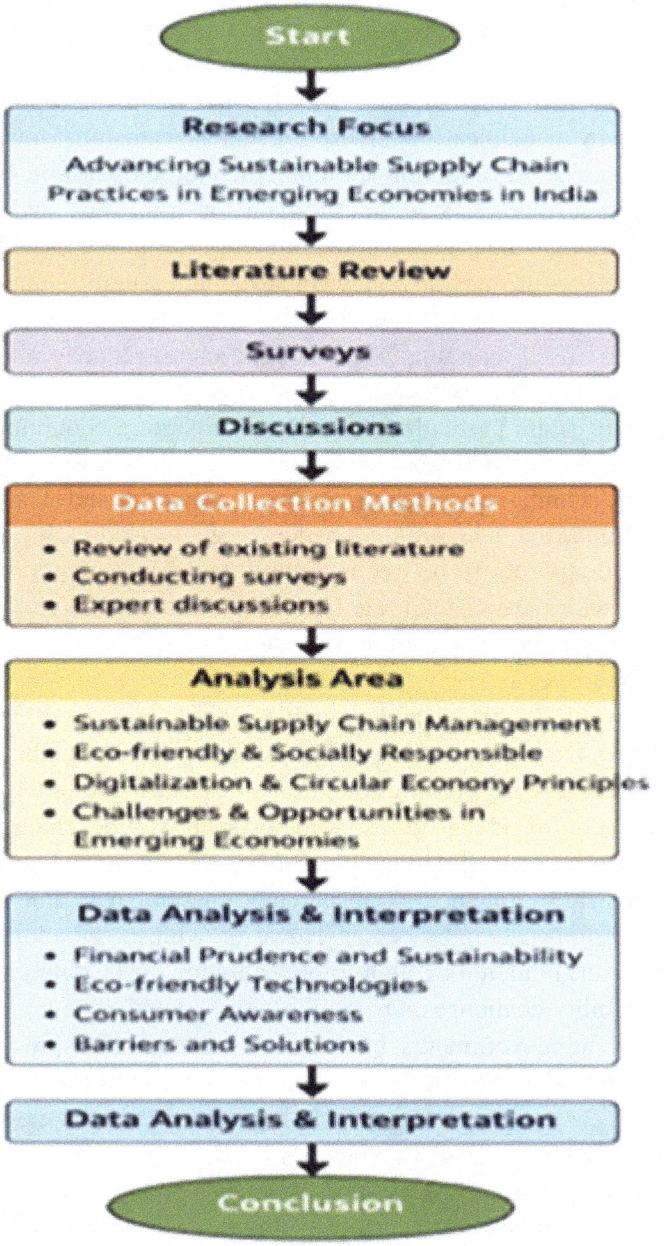

5 FINDINGS

Sustainable Supply Chain Management has emerged as a transformative approach to addressing pressing ecological, social, and economic challenges. It provides a structured framework for integrating eco-friendly practices, ethical labor standards, and efficient resource utilization across supply chains. As businesses seek to balance profitability with sustainability, this approach has gained significant traction over the past two decades, driven by key themes such as innovation, disruption management, circular economy principles, and environmental stewardship. However, despite its growing importance, the adoption and implementation of sustainable supply chain management in developing economies remain constrained by socio-economic disparities, institutional voids, and resource limitations, limiting its widespread impact and effectiveness. A primary advantage of sustainable supply chain management is its contribution to environmental sustainability. Green procurement, energy-efficient production, and closed-loop supply chains significantly reduce emissions, minimize waste, and optimize resource usage.

These practices are particularly relevant in emerging economies, where rapid industrialization often leads to severe environmental degradation. However, limited access to green technologies, weak regulatory frameworks, and insufficient financial incentives continue to hinder progress in these regions. Addressing these challenges requires collaborative efforts between the public and private sectors through targeted subsidies, stricter environmental regulations, and investments in sustainable infrastructure to unlock its full potential. Beyond environmental benefits, sustainable supply chain management plays a crucial role in social sustainability by improving labor rights, workplace safety, and equitable benefit sharing within supply chains. Ethical sourcing, fair trade practices, and corporate social responsibility initiatives are integral to fostering better working conditions and ensuring long-term sustainability.

The integration of advanced technologies such as blockchain, artificial intelligence, and the Internet of Things has further revolutionized sustainable supply chain management by enhancing transparency, enabling real-time monitoring, and improving decision-making processes. However, widespread adoption of these innovations remains hindered by high implementation costs, data privacy concerns, and interoperability challenges. Overcoming these barriers requires a coordinated approach involving governments, businesses, and technology providers to develop scalable solutions. The COVID-19 pandemic underscored the importance of sustainable supply chain management in fostering resilience, as businesses increasingly turned to digitalization, circular economy models, and flexible supply chain strategies to navigate disruptions. Despite its immense potential, it demands sustained commitment and innovative strategies to address persistent challenges, particularly in developing economies striving to balance industrial growth with environmental and social sustainability. By fostering collaboration, regulatory support, and technological innovation, sustainable supply chain management can serve as a powerful tool for achieving long-term sustainability and resilience in global supply chains. The concept extends beyond conventional supply chain management by embedding sustainability at every stage of the value chain.

From procurement to production and distribution, sustainable supply chain management emphasizes responsible sourcing, waste reduction, and energy efficiency. Companies that integrate sustainability into their supply chain operations experience long-term benefits, including improved brand reputation, cost savings, and regulatory compliance. The transition towards sustainable practices requires a shift in mindset, where organizations prioritize environmental stewardship alongside economic performance. This shift is particularly critical in industries such as manufacturing, agriculture, and logistics, where resource consumption and emissions have far-reaching consequences. One of the fundamental pillars of sustainable supply chain management is green procurement, which involves selecting suppliers based on their environmental performance and commitment to sustainability. Green procurement practices encourage businesses to source raw materials responsibly, reduce carbon footprints, and promote ethical labor practices. Companies that adopt green procurement strategies benefit from reduced risks associated with environmental regulations, enhanced operational efficiency, and improved stakeholder relationships. However, implementing green procurement can be challenging due to supply chain complexities, cost considerations, and a lack of standardized sustainability criteria.

Overcoming these challenges requires establishing clear sustainability goals, engaging with suppliers, and leveraging technology to track and measure sustainability performance. In addition to procurement, energy-efficient production processes play a crucial role in sustainable supply chain management. Energy efficiency initiatives, such as adopting renewable energy sources, optimizing production techniques, and investing in energy-saving technologies, contribute to reducing greenhouse gas emissions and operational costs. Companies that integrate energy-efficient practices into their supply chains not only achieve sustainability targets but also enhance their competitiveness in the global market. However, transitioning to energy-efficient production requires substantial capital investment, technological expertise, and regulatory incentives. Governments and industry stakeholders must collaborate to create supportive policies, provide financial incentives, and facilitate knowledge-sharing to accelerate the adoption of energy-efficient practices. Closed-loop supply chains represent another critical aspect of sustainable supply chain management, where products are designed with end-of-life considerations, enabling recycling, remanufacturing, and reuse. Closed-loop supply chains minimize waste generation, reduce dependency on virgin resources, and contribute to circular economy principles. Businesses that implement closed-loop supply chains benefit from cost savings, reduced environmental impact, and enhanced customer loyalty. However, establishing closed-loop systems requires a robust infrastructure for collection, processing, and reintegration of materials into the supply chain.

Overcoming these barriers necessitates investment in recycling technologies, collaboration with stakeholders, and consumer awareness programs to promote responsible consumption and disposal. The integration of digital technologies has further transformed sustainable supply chain management by enabling data-driven decision-making, enhancing transparency, and improving operational efficiency. Blockchain technology, for instance, enhances supply chain traceability by providing a secure and immutable record of transactions. Companies can use blockchain to verify product authenticity, track sourcing practices, and ensure compliance with sustainability standards. Artificial intelligence and machine learning facilitate predictive analytics, demand forecasting, and risk management, enabling businesses to optimize supply chain operations and mitigate disruptions. The Internet of Things enables real-time monitoring of supply chain activities, improving efficiency, reducing waste, and enhancing overall performance.

Addressing these challenges requires strategic investments, regulatory frameworks, and industry-wide collaboration to develop scalable and secure digital solutions. The role of regulatory frameworks and policy interventions in sustainable supply chain management cannot be overstated. Governments play a crucial role in shaping sustainable supply chain practices through regulations, incentives, and enforcement mechanisms. Policies that promote sustainability reporting, carbon pricing, and extended producer responsibility encourage businesses to adopt environmentally and socially responsible practices. Regulatory frameworks should be designed to provide clear guidelines, foster industry collaboration, and ensure compliance with sustainability standards. Additionally, public-private partnerships can facilitate knowledge exchange, capacity building, and infrastructure development to support implementation. Effective policy interventions create an enabling environment for businesses to integrate sustainability into their supply chain operations while maintaining economic viability. Consumer awareness and stakeholder engagement are also essential in driving sustainable supply chain management adoption. Consumers increasingly demand transparency, ethical sourcing, and sustainable products, influencing businesses to prioritize sustainability in their supply chains. Companies that engage with stakeholders, including suppliers, employees, and communities, foster a culture of sustainability and social responsibility. Corporate social responsibility initiatives, sustainability certifications, and eco-labeling programs help build consumer trust and differentiate brands in competitive markets.

Educating consumers about sustainable choices, promoting responsible consumption, and encouraging behavioral changes contribute to the success of sustainable supply chain management initiatives. Businesses must proactively communicate their sustainability efforts, engage in stakeholder dialogue, and align their strategies with consumer expectations to achieve long-term success. The future of sustainable supply chain management lies in continuous innovation, collaboration, and commitment to sustainability principles. As global challenges such as climate change, resource scarcity, and social inequalities persist, businesses must adopt forward-thinking strategies to enhance supply chain resilience and sustainability. Investing in research and development, embracing circular economy principles, and leveraging emerging technologies will drive the next phase of sustainable supply chain management evolution.

6 CONCLUSION

The study emphasizes the value-creating capability of Sustainable Supply Chain Management (SSCM) as an integrated environment to address environmental, social, and economic challenges in supply chains. Incorporating practices such as green procurement, energy efficiency, ethical labor practices, and resource optimization, SSCM demonstrates its capability to balance profitability and sustainability. SSCM has developed fast over the past two decades, with practice and research focused on challenges such as innovation, disruption management, circular economy principles, and environmental sustainability. These efforts have been instrumental in reshaping supply chain strategies, with sustainability as a core business objective rather than a secondary issue. One of the key implications of the reading is that SSCM is capable of enhancing environmental performance. Green technologies, closed-loop supply chains, and energy-efficient manufacturing have been able to check environmental degradation, particularly in fast-industrializing countries. Apart from environmental advantages, SSCM is pivotal in enhancing social sustainability. Preventing labor rights violations, occupational injuries, and uneven benefit-sharing, SSCM generates more equitable and ethical supply chains. Activities like virtuous finding, rational skill certifications, and CSR schemes have been successful in enhancing workers' satisfaction, as well as supply chain efficiency. Collaborative networks and visionary leadership are decisive facilitators in this respect, particularly in countries where socio-economic disparities are ingrained. But social sustainability is possible only if there is a change in organization culture, strong policy regimes, and active citizens' participation in ensuring that the benefits of sustainable initiatives are distributed uniformly. The contribution of advanced technologies to SSCM cannot be overstated. Blockchain, AI, and IoT are some of the technologies that have revolutionized supply chain management by offering more visibility, facilitating real observation, and improving executive. Blockchain offers transparency and accountability in procurement, while AI analytics facilitate predictive maintenance and risk management.

IoT technologies, such as sensor-based monitoring, optimize resource utilization and minimize waste.

REFERENCES

Agyabeng-Mensah, Y., Afum, E., Acquah, I. S. K., & Baah, C. (2023). How does supply chain knowledge enhance green innovation? The mediation mechanisms of corporate reputation and non-supply chain learning. *Journal of Business and Industrial Marketing*, *38*(4), 852–868. DOI: 10.1108/JBIM-04-2021-0192

Ahmed, H. N., Ahmed, S., Khan, M. A., & Ali, S. M. (2024). Sustainable supply chain in emerging economies during and post COVID-19 pandemic: A systematic literature review and future research directions. *International Journal of Emerging Markets*, *19*(9), 2472–2498. DOI: 10.1108/IJOEM-01-2022-0092

Aladaileh, M. J., Lahuerta-Otero, E., & Aladayleh, K. J. (2024). Mapping sustainable supply chain innovation: A comprehensive bibliometric analysis. *Heliyon*, *10*(7), e29157. DOI: 10.1016/j.heliyon.2024.e29157 PMID: 38623205

Alzate, I. C., Manotas, E. C., Manotas, E. M., & Boada, A. (2022). Impact of supply chain dynamic capabilities (SCDC) and horizontal collaboration over supply chain resilience for SME's sustainability in emerging economies. *Polish Journal of Management Studies, 25*.

Bhalaji, R., Bathrinath, S., Ali, S. M., & Koppiahraj, K. (2024). Risk assessment in sustainable supply chain: Theoretical and managerial implications for circular economy in emerging economies. *International Journal of System Assurance Engineering and Management*, *15*(10), 1–16. DOI: 10.1007/s13198-024-02507-4

Bhawna, Kang, P. S., & Sharma, S. K. (2024). Bridging the gap: A systematic analysis of circular economy, supply chain management, and digitization for sustainability and resilience. *Operations Management Research*, 1–19.

Carter, C. R., & Rogers, D. S. (2008). A framework of sustainable supply chain management: Moving toward new theory. *International Journal of Physical Distribution & Logistics Management*, *38*(5), 360–387. DOI: 10.1108/09600030810882816

Chardine-Baumann, E., & Botta-Genoulaz, V. (2014). A framework for sustainable performance assessment of supply chain management practices. *Computers & Industrial Engineering*, *76*, 138–147. DOI: 10.1016/j.cie.2014.07.029

Diabat, A., Govindan, K., & Panicker, V. V. (2012). Supply chain risk management and its mitigation in a food industry. *International Journal of Production Research*, *50*(11), 3039–3050. DOI: 10.1080/00207543.2011.588619

Dubey, R., Gunasekaran, A., Childe, S. J., Papadopoulos, T., Blome, C., & Luo, Z. (2017). Antecedents of resilient supply chains: An empirical study. *IEEE Transactions on Engineering Management*, *66*(1), 8–19. DOI: 10.1109/TEM.2017.2723042

Esfahbodi, A., & Zhang, Y. (2020). Sustainable supply chain management in developed vs. Emerging economies: Evidence from the UK and China's manufacturing industry. In *Encyclopedia of Renewable and Sustainable Materials* (pp. 537–549). Elsevier. DOI: 10.1016/B978-0-12-803581-8.11506-1

Esfahbodi, A., Zhang, Y., & Watson, G. (2016). Sustainable supply chain management in emerging economies: Trade-offs between environmental and cost performance. *International Journal of Production Economics*, *181*, 350–366. DOI: 10.1016/j.ijpe.2016.02.013

Geng, R., Mansouri, S. A., Aktas, E., & Yen, D. A. (2017). The role of Guanxi in green supply chain management in Asia's emerging economies: A conceptual framework. *Industrial Marketing Management*, *63*, 1–17. DOI: 10.1016/j.indmarman.2017.01.002

Govindan, K., Soleimani, H., & Kannan, D. (2015). Reverse logistics and closed-loop supply chain: A comprehensive review to explore the future. *European Journal of Operational Research*, *240*(3), 603–626. DOI: 10.1016/j.ejor.2014.07.012

Jaiswal, A., Negi, P., & Singh, N. (2024). Emerging Paradigms in Sustainable Supply Chain Management: A Comparative Study of Pre–and Post–COVID-19 Research Trends. *Abhigyan*, *42*(1), 32–42. DOI: 10.1177/09702385241233077

Karmaker, C. L., Bari, A. M., Anam, M. Z., Ahmed, T., Ali, S. M., de Jesus Pacheco, D. A., & Moktadir, M. A. (2023). Industry 5.0 challenges for post-pandemic supply chain sustainability in an emerging economy. *International Journal of Production Economics*, *258*, 108806. DOI: 10.1016/j.ijpe.2023.108806

Luthra, S., & Mangla, S. K. (2018). When strategies matter: Adoption of sustainable supply chain management practices in an emerging economy's context. *Resources, Conservation and Recycling*, *138*, 194–206. DOI: 10.1016/j.resconrec.2018.07.005

Mani, V., Gunasekaran, A., & Delgado, C. (2018). Enhancing supply chain performance through supplier social sustainability: An emerging economy perspective. *International Journal of Production Economics*, *195*, 259–272. DOI: 10.1016/j.ijpe.2017.10.025

Mishra, D., Gunasekaran, A., Papadopoulos, T., & Childe, S. J. (2018). Big Data and supply chain management: A review and bibliometric analysis. *Annals of Operations Research*, *270*(1-2), 313–336. DOI: 10.1007/s10479-016-2236-y

Mugoni, E., Kanyepe, J., & Tukuta, M. (2024). Sustainable Supply Chain Management Practices (SSCMPS) and environmental performance: A systematic review. *Sustainable Technology and Entrepreneurship, 3*(1), 100050. DOI: 10.1016/j.stae.2023.100050

Nambela, N. (2020). *The impact of adopting sustainable supply chain management practices on the performance of public sector organisations in Zambia: A case study of Zambia Air force (ZAF).*

Pakdeechoho, N., & Sukhotu, V. (2018). Sustainable supply chain collaboration: Incentives in emerging economies. *Journal of Manufacturing Technology Management, 29*(2), 273–294. DOI: 10.1108/JMTM-05-2017-0081

Palazzo, M., & Vollero, A. (2022). A systematic literature review of food sustainable supply chain management (FSSCM): Building blocks and research trends. *The TQM Journal, 34*(7), 54–72. DOI: 10.1108/TQM-10-2021-0300

Rajeev, A., Pati, R. K., Padhi, S. S., & Govindan, K. (2017). Evolution of sustainability in supply chain management: A literature review. *Journal of Cleaner Production, 162*, 299–314. DOI: 10.1016/j.jclepro.2017.05.026

Sánchez-Flores, R. B., Cruz-Sotelo, S. E., Ojeda-Benitez, S., & Ramírez-Barreto, M. E. (2020). Sustainable supply chain management—A literature review on emerging economies. *Sustainability (Basel), 12*(17), 6972. DOI: 10.3390/su12176972

Sarkis, J., Zhu, Q., & Lai, K. (2011). An organizational theoretic review of green supply chain management literature. *International Journal of Production Economics, 130*(1), 1–15. DOI: 10.1016/j.ijpe.2010.11.010

Seuring, S., & Müller, M. (2008). From a literature review to a conceptual framework for sustainable supply chain management. *Journal of Cleaner Production, 16*(15), 1699–1710. DOI: 10.1016/j.jclepro.2008.04.020

Shoomal, A., Jahanbakht, M., Componation, P. J., & Ozay, D. (2024). Enhancing supply chain resilience and efficiency through internet of things integration: Challenges and opportunities. *Internet of Things : Engineering Cyber Physical Human Systems, 27*, 101324. DOI: 10.1016/j.iot.2024.101324

Silvestre, B. S. (2015). Sustainable supply chain management in emerging economies: Environmental turbulence, institutional voids and sustainability trajectories. *International Journal of Production Economics, 167*, 156–169. DOI: 10.1016/j.ijpe.2015.05.025

Theeraworawit, M., Suriyankietkaew, S., & Hallinger, P. (2022). Sustainable supply chain management in a circular economy: A bibliometric review. *Sustainability (Basel)*, *14*(15), 9304. DOI: 10.3390/su14159304

Thomas, M. J., Veiga, M. M., Marshall, B. G., & Dunbar, W. S. (2019). Artisanal gold supply chain: Measures from the Ecuadorian Government. *Resources Policy*, *64*, 101505. DOI: 10.1016/j.resourpol.2019.101505

Walker, H., & Jones, N. (2012). Sustainable supply chain management across the UK private sector. *Supply Chain Management*, *17*(1), 15–28. DOI: 10.1108/13598541211212177

Wangsa, I. D., Vanany, I., & Siswanto, N. (2022). Issues in sustainable supply chain's futuristic technologies: A bibliometric and research trend analysis. *Environmental Science and Pollution Research International*, *29*(16), 22885–22912. DOI: 10.1007/s11356-021-17805-8 PMID: 35064513

Zamani, E. D., Smyth, C., Gupta, S., & Dennehy, D. (2023). Artificial intelligence and big data analytics for supply chain resilience: A systematic literature review. *Annals of Operations Research*, *327*(2), 605–632. DOI: 10.1007/s10479-022-04983-y PMID: 36212520

Zhu, S., Song, J., Hazen, B. T., Lee, K., & Cegielski, C. (2018). How supply chain analytics enables operational supply chain transparency: An organizational information processing theory perspective. *International Journal of Physical Distribution & Logistics Management*, *48*(1), 47–68. DOI: 10.1108/IJPDLM-11-2017-0341

Chapter 2
Crisis Preparation Strategies and Developing Resilient Supply Chains:
Future Trends in Supply Chain Resilience and Sustainability

Domnic Thavagnana Nachathiram K.
http://orcid.org/0009-0005-1213-6057
Periyar Maniammai Institute of Science and Technology (Deemed to be University), Thanjavur, India

Vijay M.
http://orcid.org/0009-0002-9291-5859
Periyar Maniammai Institute of Science and Technology (Deemed to be University), Thanjavur, India

Rosanth Ivan
http://orcid.org/0009-0009-7845-2342
Periyar Maniammai Institute of Science and Technology (Deemed to be University), Thanjavur, India, India

ABSTRACT

Globally, the supply chain is fabulous changes towards transformations. This transformation finds various challenges due to Climate changes, Political Uncertainty, technological distractions and paradise consumer demand. This chapter would like to find the link of these most prior concepts and make an analysis of new trends, innovative practices and tactics framework to be designed for eco-friendly supply

DOI: 10.4018/979-8-2600-1855-2.ch002

chain management. Prevailing trends in this supply chain management include embracing predictive analytics powered by SCM Artificial Intelligence and Machine Learning. It project future risks and respond foresightedly .It also explores how sustainability initiatives are linked across supply chain management to not only concern the fulfilment of regular compliances but also resonate with stakeholders. Governments and international organizations are driving through stringent regulations, incentives for sustainable practices, and collaborative platforms to share best practices.

1. INTRODUCTION

The multinational supply chain terrain is sustainable extraordinary modifications owing to the intersection of elements, flexible of weather changes, technical interruptions, global instability, and fluctuating customer needs and wants. These complications have required supply chain management to consider new perspectives, with durability and sustainability emerging as essential foundations. Perseverance refers to supply chain's ability to anticipate response to and overcome challenges, maintaining continuity and effectiveness of operations. Environmental responsibility on the other hand, promotes long-term profitability, reducing carbon emissions and moral standards. The reliability and operation of global supply chains are greatly impacted by the increasing frequent fundamental events in today's world that include everything from international conflicts and public health emergencies to widespread disruptions done by climate change (Kareem et al,. 2025). A theoretical framework towards integrating strong resilience methods into supply chain fundamentals are required because of increasing instability in order to assure continues operations and sustained performance in the face of many challenges (Anagnostakos,2024;Bamia & Bamia, 2025). For the purpose to address this an increasing alignment between research and industry practices on the development of integrated framework that encompass agility, systemic reliance and adaptability as well as traditional risk management (Karanam et al.,2024). In global, Supply chain is being fabulous changes towards transformations. This transformation finding various challenges due Climate changes, Political Uncertainty, technology distractions and paradise consumer demand. The industries strive to adhere this disruption by following dual aspect of concepts as Resilience and sustainability have emerged as critical concepts for shaping future trends in supply chain management. Developing an in-depth understanding of supply chain resilience is part of this re-evaluation that goes beyond isolated techniques to include fundamental features like improved collaborative connections, sustainable practices and transparency supported by technology (Faggioni et al.,2024). This book chapter would like to find the link of these most prior concepts and make analysis of neo trends, innovative practices, tactics framework to be designed for eco-friendly supply chain management. It examines emerging trends, creative methods and essential framework that enable organisations to have dynamic supply chains. This chapter also highlights how management partnership eco-system and modern technologies enable sustainable results. Additionally the discussion regarding supply chain resilience emphasizes how important these innovations for anticipating, persisting and adjusting to incidents, which promotes a proactive rather than reactive approach (Karanam et al., 2024;Mahdiraji et al., 2024). The tactical use of modern digital technologies such as block chain, artificial intelligence and the internet of things which offer enhance visibility and operational optimization abilities, further supports this proactive strategy (Enyejo et al.,2024). A Resilient concept is enumerated by its ability to expect, stance and recover from those disruptions while ensuring uninterrupted operations and keeping operation running smoothly.

1.1 Resource Purpose and Scope

This study aims to examine how resilience and sustainability collaborate to impact on existing supply chain trends which are AI driven. It examines into the economic, technological and political factors that are contribute to these changes, providing insights into best practices for sustainable supply chain in carbon-free settings. Prevailing trends in this supply chain management include embracing of predictive analytics powered by SCM artificial Intelligence and Machine Learning. These enable the industries to project the future risks and respond foresightedly.

1.2 Importance of Resilience and Sustainability in Supply Chain Management

Resilience and sustainability have to be addressed owing to the increasing complexity of supply chain networks. These two related ideas offer business a framework to deal with interruptions while maintaining long-term operational efficiency and environmental responsibility. Virtual replica of Physical object and system allowing supply chain management to simulate the various scenarios, streamline operations, and enhance rational decision making in this real time digital transformation. The involvement and projections of block chain technology in improves the transparency and deductibility in supply chain management. .

1. The ability of supply chain to anticipate, withstand and recover from incidents is referred to as resilience. It involves maintaining adaptable logistic networks, using technology for predictive analytics and changing suppliers. Reducing car-

bon emission, optimizing resource uses, minimizing environmental effect, and promoting social responsibility are the main goal of supply chain sustainability.

2. Business are able to operate effectively while reducing financial, environmental, and reputational risk due to strong and sustainable supply chain.

1.3 Objectives of This Research

1. To identify the major problems and challenges affecting global supply chain
2. To examine how resilience and sustainability may improve the effectiveness of the supply chain
3. To examine the new technologies that support risk management, transparency and predictive analysis

1.4 Research Gap

Despite supply chain sustainability and resilience are growing important in emerging corporate setting; the majority of the literature that is currently available at these ideas are independently rather than collectively. Few investigations examine how supply chains might be made stronger and sustainable by integrating emerging technology, digital transformation and circular economy principles. Additionally empirical finding in emerging economics and specific industry are limited. Further research is needed to understanding the strategic methods and future trends that will enable business to create supply chain system that are sustainable and resilient.

1.5 Fundamental Elements

Redundancy: To decrease the effects of disruptions, buffer stocks should be built, different vendors should be maintained and other logistic paths should be established.

Agility: The capacity to easily modify operations in response to unexpected circumstances by utilizing adaptable methods of productions, inventory plans, and responding logistics.

Visibility: The entire process of supply chain operations using digital technologies especially block chain, IoT, and AI to improve reduction of risk and real-time decision-making.

Collaboration: Building powerful connection with distributor, suppliers and other stakeholders to build a cooperative network that promotes reciprocal developments and adoptions.

Risk Management: Proactive identification of possible risk using predictive analytics and establishment of backup plans.

1.6 Various Strategies to Build Resilience and Supply Chain

a) Supply chain diversification – Using a variety of possibilities to prevent being relevant on geographical area
b) Digital Transformation- Enhancing supply chain implementation by block chain, AI, and machine learning.
c) Scenario Planning: Backup plans and stress test to provide apt planning
d) Sustainable Practices: Addressing environmental issues through the use of sustainable practices.
e) Strengthening Supplier Relationship: Implementing long-term relationship cooperation with them.

1.7 The Role of Technology in Implementing Supply Chain Resilience

a) Predictive and reduce risk management- It plays a vital role in supply chain by implementing organisation bare potential risk. By analysing historical data, external forces and market trends such as fluctuation of technology lacking. Optimize the inventory level to predict storage condition. It enhances demand forecasting accuracy; improve prompt planning, manipulating risk management and forecast of AI & ML application.
b) AI & ML – Artificial Intelligence (AI) and Machine Learning (ML) have modified supply chain forecasting by improvement of accuracy and efficiency. These technologies indicate: automated demand forecasting- AI driven models gives consumer behaviour, market condition economic environment. Decision making: ML indicates vast amount of data in real time business. Optimizing logistics: AI powered reduces delivery efficiency and reduce transportation cost. Supplier performance: AI evaluates supplier reliability and external risk factor.

2. LITERATURE REVIEW

Recent investigation emphasis the combination of emerging technologies such as artificial intelligence and blockchain technology to enhance real time monitoring and adaptive decision-making (Faggioni et al.,2024). Additionally predictive analytics and machine learning techniques are often utilized in this collaboration to effective manner (Jayadi et al., 2024). Enabling proactive rather than reactive responses to unexpected challenges. Improving event handling capabilities and effective response mechanism that enable supply chains to return to regular operational performance after interruption further supports this proactive approach (Odulaja et al., 2023). The relationship between sustainable practices and supply chain adaptability, especially in decreasing environmental uncertainties, has also receiving recognition, insisting the need for detailed empirical analysis of the relationship (Adeleye et al., 2024). The growing complexity of supply chain networks is focus on sustainability to increase the frequency of global interruption such as climate change, political conflicts and pandemic (Bamia & Bamia, 2025). In order to generate supply chain ecosystem which are more durable and resilient by encouraging improved awareness, predictive analytics and accessible stakeholder interactions, it is essential that digital transformation strategies be incorporated. This can be done by using technologies like block chain, and internet of things (Faggioni et al.,2024; Karanam et al., 2024; Samuels,2025). Vital part supply chain durability has been shown to be a systems own ability to adapt its operation, before during and after a distribution in order to continue essential operation under both anticipated and unexpected circumstances (Choi et al., 2023). It examines how the supply chain management currently takes orders manually. The availability and cognitive requirements on employees are mentioned. Semi-structured interviews were used to collect data. These studies investigate how AI-driven will use in the society (Shamsuzzoha & Pelkonen, 2025). This research examines at an organisational performance in connection with agile techniques. Data collection from 340 manufacturing company responsibility. Components and reliability analysis were connected in this study. The necessity of understanding the green supply chain management with agile methods (Akhil NSB et,al 2025). The main supply chain process and modified performance are focus of this study. Data collection from 71 respondents of agile team. It investigate improved result and adaptability of technology-driven (Steegh, et,al 2025). The complete digital transformation of supply chain, which makes use of modern digital technologies to strengthen decision-making and operational effectiveness, significantly enhance their transformational efficiency (Samuels,2025; Singh, 2024). Specifically the combination of artificial intelligence and machine learning technologies provides forecasting capabilities that enable businesses anticipate possibilities disruptions and effectively optimize operations (Enyjeo et al,. 2024). Block chain technology improves supply chain stakeholders' transparency and confidence by maintaining irreversible records, which renders it possible to quickly identify and address the problem (Singh, 2024). At the same time internet of things offers real time information on the position and state of assets, enabling faster response to unforeseen events and improving inventory control (Holloway, 2025). Furthermore, by establishing trust and reputation which are consider for promoting common objective among stakeholders and minimizing negative impacts on vulnerable groups during disruptions in technical advantages promote strong corporate social responsibility policies (Mathiyazhagan et,al., 2023). Furthermore accomplishing comprehensive sustainability across environmental, social and economic factors with the global supply chain networks is dependent on the collaborative application of these specialised technologies such as block chain for an enhanced transparency and ethical sourcing, IoT for regular continuous surveillance and AI for predictive analysis (Samuel, 2025 Tariq, 2025; Vadigicherla, 2024). In combination digital technologies strengthen accountability, efficiency and transparency enabling organisations to handle challenging task makes quick choices and respond to challenges more skilfully (Halloway,2025; Tariq, 2025). By maximising utilisation of resources and reducing waste throughout the value chain, this incorporation of digital technologies not only improves resilience but also greatly the overall objectives of supply chain sustainability (Alquarish, 2025). The projection of green based renewable energy sources and innovative packaging solutions also underscores effort to reduce the environmental impact. Socially, the focus has transformed to ethical concern, fair labour practices and committed based community engagement with the principles of corporate social responsibilities.

2.1 Strengthening Supply Chain Resilience

Key components of modern supply chain management and resilience, it enables business. The following key elements are: Predictive analytics powered AI: In supply chain merging of AI and ML enhances business to anticipate possible risk, improved productivity and predictive disruption. Real-time decision-making made prevent disruption.

Digital-Twins: Organisation can create several scenarios uncover bottlenecks and effectiveness by using digital twins.

Block chain Technology: By providing permanent record of the transaction enhances supply chain accuracy and reliability.

2.2 Green Supply Chain Management

Business efforts are helps to reduce the environmental impact of stakeholders, and sustainability.

1. Renewable energy and Green Practices:

Initiative to reduce environmental impact is brought out by the use of renewable energy sources and environmentally practices such as innovative solutions.

2. Ethical Labour Practice and Corporate Social Responsibilities (CSR):

In order to conform that CSR principle, organisations placed a strong focus on community involvement, strong practices and responsible sources.

3. Strategies:

Globalisation reduces carbon emission through decrease dependencies on international transportation, it will improve responsiveness.

3. CONCEPTUAL FRAMEWORK FOR RESILIENCE AND SUSTAINABLE SUPPLY CHAIN

Figure 1. Conceptual Framework for Resilience and Sustainable Supply chain

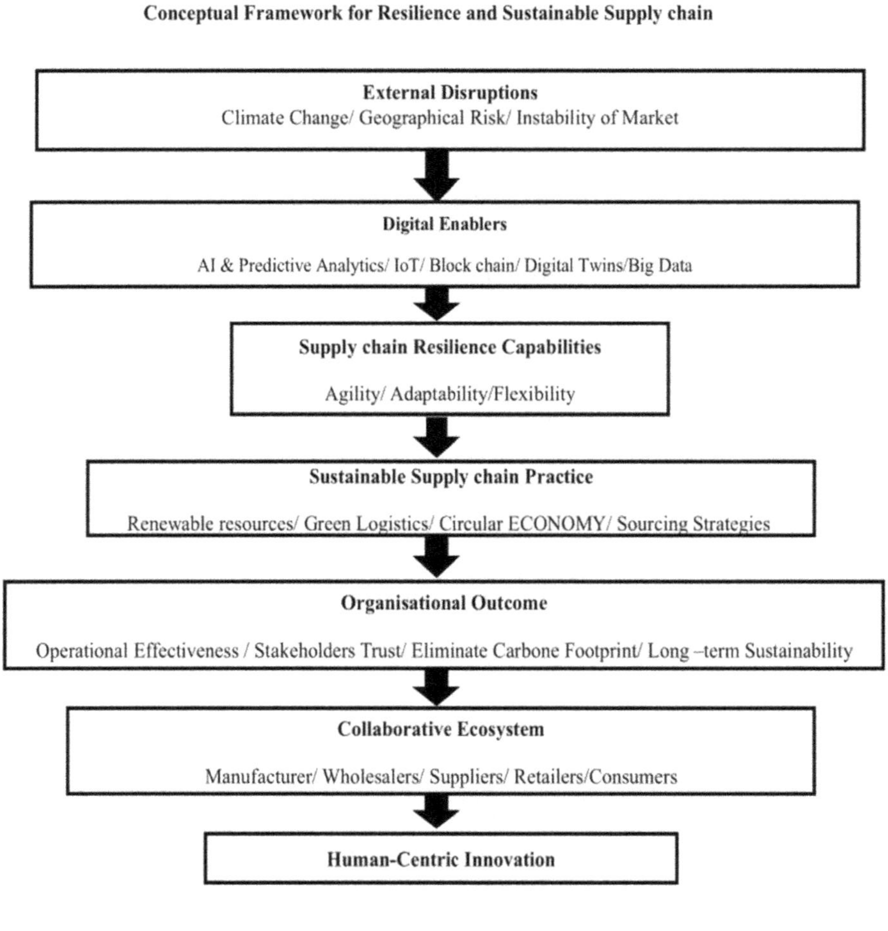

The conceptual framework indicates how technical facilitators, resilience capacities, outside forces and sustainable supply chain are progressively related. Typical supply chain operations are challenged by outside forces like market swings, geographical risk and climate change. Organisations use digital enablers like block chain, AI, digital twins, predictive analysis, IoT, and big data technologies to rectify these risks. By enhancing operational efficiency, agility and improve supply chain resilience. It also emphasis green logistics, circular economy, and ethical sourcing. In combination these strategies support corporate objectives like improve operational efficiency, stakeholder confidence and long-term sustainability. It promotes human-centric development in contemporary supply chain concludes by cooperative system of manufacturers, suppliers, wholesalers, retailers and customers.

4. METHODOLOGY

This study examines at recent developments in resilience and sustainable supply chain management using conceptual research methodology. This study focuses on a clear analysis of research on supply chain and as well as case studies. Secondary data were collected from books, journals, conference papers and report of top international companies. A concept oriented review technique was implemented to analyse an important themes like, resilience, supply chain and digital transformation technologies like, and block chain, digital twins and AI. Additionally selected case study from global sustainable supply chain practice was additionally examined.

This section explains the methodological strategies used to collect and analyse relevant data using both quantitative and qualitative data methods are in order to investigate the consequences of emerging technologies on supply chain durability and resilience sustainability. In specifically, the methodology uses case studies and expert professional interviews to gain insight into the real-world uses and challenges of incorporating modern technologies like block chain, artificial intelligence and the internet of things into complicated in supply chain operations (Halloway, 2025a, 2025b).

5. EMERGING TRENDS IN SUPPLY CHAIN MANAGEMENT

Emerging supply chains are leading constantly due to technological advances, concern about sustainability and global challenges. The future of supply chain management is changing by a number of emerging trends that help business become more resilient and sustainable. At the important serious of resilience and sustainability lies the concept of collaborative ecosystems, where alliance between suppliers, product manufacturers and consumers drive mutual growth. The emergence of industry 5.0 notifying human centric approaches, leveraging advanced technologies along with human creativity to get sustainable outcomes. This chapter dives into the convergence and eco-friendliness, delving into how this concept builds the next era of supply chain management. It assesses the upcoming trends cutting-edge methods and critical framework that empower the organisations to agile supply chains. This chapter also indicate the role of modern technologies, partnership driven ecosystem, and governance in driving sustainable outcomes.

5.1 Predictive Analysis and AI/ML

Supply chain decision-making has been significantly improved by the integration of AI, machine learning and predictive analytics. Organisations are able to predict demand fluctuations, identify potential problems, analyse enamours quantities of real time data and make proactive data.

Digital twin technology creates virtual models of supply chain system including logistic networks and operational procedures through digital twin technology. Organisations can identify operational barriers, efficient planning and stimulate various circumstances with the help of digital representations. Digital twin improves supply chain resilience while enabling effective decision making.

5.2 Block Chain Technology

It produce safe digital ledger for documenting supply chain transactions is made available by block chain technology. It reduces the possibility of threats and fraud and improves trust and stability. It makes digital ledger for documentation and confirming supply chain methods is made possible by block chain technology. It improves responsibility stability, security, confidence and transparency of suppliers.

5.3 Low Carbon Energy and Ethical Consideration

For the purpose of carbon emission, businesses are quickly implementing eco-friendly practices and renewable energy sources. Green logistic, energy efficient transportation and sustainable packaging are enhancing company reputation. These programme enhance ethical corporate practices and environmental sustainability. Green logistic provide to reducing environmental outcome through efficient distribution network and transportation. Sustainable options for packaging also encourage resource management and waste reduction.

5.4 Social and Ethical Consideration

Ethical labour policies, community involvement and ethical sourcing are growing more important in modern supply chain. In order to promote stakeholder trust and long –term sustainability are integrating corporate social responsibility. Ensuring fair working conditions and proper handling of employees through the supply chain is an important to organisation. Initiative of community involvement also supports social progress and moral business practices. Transparency and social responsibility in the purchase of raw material are made possible by ethical sourcing. Incorporating corporate social responsibility into their supply chain strategy is an effort to improve stakeholder confidence. It will enhance the standard and loyalty of supplier and customer.

5.5 Collaborative Ecosystem and Industry 5.0

Increasing effectiveness of innovation in the sustainable supply chain requires correlation between manufacturer, wholesaler, supplier and customer. Industry 5.0 is expansion of combine cutting edge technology with human creativity. Information exchange of data and operational effectiveness throughout the supply chain network are enhanced by efficient collaboration among various parties. Innovation and sustainable business practices are promoted by this kind of cooperation. Industry 5.0 further facilities this change. The human centred strategy increases supply chain system overall resilience and sustainable innovation.

5.6 Government and Regulations

Government plays an important role to promoting sustainable supply chain management through the way of regulations and collaborative systems. They establish environmental norms and regulations that motivate companies to implement ethical supply chain methods. Government programs indicate cooperation between institutions, business and stakeholders. Furthermore regulatory oversight ensure to sustainable standards. It will leads the sustainable standards and creation of coordination. Governments and international organisational play a crucial role in enforcing sustainability regulations and promoting responsible supply chain practices.

6. SUSTAINABLE SUPPLY CHAIN MANAGEMENT

SSCM integrates reduce negative environmental factors into supply chain operations and improve social and economic considerations. It places a strong emphasis on feasible operations, resource consumption and ethical labour standards. SSCM principles are cutting carbon emission, reducing waste production and optimum utilization of resources. To enhances sustainable and ethical supply chain operations, organisation promote aligning their supply chain policies with globally sustainable programs like the United Nations sustainable development goals and environmental management standards like ISO 14001.

6.1 Green Logistics and Energy Integration

Reducing the environmental impact of transport, distribution activities along the supply chain is the primary objective of green logistics. In an effort to reduce operating expenses and greenhouse emission, organisation are slowly implementing renewable energy sources and energy-efficient technologies. Organisation can enhance their environmental performance while maintaining operational efficiency by incorporating energy efficient stores, efficient logistic networks and emission of transport system. With the goal to reduce fuel consumption and improve delivery efficiency, modern technologies like AI are being appoint for improve logistic planning. By enabling it possible to recover recycle returned goods contribute sustainability.

6.2 Ethical Sourcing

Sustainable purchasing involved choosing supplier who commit with socially and environmentally conscious practices. Organisations are increasingly evaluate sustainable supplier such as ethical labour standards, responsible resource utilization and adherence with environmental regulation, ethical purchasing, fair wage, good working condition and raw material usage across global supply chain technologies like, block chains are also adapted to enhance transparency.

6.3 Circular Economy Model and Reduce Wastage

By promoting recycling, reuse and remanufacturing strategy is circular economy model. Supply chain improves the extending product life cycle and reclaiming value from used products as opposed to the linear model of manufacturing. Companies are following some strategies like product as a service model that promotes reuse, recycle and remanufacture and creating biodegradable packaging. Furthermore waste to energy helps with industrial waste into renewable energy sources. Which reduces garbage going to landfill, and it improves the production of sustainable energy.

6.4 The Role of AI in Sustainability

Supply chain operations are becoming eco-friendly in large part to automation technologies. In manufacturing and logistic processes, robotics and AI automation system improve operational efficiency, reduce waste and eliminate human error. Drone technology and self-driving cars are being have been used more and more to increase the final- mile delivery efficiency while reducing carbon and fuel consumption. Recycling facilities also make significant use of robotic separation devices to enhance material management procedures.AI-powered inventory management system also assist in businesses in reducing surplus inventory and improving production process.

6.5 Localisation Strategies and Sustainability

The process of adapting business operations goods and services to fix the cultural, economic and legal requirements of a particular local market is known as globalisation strategies. Employing the local workforce obtaining raw materials regionally and modifying products to regional preferences are all methods that apply localisation. This strategy increases market acceptance and strengthen with nearby communities. Localisation reduces transportation distance which reduces carbon emission and the impact on the environment from the perspective of sustainability. Additionally it supports regional economic development and support the proper use of regional asset. Business may affect the balance between ethical behaviour, environmental preservation and revenue growth by incorporating sustainability concept into localisation concept. It will support sustainable supply chain and long-term company resilience.

6.6 The Role of Robotics and Automation in Sustainability

Reducing carbon emission associated with long-distance transportation and logistics operation, local manufacturing are significantly promotes environmental sustainability. Faster supply chain promotes delivery efficiency while reducing fuel usage and greenhouse gas emission. Additionally local suppliers can use easily accessible renewable energy sources and implement circular economy techniques more successfully. Shorter time for journey also reduce product damage and degradation especially in perishable field like agriculture and food. Localised supply chain ideas that promotes both environmental sustainability and operational effectiveness.

6.7 Governance, Collaborations and Challenges in Sustainable Supply chain Management

In legislative framework, policy incentive programme and environmental guidelines, government and multinational organisations are permitted to implement responsible supply chain practices that reduce carbon emission while encouraging sustainable resources used by programs like the Paris of convention and the United Nations sustainable development goals. Sustainability certification and conformity to global standards like ISO 14001 promote ethical sourcing and environmental management. At the same time supply chain system are increasingly using digital technologies include blockchain, internet of things-based monitoring system and analytics driven by AI to improve transparency and compliance monitoring. Strong relationship between important parties that includes manufacturers, suppliers, and logistic companies are necessary for sustainable supply chain. Organisation can increase effectiveness of resource and encourage sustainable production and consumption methods through collaborative sustainable programs, circular economy projects and shared digital platforms.

However, there are a number of interruptions in the way of creating stable and sustainable supply chains. It deals with high initial expenditure for green technologies, uncertainty about return on investment. Sustainable practices is further complicated by organisational resistant to change, a shortage of technology know-how and the difficulty of supplier networks. Despite these obstacles, efficient governance, collaborative ecosystem and technological incorporation are essentials for establishing resilience and sustainable supply chain.

6.8 Implementation of Sustainable Supply Chain and Resilience

In the current global supply chains are vital channel for trade in the contemporary world, which is marked by extensive interconnected and quick challenges. They facilitate the continuous moments of goods and services among many geographical and economic system (SAIDI et, al 2024). Regarding business functioning in an increasingly unpredictable global context, developing resilience and sustainable supply chain processes has emerged as an essential strategic goal. Supply chain must be flexible and environmentally conscious due to rapid advances in technological breakthroughs, climate related challenges, political disputes and changing customer expectations. In order to promote real time monitoring, predictive analytics and agile technical procedures for greater responsiveness and flexibility, this is required for the need of integration with cutting edge technological solutions such as block chain, machine learning and artificial intelligence (Karanam et al 2024). By providing proactive risk reduction, resource allocation optimization and adhering to environmental, social and economic standard this dynamic integration improve supply chain operations economic viability and ethical reputation (Kazancoglu et al,. 2023; Samuels, 2025). The goal of supply chain management is to integrate factors while making certain that the system can withstand interruptions and bouncing from unforeseen events. The goal of this method reduce negative effects on the environment and improve social responsibility (Villar et al, 2023). This comprehensive strategies guarantees that business may utilize their supply chain as a strategic advantages instead of logical channels by finding a balance between profitability, social responsibility, and environmental responsibility (Zejjari & Benhayoun, 2024). Implementing innovative digital technologies is essential to building dependable and sustainable supply chains. To improve visibility and as well as coordination throughout supply chain system, are increasingly utilizing technologies like block chain, artificial intelligence and predictive analytics. In complicated global business environments, these technologies allow for optimum resource efficiency and risk mitigation through improved transparency and accountability (Ameh, 2024). The real-time activities are tracking, early interruption deduction and data-driven decision making become possible by these technologies. Organisation may adopts to hazard and unpredictability to transparency and exchange of information which stimulate resilience. Specifically AI makes real time data analysis to feasible environment for business and improving operational effectiveness and promoting sustainable objectives (Esan et al,. 2024). The development of adaptable and various sourcing techniques is another critical component of supply chain implementation. Businesses that concentrate significantly on small number of suppliers are more exposable to disruptions. In order to reduce resilience on a single supplier are increasingly implement multi sourcing methods and creating geographical supply networks. By cutting edge method enhance low risk, carbon emission and reduce waste. This chapter also explore the how sustainability initiatives are linked across supply chain management to not only concerning the fulfilment of regular compliances but also resonate with stakeholders. Additionally enabling real-time decision making and adaptive capabilities, the strategic incorporation of digital transformation efforts which include block chain, AI and agility (Enjeyo et al,. 2024, Halloway, 2025, Tariq 2025). Machine learning and artificial intelligence optimize transportation by forecasting demand and enhancing planning routes which lower than fuel consumption and cost (AI-Faouri et al, 2025). Another vital component of supply chain formulation strategies helps to improve sustainability. It will enhance the stand able method in globally. If these methods are following in prompt manner, the company will achieve their objectives, mission and vision without any interruptions. Sustainable procurement ensures that suppliers use production techniques that uphold the environment and logical labour standards. These initiatives improves stake holder trust and the company royalty while also when they reducing their efficiency.

7. CASE STUDIES

Case Study 1: Predictive Analysis in Retail Supply Chain

This case study examines at how a major retailer enhanced supply chain sustainable and resilience by using AI and predictive analytics. The business used real-time data analytics technologies to maintain on inventory levels, demand trends and possible supply network interruptions. By using risk assessment techniques, managers where able to make proactive and educated decisions that reduced operational disruptions, the system also improved inventory allocation and transportation planning, reduces overstock and unnecessary shipments and predictive models assisted the organisation to predict supply shortage, demand fluctuations and logical challenges before they developed.

Case Study 2: Block Chain for Zero Carbon Sustainability

IBM and Maersk worked together to build TradeLens, block chain enabled digital platform designed to improved transparency in international shipping processes. Block chain is used by the system to safely record and manage shipping operations among various logistics network stakeholders. The technology helps improve shipping transaction and cut down on needless transportation task by increasing data availability and decreasing inefficient documentation. These improvements assist in reducing carbon emission in worldwide supply system. Additionally, the platform stimulates cooperation between ports, shipping firms and logistic suppliers. Improve the openness lowers of possibility in corruption and enhances accountability. Therefore the international trading networks, block chain technology improves both environmental sustainability and operational effectiveness is stabled.

Case Study 3: Renewable Energy in the Manufacturing Supply Chain

The present investigation highlights how manufacturing companies are utilize renewable energy sources to improve supply chain sustainability. To reduce their dependence on oil and gas, businesses are increasingly incorporating solar and wind energy into their production facilities. These programs substantially improve manufacturing energy efficiency. Adoption of renewable energy additionally supports environmental goals. The establishment of clean energy technology improves supply chain resilience and encourages green manufacturing process. Businesses are better equipped to deal with changes in energy prices when they are less dependent and traditional sources of energy. This example demonstrates that renewable energy may be utilised to build supply chain that are sustainable.

Case Study 4: Localised Productions in Tesla Gigafactories

Tesla has deliberately built Gigafactories in several locations, in order to promote localised promotion and sustainable supply chain operations. Tesla reduces transportation distances and as well as carbon emission its locating its manufacturing factories nearer to important consumer market. This localisation reduces time to delivery and improves supply chain agility. Additionally the Gigafactories are constructed to run on energy-efficient technology and energy from sustainable. These methods significantly improve the manufacturing environmental sustainability. Additionally reducing resilience on extensive multinational logistic systems localised manufacturing and increasing supply chain resilience. This plan promotes employability, and regional development growth. Tesla strategy indicates localised manufacturing can improve both sustainability and organisational effectiveness. Tesla strategy shows how regional manufacturing can stimulate both operational effectiveness and sustainability for the environment.

Case Study 5: Sustainable Sourcing in Unilever

To encourage environmental and social responsibility, Unilever has implemented sustainable sourcing techniques across its worldwide supply chain. Acquiring raw materials from regional suppliers and small-scale producers is the primary objectives for the organisation. This approach promotes sustainable farming methods and reduces carbon emission caused by transportation. In order to make sure equal working conditions and suitable resource uses. Unilever also maintain close relationship with their suppliers. This cooperation will lead to maintain supply networks and sustainability certificate programs. This program promotes long term supply chain sustainability and increase trust of stakeholders. It demonstrates how the Unilever stand in market and its sustainability of supply chain.

Case Study 6: Localised Automated Production in Adidas Speed Factories

Adidas introduced to implements localized and highly automated manufacturing methods. These factories produced shoes closer to important customer markets through the cutting-edge robotics and automation technologies. Adias minimises needs to transportation and reduce carbon emission relates to global shipping by reduce dependence on faraway manufacturing hubs. The automation driven production system increases the efficiency of manufacturing and effectiveness of operations. Reduce production cycle enable the business to react quickly satisfy customer needs. By reducing the disruptions produced on international networks and increase resilience and supply chain. Using effective resources in speedfactory idea also promotes sustainable production methods. This example shows localization and technology may support resilient and supply chain management.

8. OUTCOME OF THE STUDY

Figure 2. Implementation of Resilience and Sustainable Supply Chain Practices

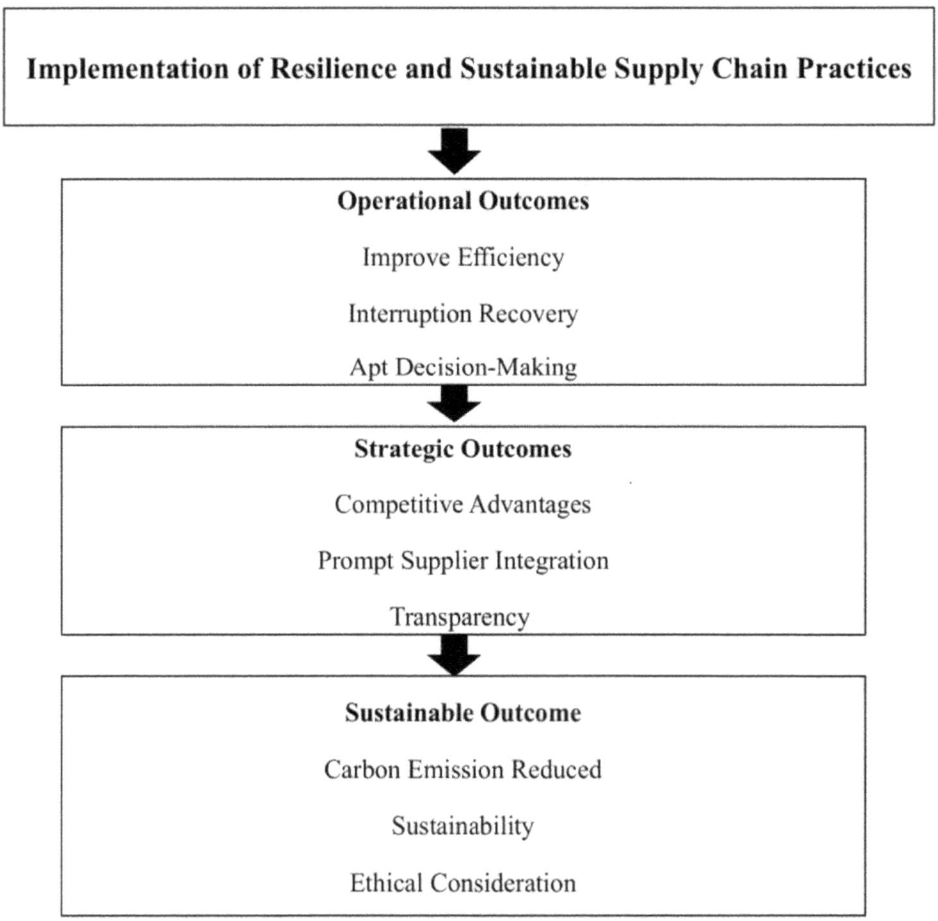

This diagram interprets the result of implementing resilience and sustainable supply chain practices. It suggest that companies who use strong and environmentally responsible supply chain strategies initially attain operational results such as increase productivity, faster recovery from interruptions and improve decision-making skills. The overall effectiveness and adaptability of supply chain system are enhanced by these operational innovations. Organisations gain benefit economically as a result, obtaining a competitive edge increasing supplier integration and improving supply chain network accessibility. Businesses may effectively react market fluctuation and global instability due to these strategic advantages. Implementing resilient and sustainable methods eventually results in sustainable outcomes including minimised carbon emission, better sustainability performance and increasingly ethical business practices.

9. FUTURE RESEARCH

The future research may investigate improve the resilience and supply chain sustainability process the incorporation of advanced digital technologies like block chain, AI, digital twins, and the IoT. Researcher can look into the ways that predictive analysis and continuous monitoring system assist proactive risk control and operational effectiveness. Further research may focus on how controlled inventory system and smart storage facilities may reduce waste and improve efficiency of resource use. In addition, future research may examine how well circular economy techniques such as recycling, up cycling and green logistic enhance the performance of sustainable supply chain.

Finding

The report highlights how supply chain management practices have greatly impacted in global interruptions like climate change, economy crises, political instability, and market volatility. Modern concerns are unable to be adequately addressed by traditional supply chain model that exclusively focus on efficiency. The outcomes indicate that in addition to maintain continues and long term stability; businesses are progressively incorporating sustainability and resilience into their supply chain strategy.

The growing significance of digital technology in strengthening supply chain resilience is one of the main finding of this study. Organisation can monitor supply chain activity within real time predict, disruption, and make data driven decision by increased visibility, transparency and collaborative work with supply chain networks. This study also finds that organisational effectiveness like flexibility, agility and modification of supply chain models. Businesses are better equipped with unexpected disturbances when they establish modified sourcing strategies, supplier system and logical networks. When faced the discomfort of this situation in business to quickly modify their manufacturing, sourcing and distribution of goods.

The growing importance of sustainability supply chain management process in real business world. Businesses have accepted eco-friendly tactics like sustainable buying, circular economy model, green logistics and the combination of renewable energy. It indicates stakeholders' trust and company reputation in the business environment. The result also shows that collaborative eco systems are essentials for enhancing resilience and sustainable supply chain. It encourages transparency, knowledge sharing, and risk bearing are best example to effective relationship between supplier and manufacturer. This kind of relationship will ensure the effective supply chain operations in the environment. Finally this study shows that implementing resilience and supply chain practices enhances several advantages to the company. It includes better supply chain transparency, carbon emission and effective competitive advantages. Overall, the result shows that creating supply chain that have been prepared for future calls for integrating technology innovation with surrounding activities.

Suggestion

Based on the finding of this study, number of strategic recommendations placed for companies seeking to improve sustainable supply chain management. To improve supply chain visibility, and predictive capabilities businesses should give top priority to using cutting edge digital technologies. AI identifies future hazards and interruption in supply chain operations.

Secondly, companies should focus on creating supply chain system that are flexible and varied. Sometimes, suppliers and political are make interruption between the smooth function of sustainability.

Thirdly, companies should integrate eco-friendly practices across their supply chain activity to further establishment of sustainability. It involves employing renewable energy sources, formulating green logistic solutions, cutting waste through circular economy models and supplying raw material are ethically.

Another important recommendation is to enhance collaboration among supply chain stakeholders. To promote information sharing co-ordinate decision making organisation should develop strong relationship with companies, suppliers and government. Digital eco system and collaborative platforms might improve supply networks and improve transparency.

Company want to invest in human-centred innovations and organisation development. Employees who receive training in digital technology, sustainable practices and risk management techniques will be more able to handle in supply chain systems.

Lastly, through international collaboration, incentives and legal frameworks, policy makers and government may promote supply chain efforts. Organisation may move toward more resilient and supply chain system with the support of green technologies carbon reduction and technology innovation.

10. CONCLUSION

Supply chains are increasingly embracing localization strategies to mitigate the risks, improve responsiveness, and reduce environmental impact by reducing global transportation requirements. The massive significant of global supply chain is undergoing transformation, climate change, political instability, technological improvements and fluctuating customer needs. In order to manage these issues and influence supply chain management going forward the concept of sustainable supply chain and resilience become essential ideas. It also combines with new developments, innovative methods and strategic framework for sustainable development. Collaborative system of industry 5.0 and data-driven decision-making which is ensures satisfaction of stakeholders and their long term survival. This Chapter also discusses the pivotal role of governance and sustainable supply chain. Governments and international organizations are driving agenda through stringent regulations, incentives for sustainable practices, and collaborative platforms to share best practices. The role of data-driven decision-making in compliance monitoring and reporting further enhances accountability and transparency across the supply chain. The incorporation of flexibility and sustainability in supply chain management is mandatory for managing the complexities of the modern business environment. By embracing innovative practices, advanced technologies, and collaborative approaches, organisations can build eco-friendly and resilient supply chain that meet stakeholder expectations and contribute to long-term viability.

REFERENCES

Al-Faouri, E. H., Huson, Y. A., Alkrarha, A. S., Aljawarneh, N. M., & Alqmoo, T. J. (2025). Mapping the landscape: A bibliometric analysis of digital leadership, service quality, and supply chain management. *Uncertain Supply Chain Management, 13*(3), 543–556. DOI: 10.5267/j.uscm.2024.8.013

Ameh, B. (2024). Technology-integrated sustainable supply chains: Balancing domestic policy goals, global stability, and economic growth. *International Journal of Science and Research Archive, 13*(2), 1811–1828. DOI: 10.30574/ijsra.2024.13.2.2369

Amoozad Mahdiraji, H., Yaftiyan, F., Garza-Reyes, J. A., Razavi Hajiagha, S. H., & Kazancoglu, Y. (2024). Decarbonised closed-loop supply chains resilience: Examining the impact of COVID-19 toward risk mitigation by a fuzzy multi-layer decision-making framework. *Annals of Operations Research*. Advance online publication. DOI: 10.1007/s10479-024-06093-3

Anagnostakos, P. (2024). *Balancing resilience and sustainability: Tensions, trade-offs, and strategies for multinational enterprises in a complex global landscape*. https://doi.org/DOI: 10.2139/ssrn.5074123

Bamia, A., & Bamia, F. (2025). SCRGD: Supply chain resilience in the face of global disruptions. *International Business Research, 18*(2), 80. DOI: 10.5539/ibr.v18n2p80

Choi, T.-M., Dolgui, A., Li, G., Sethi, S. P., & Yue, X. (2023). Special issue: Advancing supply chain resilience for excellence in the post-pandemic era. *Frontiers of Engineering Management, 10*(1), 1–4. DOI: 10.1007/s42524-022-0246-9

Enyejo, J. O., Adeyemi, A. F., Olola, T. M., Igba, E., & Obani, O. Q. (2024). Resilience in supply chains: How technology is helping USA companies navigate disruptions. *Magna Scientia Advanced Research and Reviews, 11*(2), 261–277. DOI: 10.30574/msarr.2024.11.2.0129

Esan, O., Ajayi, F. A., & Olawale, O. (2024). Supply chain integrating sustainability and ethics: Strategies for modern supply chain management. *World Journal of Advanced Research and Reviews, 22*(1), 1930–1953. DOI: 10.30574/wjarr.2024.22.1.1259

Faggioni, F., Rossi, M. V., & Sestino, A. (2024). Conceptualizing supply chain resilience in exogenous crisis times: Toward a holistic definition. *Journal of the Knowledge Economy, 15*(4), 17308–17332. Advance online publication. DOI: 10.1007/s13132-024-01816-0

Kareem, S., Fehrer, J. A., Shalpegin, T., & Stringer, C. (2025). Navigating tensions of sustainable supply chains in times of multiple crises: A systematic literature review. *Business Strategy and the Environment*, *34*(1), 316–337. DOI: 10.1002/bse.3990

Kazancoglu, I., Ozbiltekin-Pala, M., Mangla, S. K., Kumar, A., & Kazancoglu, Y. (2023). Using emerging technologies to improve the sustainability and resilience of supply chains in a fuzzy environment in the context of COVID-19. *Annals of Operations Research*, *322*(1), 217–240. DOI: 10.1007/s10479-022-04775-4 PMID: 35789688

Mathiyazhagan, K., Majumdar, A., & Appolloni, A. (2023). Guest editorial: Resilience in sustainable supply chain post-COVID-19: future pathways. *International Journal of Logistics Management*, *34*(4), 873–878. DOI: 10.1108/IJLM-07-2023-603

Odulaja, B. A., Oke, T. T., Eleogu, T., Abdul, A. A., & Daraojimba, H. O. (2023). Resilience in the face of uncertainty: A review on the impact of supply chain volatility amid ongoing Geopolitical Disruptions. *International Journal of Applied Research in Social Sciences*, *5*(10), 463–486. DOI: 10.51594/ijarss.v5i10.634

Odulaja, B. A., Oke, T. T., Eleogu, T., Abdul, A. A., & Daraojimba, H. O. (2023). Resilience in the face of uncertainty: A review on the impact of supply chain volatility amid ongoing Geopolitical Disruptions. *International Journal of Applied Research in Social Sciences*, *5*(10), 463–486. DOI: 10.51594/ijarss.v5i10.634

Saidi, D., Bassou, A. A., Alami, J. E. L., & Hlyal, M. (2024). Sustainability and resilience analysis in supply chain considering pricing policies and government economic measures. *International Journal of Advanced Computer Science and Applications*, *15*(1). Advance online publication. DOI: 10.14569/IJACSA.2024.0150127

Samuels, A. (2025). Digital transformation in supply chains: Improving resilience and sustainability through AI, Blockchain, and IoT. *Frontiers in Sustainability*, *6*(1584580), 1584580. Advance online publication. DOI: 10.3389/frsus.2025.1584580

Samuels, A. (2025). Digital transformation in supply chains: Improving resilience and sustainability through AI, Blockchain, and IoT. *Frontiers in Sustainability*, *6*(1584580), 1584580. Advance online publication. DOI: 10.3389/frsus.2025.1584580

Shamsuzzoha, A., & Pelkonen, S. (2025). A robotic process automation model for order-handling optimization in supply chain management. *Supply Chain Analytics*, *9*(100102), 100102. DOI: 10.1016/j.sca.2025.100102

Singh, P. K. K. (2024). Measuring the broader value proposition of digital transformation in supply chains. *International Journal of Supply Chain Management*, *13*(1), 16–24. DOI: 10.59160/ijscm.v13i1.6222

Steegh, R., Van De Voorde, K., Paauwe, J., & Peeters, T. (2025). The agile way of working and team adaptive performance: A goal-setting perspective. *Journal of Business Research, 189*, 115163.

Vadigicherla, M. S. (2024). Enhancing Supply Chain Resilience through Emerging Technologies: A Holistic Approach to Digital Transformation. *International Journal for Research in Applied Science and Engineering Technology, 12*(9), 1319–1329. DOI: 10.22214/ijraset.2024.64326

Villar, A., Paladini, S., & Buckley, O. (2023). Towards supply chain 5.0: Redesigning supply chains as resilient, sustainable, and human-centric systems in a post-pandemic world. *Operations Research Forum, 4*(3). https://doi.org/DOI: 10.1007/s43069-023-00234-3

Zejjari, I., & Benhayoun, I. (2024). The use of artificial intelligence to advance sustainable supply chain: Retrospective and future avenues explored through bibliometric analysis. *Discover Sustainability, 5*(1), 174. Advance online publication. DOI: 10.1007/s43621-024-00364-6

Chapter 3
The Role of Artificial Intelligence in Transforming Global Supply Chains

D. Ramkumar
http://orcid.org/0000-0001-9706-4980
Sri Meenakshi Government Arts College for Women, India

N. Poorna Chelvan
http://orcid.org/0000-0002-6424-2514
NMS S. Vellaichamy Nadar College, India

S. Vijayanand
http://orcid.org/0000-0002-3754-471X
Government Arts and Science College, Idappadi, India

ABSTRACT

This chapter investigates the transformative impact of Artificial Intelligence (AI) on global supply chains, highlighting its role as a catalyst for innovation and efficiency. It begins with an overview of the complexities and evolution of supply chain management, setting the stage for AI's emergence as a disruptive technology. By examining key AI technologies such as machine learning, natural language processing, and robotics, the chapter illustrates how AI enhances demand forecasting, inventory optimization, logistics, and predictive maintenance. The integration of Big Data and the Internet of Things (IoT) further amplifies AI's capabilities, enabling real-time insights and end-to-end operational visibility. While discussing the benefits—such as cost reduction, risk mitigation, and sustainability—the chapter

DOI: 10.4018/979-8-2600-1855-2.ch003

also addresses challenges like data privacy concerns, high implementation costs, and ethical considerations. Concluding with actionable recommendations, it underscores the urgency for organizations to embrace AI to remain competitive in a dynamic global marketplace.

1. INTRODUCTION

The introduction sets the foundation for understanding the transformative role of Artificial Intelligence (AI) in global supply chains. It explores how supply chains operate in an interconnected world, traces their historical evolution, highlights the emergence of AI as a game-changing technology, and defines the scope and objectives of the chapter.

1.1 Overview of Global Supply Chains

Global supply chains are the backbone of modern economies, facilitating the production, transportation, and delivery of goods and services across regions. These networks interconnect manufacturers, suppliers, distributors, and retailers to ensure seamless operations and customer satisfaction. Over time, global supply chains have grown increasingly complex, with companies relying on international sourcing and just-in-time inventory systems. However, challenges such as fluctuating demand, geopolitical tensions, and disruptions like pandemics have exposed vulnerabilities in traditional supply chains. This section provides a complete overview of how global supply chains function and the pressing need for innovation to address inefficiencies and disruptions.

1.2 Evolution of Supply Chain Management

Supply chain management (SCM) has undergone significant evolution, from manual tracking and planning to digitized and data-driven operations. In the 20th century, the focus was on improving logistics and inventory management. The advent of computers and Enterprise Resource Planning (ERP) systems marked the digitalization of supply chains, enabling better coordination and resource utilization. Over the past two decades, advancements in analytics, cloud computing, and the Internet of Things (IoT) have further enhanced supply chain efficiency. This section traces the milestones in SCM's journey and highlights the limitations of traditional methods, which have paved the way for AI-driven innovations (Parkhi, *et al.* 2015).

1.3 The Emergence of Artificial Intelligence (AI)

AI has emerged as a transformative force in supply chain management, offering unprecedented capabilities in data processing, predictive analytics, and automation. By leveraging machine learning, natural language processing, and computer vision, AI enables organizations to predict demand patterns, optimize inventory, and enhance decision-making processes. The integration of AI into supply chains addresses critical challenges such as inefficiencies, delays, and resource misallocation. This section examines the rise of AI as a disruptive technology, showcasing its potential to revolutionize global supply chains and meet the demands of an increasingly everchanging and competitive business environment (Goul, *et al.* 1992).

1.4 Objectives and Scope of the Chapter

The chapter aims to explore the multifaceted role of AI in transforming global supply chains, focusing on its applications, benefits, and challenges. It provides an in-depth analysis of how AI technologies are reshaping supply chain operations, improving efficiency, and addressing real-world challenges such as supply chain disruptions, sustainability concerns, and shifting consumer expectations. The chapter also discusses case studies and future trends to highlight the potential of AI-driven supply chains. By offering actionable insights and recommendations, this chapter seeks to inform academics, practitioners, and policymakers about the critical role of AI in shaping the future of global supply chain management.

2. UNDERSTANDING ARTIFICIAL INTELLIGENCE IN THE SUPPLY CHAIN CONTEXT

Artificial Intelligence (AI) has become a cornerstone of modern supply chain management, offering innovative solutions to enhance efficiency, reduce costs, and improve decision-making processes. This section investigates into the definition of AI in supply chains, examines the key AI technologies transforming the industry, and explores the role of Big Data and the Internet of Things (IoT) in enhancing AI integration.

2.1 Defining Artificial Intelligence in Supply Chains

Artificial Intelligence in supply chains refers to the application of intelligent algorithms, machine learning models, and automated systems to optimize and streamline supply chain processes. Unlike traditional supply chain management, which relies heavily on manual intervention and static decision-making, AI introduces active, data-driven approaches that adapt to changing market conditions in real-time. AI in this context is used for tasks such as demand forecasting, route optimization, inventory management, and anomaly detection. By leveraging AI, organizations can predict disruptions, improve operational efficiency, and achieve greater resilience in their supply chains.

2.2 AI Technologies Relevant to Supply Chains

AI's transformative impact on supply chains is driven by a suite of advanced technologies. Each plays a unique role in addressing specific challenges within the supply chain ecosystem:

- **Machine Learning (ML):**

ML enables systems to learn from historical data and improve their performance over time. In supply chains, ML is widely used for demand forecasting, inventory optimization, and identifying patterns in supplier performance. It helps in making accurate predictions about future trends and minimizing inefficiencies (Daios, *et al.* 2025).

- **Natural Language Processing (NLP):**

NLP is utilized for processing and analyzing text or speech data. In supply chains, it powers chatbots, customer service automation, and contract analysis. For example, NLP can streamline communication between suppliers, customers, and logistics providers by extracting key insights from emails, invoices, or procurement documents (Aslam & Calghan, 2023).

- **Robotic Process Automation (RPA):**

RPA automates repetitive and rule-based tasks such as order processing, invoice generation, and shipment tracking. By reducing manual errors and accelerating these processes, RPA enhances efficiency and allows supply chain professionals to focus on strategic tasks (Stevens, 2023).

- **Computer Vision:**

Computer vision uses image and video recognition to monitor physical assets in real-time. In warehouses and production facilities, it is used for quality control, inventory counting, and ensuring compliance with safety standards. It can also track shipments and detect damages during transit (Polo, 2025).

- **Predictive Analytics:**

Predictive analytics uses AI algorithms to analyse historical data and forecast future outcomes. In supply chains, it predicts demand fluctuations, identifies potential bottlenecks, and recommends proactive solutions to mitigate risks. This ensures smoother operations and improved customer satisfaction (Adewusi, *et al.* 2024).

2.3 Role of Big Data and IoT in Enhancing AI Integration

The integration of AI into supply chains is significantly enhanced by the availability of Big Data and the connectivity enabled by the Internet of Things (IoT) (Susatyono, *et al.* 2024).

- **Big Data:**

Modern supply chains generate vast amounts of data from various sources, including sales records, transportation logs, and customer feedback. Big Data analytics processes this information to uncover trends, patterns, and insights. AI algorithms thrive on these large datasets, using them to train models and improve decision-making accuracy. For example, analysing Big Data allows AI systems to predict demand surges during peak seasons and optimize inventory accordingly.

- **Internet of Things (IoT):**

IoT devices, such as smart sensors and connected machinery, provide real-time data on the condition, location, and status of goods and equipment. This data feeds into AI systems, enabling real-time monitoring and proactive management. For instance, IoT sensors in shipping containers can alert managers about temperature changes, allowing immediate corrective action to prevent spoilage of perishable goods.

Together, Big Data and IoT create a robust foundation for AI to deliver actionable insights and transformative solutions in supply chain management, ensuring efficiency, resilience, and customer satisfaction.

3. APPLICATIONS OF AI IN SUPPLY CHAIN TRANSFORMATION

Artificial Intelligence (AI) has revolutionized supply chain management by offering innovative solutions to longstanding challenges. By automating processes, providing real-time insights, and enabling data-driven decision-making, AI applications are transforming every stage of the supply chain. This section explores the key areas where AI is making a significant impact.

3.1 Demand Forecasting and Inventory Optimization

AI enhances demand forecasting by analysing large datasets from various sources, including historical sales, market trends, weather patterns, and customer behavior. Machine learning algorithms identify patterns and predict future demand with high accuracy, helping organizations avoid overstocking or understocking. For inventory optimization, AI dynamically adjusts stock levels based on predicted demand, reducing holding costs and ensuring product availability. For example, retail giants like Amazon use AI to optimize inventory placement in warehouses, improving fulfilment speed and customer satisfaction (Nweje & Taiwo, 2025).

3.2 Supply Chain Planning and Scheduling

AI-powered tools enable precise and well-organized supply chain planning by integrating real-time data from suppliers, manufacturers, and logistics providers. These systems use optimization algorithms to balance supply and demand, allocate resources effectively, and minimize delays. In scheduling, AI automates complex processes such as production sequencing and workforce allocation. For instance, AI can predict delays in manufacturing due to material shortages and suggest alternative plans, ensuring uninterrupted operations (Dash, *et al.* 2019).

3.3 Predictive Maintenance of Equipment

AI is critical in predictive maintenance, where sensors and IoT devices collect real-time data on equipment performance. Machine learning models analyze this data to predict potential failures before they occur, reducing downtime and repair costs. Predictive maintenance is particularly beneficial in manufacturing and logistics, where unplanned equipment failures can disrupt the entire supply chain. For example, in a factory setting, AI can detect anomalies in machine vibrations and recommend maintenance actions to prevent breakdowns (Ucar, *et al.* 2024).

3.4 Logistics and Transportation Management

AI optimizes logistics and transportation by improving route planning, load optimization, and delivery schedules. Algorithms analyse traffic patterns, weather conditions, and delivery constraints to identify the most efficient routes, reducing fuel consumption and delivery times. AI also enables real-time tracking of shipments, enhancing visibility and customer satisfaction. Autonomous vehicles and drones, powered by AI, are becoming increasingly common for last-mile delivery, offering cost-effective and faster solutions. Companies like UPS and DHL leverage AI to streamline their logistics operations and improve delivery reliability (Bhargava, *et al.* 2022).

3.5 Warehouse Automation and Robotics

AI is transforming warehouses into smart, automated environments. Robotic systems equipped with AI manage tasks such as sorting, picking, and packing goods with high speed and precision. AI also optimizes warehouse layout and operations by analysing data on item movement and storage patterns. For instance, Amazon's AI-powered robotic systems efficiently manage inventory and reduce processing times, enabling faster order fulfilment. Also, computer vision technologies assist in inventory tracking and quality control (Sodiya, *et al.* 2024).

3.6 Supplier Relationship Management and Risk Assessment

AI enhances supplier relationship management by analysing supplier performance data and providing insights into reliability, quality, and delivery times. This helps organizations select the best suppliers and negotiate favourable terms. AI also plays a crucial role in risk assessment by monitoring geopolitical events, economic trends, and supplier-specific risks. For example, AI systems can predict supply chain disruptions caused by natural disasters or political instability and recommend alternative sourcing strategies. By proactively identifying and mitigating risks, organizations can maintain resilient supply chains (Nasir & Butt, 2025).

The applications of AI in supply chain management are vast and transformative, driving efficiency, reducing costs, and improving decision-making across all levels. From predicting demand to optimizing logistics, AI has become an indispensable tool for organizations looking to maintain a competitive edge in the global market. These advancements not only streamline operations but also enhance resilience and adaptability, ensuring supply chains are future-ready.

4. BENEFITS OF AI IN GLOBAL SUPPLY CHAINS

The integration of Artificial Intelligence (AI) into global supply chains has led to significant advancements, addressing long-standing challenges while unlocking new opportunities for growth, efficiency, and customer satisfaction. This section highlights the key benefits AI offers in transforming global supply chains.

4.1 Improved Efficiency and Cost Reduction

AI-powered automation significantly improves efficiency by streamlining repetitive tasks, such as order processing, inventory management, and scheduling. By reducing manual intervention, AI minimizes errors and accelerates operations. Predictive analytics optimizes production schedules and inventory levels, ensuring that resources are utilized efficiently and waste is minimized. Furthermore, AI enhances transportation management through route optimization, reducing fuel consumption and delivery times. Collectively, these improvements lead to substantial cost savings for organizations, allowing them to allocate resources to strategic initiatives (Shil, *et al.* 2024).

4.2 Enhanced Decision-Making Through Real-Time Data Insights

AI leverages real-time data from IoT devices, sensors, and external sources, such as market trends and weather forecasts, to provide actionable insights. Advanced algorithms analyze this data to identify patterns, forecast demand, and predict potential disruptions. This enables supply chain managers to make informed, data-driven decisions that enhance operational agility and responsiveness. For example, AI can identify a sudden spike in demand for a product and trigger adjustments in production and logistics to meet customer needs without delays (Alonge, *et al.* 2023).

4.3 Mitigating Risks and Enhancing Resilience

AI enhances supply chain resilience by identifying and mitigating risks before they escalate into disruptions. Machine learning models analyse historical data and external factors, such as geopolitical events and natural disasters, to predict potential risks. AI also provides organizations with contingency plans by recommending alternative suppliers, routes, or inventory strategies. For instance, during the COVID-19 pandemic, AI-enabled supply chains were better equipped to adapt to sudden changes in demand and supply, minimizing the impact of disruptions (Riad, *et al.,* 2024).

4.4 Sustainability and Waste Reduction

Sustainability is a growing priority for organizations, and AI plays a critical role in achieving this goal. AI-driven solutions optimize resource utilization, reduce energy consumption, and minimize waste across supply chain operations. For example, AI can identify inefficiencies in production processes, such as overproduction or excessive energy use, and suggest corrective measures. Also, AI enhances reverse logistics, enabling efficient recycling and reuse of materials, contributing to a circular economy. These efforts not only reduce the environmental footprint but also align with consumer demand for eco-friendly practices (Dauvergne, 2022).

4.5 Personalization and Customer-Centric Supply Chains

AI empowers organizations to create more personalized and customer-centric supply chains by analysing customer preferences, purchasing behavior, and feedback. Machine learning models segment customers based on their needs and recommend tailored products, delivery options, and services. AI also enables dynamic pricing strategies and personalized marketing campaigns, enhancing customer satisfaction and loyalty. For example, e-commerce platforms use AI to recommend products and optimize delivery timelines based on individual customer preferences, creating a seamless and satisfying shopping experience (Charles, *et al.* 2023).

The benefits of AI in global supply chains extend beyond operational improvements, fostering resilience, sustainability, and customer satisfaction. By integrating AI, organizations can achieve a competitive edge in an increasingly dynamic and demanding global market. These advancements not only address immediate challenges but also position businesses for long-term success by building agile, efficient, and customer-focused supply chains.

5. CHALLENGES IN AI IMPLEMENTATION

While Artificial Intelligence (AI) offers transformative potential for global supply chains, its implementation is not without challenges. Organizations must address several technical, financial, and ethical barriers to fully harness AI's capabilities. This section explores the key challenges that organizations face when integrating AI into supply chain operations.

5.1 Data Privacy and Security Concerns

AI relies heavily on vast amounts of data to function effectively, and this dependence raises significant concerns about data privacy and security. Supply chains often handle sensitive data, including customer information, supplier details, and financial records. Ensuring this data is securely stored, transmitted, and processed is critical, as any breach could lead to significant reputational and financial losses. Furthermore, adhering to stringent data privacy regulations, such as GDPR in Europe and CCPA in California, adds complexity to AI implementation. Organizations must invest in robust cybersecurity measures to protect their data ecosystems while maintaining compliance with regional and global standards (Devineni, 2024).

5.2 High Implementation Costs and ROI Issues

The initial investment required for AI implementation is often a significant barrier, particularly for small and medium-sized enterprises (SMEs). Costs include acquiring AI technologies, upgrading infrastructure, and training employees. Also, organizations may face challenges in quantifying the return on investment (ROI) from AI projects, especially in the early stages. The benefits of AI, such as improved efficiency and cost savings, may take time to materialize, leading to hesitation among businesses to commit to large-scale AI adoption (Mun, *et al.* 2020).

5.3 Skills Gap and Workforce Resistance

The successful deployment of AI requires a workforce skilled in data analytics, machine learning, and AI programming. However, many organizations face a shortage of such expertise, creating a skills gap that hinders AI adoption. Furthermore, workforce resistance to AI is a common challenge, as employees may fear job displacement or struggle to adapt to new technologies. Addressing these concerns requires organizations to invest in upskilling programs and create a culture of collaboration where AI is viewed as an enabler rather than a threat to jobs (Babashahi, *et al.* 2024).

5.4 Integration With Legacy Systems

Many organizations operate on legacy systems that lack the infrastructure and compatibility to support AI technologies. Integrating AI into these outdated systems is often a complex and costly process. Legacy systems may not have the necessary data storage, processing capabilities, or connectivity required for AI operations. Also, the lack of standardization across different systems further complicates integration.

Organizations must modernize their IT infrastructure and adopt interoperable systems to enable seamless AI deployment (Singh & Adhikari, 2023).

5.5 Ethical and Regulatory Issues

AI introduces ethical challenges, such as bias in algorithms, lack of transparency, and the potential misuse of data. For example, biased AI models can result in unfair supplier evaluations or discriminatory pricing strategies. Besides, regulatory frameworks for AI are still evolving, creating uncertainty for businesses regarding compliance. Organizations must adopt ethical AI practices, such as ensuring fairness, accountability, and transparency in their algorithms, and stay informed about emerging regulations to mitigate risks (Mennella, *et al.* 2024).

The challenges in implementing AI in supply chains are multifaceted, ranging from technical barriers to ethical dilemmas. Addressing these issues requires a strategic approach, including investments in infrastructure, workforce development, and robust governance frameworks. By overcoming these challenges, organizations can unlock the full potential of AI and drive sustainable, efficient, and innovative supply chain transformation.

6. FUTURE TRENDS AND OPPORTUNITIES IN AI-DRIVEN SUPPLY CHAINS

The future of global supply chains is being reshaped by advancements in Artificial Intelligence (AI), which is creating opportunities for unprecedented innovation, efficiency, and sustainability. As organizations embrace AI-driven solutions, new trends and technologies are emerging that will further revolutionize supply chain management. This section explores the key trends and opportunities that lie ahead in AI-driven supply chains.

6.1 Role of AI in Enabling Autonomous Supply Chains

The concept of fully autonomous supply chains is rapidly gaining traction, where AI systems manage end-to-end processes with minimal human intervention. Autonomous supply chains leverage AI to automate tasks such as demand forecasting, procurement, production scheduling, and delivery. These systems can dynamically adapt to changes in real-time, ensuring resilience and efficiency. For instance, AI-driven predictive analytics can detect disruptions in supply, automatically reconfigure routes, and place orders with alternative suppliers. As AI technologies mature, autonomous supply chains are expected to become the standard, enabling businesses to operate seamlessly in an increasingly volatile global environment (Radhakrishnan, *et al.* 2025).

6.2 Blockchain and AI Integration for Transparent Supply Chains

The integration of blockchain technology with AI presents a powerful solution for enhancing transparency and traceability in supply chains. Blockchain provides a secure and immutable ledger for recording transactions, while AI analyses this data to detect patterns, predict risks, and optimize operations. Together, these technologies enable end-to-end visibility, ensuring accountability across the supply chain. For example, in the food industry, blockchain and AI can trace the journey of products from farm to table, ensuring quality and authenticity. This integration also helps combat fraud, reduce counterfeiting, and build consumer trust (Talla, 2022).

6.3 AI-Powered Circular Economy Models

AI is playing a pivotal role in advancing circular economy models, which aim to minimize waste and maximize resource efficiency. AI technologies enable organizations to design sustainable supply chains by optimizing product lifecycles, facilitating recycling, and reducing energy consumption. For instance, AI-powered reverse logistics systems can identify reusable materials and streamline their recovery and reintegration into production processes. By leveraging AI to monitor and manage resources, businesses can achieve greater sustainability while reducing costs and meeting environmental regulations (Sikander, 2024).

6.4 Advancements in AI-Powered Robotics and Drones

The adoption of AI-powered robotics and drones is revolutionizing supply chain operations, particularly in warehousing and logistics. Robots equipped with AI are being used for tasks such as sorting, packing, and transporting goods with unmatched precision and speed. Drones are increasingly being deployed for last-mile delivery, offering faster and more cost-effective solutions. AI also enables these technologies to operate autonomously, making real-time decisions based on data inputs. For example, drones equipped with computer vision can identify the optimal delivery route, avoiding obstacles and reducing delivery times. As these technologies continue to advance, they promise to significantly enhance efficiency and reduce labour-intensive processes (George, 2025).

6.5 The Role of Quantum Computing in Supply Chain Optimization

Quantum computing represents the next frontier in supply chain optimization. By leveraging quantum algorithms, businesses can solve complex problems that are currently beyond the reach of classical computing. For instance, quantum computing can optimize logistics networks, reduce transportation costs, and improve production schedules by processing vast amounts of data simultaneously. Quantum-enabled AI systems can also enhance predictive analytics, providing more accurate forecasts and enabling proactive decision-making. While still in its early stages, quantum computing holds immense potential to transform supply chains by unlocking levels of efficiency and accuracy previously unimaginable (Hassan, *et al.* 2024).

The future of AI-driven supply chains is characterized by innovation, sustainability, and adaptability. Technologies such as autonomous systems, blockchain integration, circular economy models, robotics, and quantum computing are redefining the boundaries of what is possible in supply chain management. By staying ahead of these trends and embracing these opportunities, businesses can create resilient, efficient, and sustainable supply chains that are well-equipped to meet the demands of a rapidly evolving global scenario.

7. RECOMMENDATIONS FOR SUCCESSFUL AI ADOPTION IN SUPPLY CHAINS

Adopting AI in supply chains is not merely about implementing advanced technology; it requires a holistic transformation of processes, culture, and strategic planning. Below are detailed recommendations to ensure the successful adoption of AI in supply chains.

7.1 Building an AI-Ready Organizational Culture

Creating a culture that embraces AI is fundamental for smooth adoption. Organizations must:

- **Foster Awareness and Acceptance:** Educate employees about the benefits of AI and its potential to enhance productivity rather than replace jobs.
- **Encourage Innovation:** Promote a mindset that values experimentation, agility, and resilience in adapting to new technologies.

- **Facilitate Cross-Functional Collaboration:** Encourage teams from IT, operations, and supply chain management to work together to understand AI's capabilities and limitations.
- **Communicate a Clear Vision:** Align AI initiatives with the organization's broader strategic goals, ensuring stakeholders at all levels understand the purpose and expected outcomes.

7.2 Investment in AI Skills Development and Talent Acquisition

For AI to thrive in supply chain management, organizations must address the human capital component by:

- **Upskilling the Workforce:** Offer training programs in AI-related skills, such as data analytics, machine learning, and programming, to existing employees.
- **Hiring Specialized Talent:** Recruit experts in AI, data science, and supply chain analytics to fill critical skill gaps.
- **Partnering with Educational Institutions:** Collaborate with universities and technical schools to develop tailored programs that prepare future employees for AI-centric roles.
- **Encouraging Continuous Learning:** Create a culture of lifelong learning to ensure employees remain adept at leveraging emerging AI technologies.

7.3 Leveraging Collaborative AI Ecosystems

No single organization can unlock the full potential of AI in isolation. Collaboration is key, and businesses should:

- **Engage with Technology Partners:** Partner with AI solution providers to customize and implement technologies suited to specific supply chain needs.
- **Participate in Industry Consortia:** Join industry groups to share knowledge, best practices, and case studies regarding AI applications in supply chains.
- **Integrate Supply Chain Stakeholders:** Collaborate with suppliers, distributors, and logistics providers to ensure AI solutions optimize the entire value chain.
- **Adopt Open Innovation Models:** Encourage co-creation of AI-driven solutions by involving external innovators and startups.

7.4 Addressing Ethical and Legal Implications

AI adoption comes with ethical and legal considerations that organizations must proactively address:

- **Ensure Data Privacy and Security:** Establish robust protocols to protect sensitive supply chain data and comply with global regulations such as GDPR and CCPA.
- **Promote Transparency and Fairness:** Design AI systems to avoid biases in decision-making processes, ensuring fair treatment across all supply chain stakeholders.
- **Define Accountability:** Clearly outline responsibility for AI-driven decisions to prevent ambiguity and build trust in the system.
- **Assess Environmental Impact:** Implement AI solutions that align with sustainability goals, such as optimizing transportation routes to reduce carbon emissions.

7.5 Developing Scalable and Flexible AI Solutions

AI solutions should be designed with long-term scalability and adaptability in mind to accommodate future needs. Organizations can achieve this by:

- **Implementing Modular Architectures:** Build AI systems with modular components that can be updated or expanded as new capabilities emerge.
- **Prioritizing Interoperability:** Ensure AI technologies seamlessly integrate with existing supply chain management systems and future technologies.
- **Emphasizing Real-Time Analytics:** Use AI for real-time monitoring and predictive analytics to respond swiftly to market changes or disruptions.
- **Testing and Iterating:** Pilot AI projects in controlled environments, gather feedback, and refine solutions before scaling across the supply chain.

By embracing these recommendations, organizations can harness the transformative power of AI to enhance supply chain efficiency, agility, and resilience in a competitive global market.

8. CONCLUSION

The conclusion ties together the key insights into how AI is transforming supply chains and outlines the broader implications for businesses and the global economy. It also serves as a rallying call for organizations to embrace AI to remain competitive in an increasingly digital world.

8.1 Summary of AI's Transformative Role in Supply Chains

AI has emerged as a critical enabler of efficiency, agility, and innovation in supply chain management. By leveraging AI-driven solutions, businesses can:

- **Enhance Decision-Making:** AI provides predictive analytics and real-time insights, allowing organizations to anticipate and respond to supply chain disruptions more effectively.
- **Optimize Operations:** AI-powered automation streamlines processes, reduces human error, and enhances productivity across procurement, logistics, and inventory management.
- **Improve Customer Satisfaction:** Personalization enabled by AI ensures timely delivery and tailored solutions, boosting customer loyalty.
- **Promote Sustainability:** AI helps minimize waste and optimize resource usage, aligning with global sustainability goals.

Through these applications, AI is not just a tool but a transformative force reshaping the way supply chains operate, making them more resilient and responsive to everchanging market demands.

8.2 Long-Term Implications for Businesses and the Global Economy

The adoption of AI in supply chains has far-reaching implications that extend beyond individual organizations to the global economy:

- **Competitive Advantage:** Early adopters of AI in supply chains will likely achieve a competitive edge through cost savings, improved efficiency, and faster time-to-market.
- **Economic Growth:** By enhancing productivity and enabling innovative business models, AI contributes to economic growth on a macro scale.
- **Job Evolution:** While AI may automate routine tasks, it creates opportunities for higher-skilled roles, fostering the evolution of the workforce.
- **Global Supply Chain Integration:** AI facilitates better coordination and transparency across international supply chains, improving trade flows and fostering economic globalization.

- **Risk Mitigation:** With predictive analytics and real-time monitoring, AI enables organizations to mitigate risks related to supply chain disruptions, such as those caused by geopolitical tensions or natural disasters.

8.3 Call to Action for AI Adoption in Supply Chains

To fully realize the transformative potential of AI, businesses must take proactive steps toward adoption:

- **Embrace Innovation:** Organizations should view AI as a strategic priority, embedding it into their long-term vision and operational strategies.
- **Invest in People and Technology:** Commitment to upskilling employees and investing in state-of-the-art AI technologies is essential to build a robust foundation for AI integration.
- **Collaborate Across Ecosystems:** Businesses must engage with partners, suppliers, and technology providers to create collaborative ecosystems that amplify the benefits of AI.
- **Act Responsibly:** Ethical considerations, including data privacy, fairness, and sustainability, should guide the deployment of AI solutions to ensure trust and accountability.
- **Start Small but Scale Quickly:** Organizations should initiate AI projects with manageable pilots to demonstrate value before scaling across the supply chain.

The path forward requires courage, innovation, and collaboration. Businesses that take decisive action to adopt AI today will not only enhance their operational efficiency but also secure their position as leaders in the supply chains of tomorrow. The future of supply chain management lies in AI, and the time to act is now.

REFERENCES

Adewusi, A. O., Komolafe, A. M., Ejairu, E., Aderotoye, I. A., Abiona, O. O., & Oyeniran, O. C. (2024). The role of predictive analytics in optimizing supply chain resilience: A review of techniques and case studies. *International Journal of Management & Entrepreneurship Research*, *6*(3), 815–837. DOI: 10.51594/ijmer.v6i3.938

Alonge, E. O., Eyo-Udo, N. L., Ubanadu, B. C., Daraojimba, A. I., Balogun, E. D., & Ogunsola, K. O. (2023). Real-time data analytics for enhancing supply chain efficiency. *Journal of Supply Chain Management and Analytics*, *10*(1), 49–60.

Aslam, F., & Calghan, J. (2023). Using NLP to enhance supply chain management systems. *Journal of Engineering Research and Reports*, *25*(9), 211–219. DOI: 10.9734/jerr/2023/v25i9994

Babashahi, L., Barbosa, C. E., Lima, Y., Lyra, A., Salazar, H., Argôlo, M., Almeida, M. A., & Souza, J. M. D. (2024). AI in the workplace: A systematic review of skill transformation in the industry. *Administrative Sciences*, *14*(6), 127. DOI: 10.3390/admsci14060127

Bhargava, A., Bhargava, D., Kumar, P. N., Sajja, G. S., & Ray, S. (2022). Industrial IoT and AI implementation in vehicular logistics and supply chain management for vehicle mediated transportation systems. *International Journal of System Assurance Engineering and Management*, *13*(S1, Suppl 1), 673–680. DOI: 10.1007/s13198-021-01581-2

Charles, A. N., Akinyemi, O. V., & Blessing, C. (2023). Leveraging Artificial Intelligence and Communication Strategies to Optimize Supply Chains, Marketing Performance, and Customer-Centric Business Decision Making. *Communication In Physical Sciences*, *9*(4), 1101–1118.

Daios, A., Kladovasilakis, N., Kelemis, A., & Kostavelis, I. (2025). AI applications in supply chain management: A survey. *Applied Sciences (Basel, Switzerland)*, *15*(5), 2775. DOI: 10.3390/app15052775

Dash, R., McMurtrey, M., Rebman, C., & Kar, U. K. (2019). Application of artificial intelligence in automation of supply chain management. *Journal of strategic innovation and sustainability, 14*(3), 43-53.

Dauvergne, P. (2022). Is artificial intelligence greening global supply chains? Exposing the political economy of environmental costs. *Review of International Political Economy*, *29*(3), 696–718. DOI: 10.1080/09692290.2020.1814381

Devineni, S. K. (2024). AI in data privacy and security. [IJAIML]. *International Journal of Artificial Intelligence and Machine Learning*, *3*(01), 35–49.

George, A. S. (2025). Advancements in Artificial Intelligence for Industrial Robotics and Intelligent Drones: A Comprehensive Review. *Partners Universal Innovative Research Publication*, *3*(1), 44–51.

Goul, M., Henderson, J. C., & Tonge, F. M. (1992). The emergence of artificial intelligence as a reference discipline for decision support systems research. *Decision Sciences*, *23*(6), 1263–1276. DOI: 10.1111/j.1540-5915.1992.tb00448.x

Hassan, A., Bhattacharya, P., Dutta, P. K., Verma, J. P., & Kundu, N. K. (Eds.). (2024). *Quantum computing and supply chain management: A new era of optimization: A new era of optimization*. IGI Global.

Mennella, C., Maniscalco, U., De Pietro, G., & Esposito, M. (2024). Ethical and regulatory challenges of AI technologies in healthcare: A narrative review. *Heliyon*, *10*(4), e26297. DOI: 10.1016/j.heliyon.2024.e26297

Mun, J., Housel, T., Jones, R., Carlton, B., & Skots, V. (2020). Acquiring artificial intelligence systems: Development challenges, implementation risks, and cost/ benefits opportunities. *Naval Engineers Journal*, *132*(2), 79–94.

Nasir, M. S., & Butt, S. A. (2025). The Role of Supplier Relationship Management in Reducing Operational Risks. *Economic Trends and Business Review*, *3*(1), 34–49.

Nweje, U., & Taiwo, M. (2025). Leveraging Artificial Intelligence for predictive supply chain management, focus on how AI-driven tools are revolutionizing demand forecasting and inventory optimization. *International Journal of Science and Research Archive*, *14*(1), 230–250. DOI: 10.30574/ijsra.2025.14.1.0027

Parkhi, S., Joshi, S., Gupta, S., & Sharma, M. (2015). A Study of Evolution and Future of Supply Chain Management. *AIMS International Journal of Management*, *9*(2), 95–106.

Polo, L. (2025). A Supply Chain Approach Highlighting the Use of Artificial Intelligence and Computer Vision to Improve the Efficiency of Food Supply Chains in the United States. *International Journal for Multidisciplinary Research*, *7*(2), 1–24.

Radhakrishnan, G. V., Gabhane, M., Jha, S., Al Said, N., & Murthy, B. S. R.G V Radhakrishnan. (2025). AI and IOT in supply chains: Creating intelligent and autonomous business operations. *Journal of Information Systems Engineering & Management*, *10*(11s), 625–632. DOI: 10.52783/jisem.v10i11s.1664

Riad, M., Naimi, M., & Okar, C. (2024). Enhancing supply chain resilience through artificial intelligence: Developing a comprehensive conceptual framework for AI implementation and supply chain optimization. *Logistics (Basel)*, *8*(4), 111. DOI: 10.3390/logistics8040111

Shil, S. K., Islam, M. R., & Pant, L. (2024). Optimizing US supply chains with AI: Reducing costs and improving efficiency. *International Journal of Advanced Engineering Technologies and Innovations*, *2*(1), 223–247.

Sikander, A. (2024). Artificial intelligence and the circular economy: How AI advances waste reduction. *Green Environmental Technology*, *1*(2), 23–34.

Singh, N., & Adhikari, D. (2023). Challenges and solutions in integrating AI with legacy inventory systems. *International Journal for Research in Applied Science and Engineering Technology*, *11*(12), 609–613. DOI: 10.22214/ijraset.2023.57376

Sodiya, E. O., Umoga, U. J., Amoo, O. O., & Atadoga, A. (2024). AI-driven warehouse automation: A comprehensive review of systems. *GSC Advanced Research and Reviews*, *18*(2), 272–282. DOI: 10.30574/gscarr.2024.18.2.0063

Stevens, W. (2023). Robotic process automation in supply chain. *European Journal of Supply Chain Management*, *1*(1), 1–10.

Susatyono, J. D., Suasana, I. S., & Rozikin, K. (2024). Integrating Big Data and Edge Computing for Enhancing AI Efficiency in Real-Time Applications. *Journal of Technology Informatics and Engineering*, *3*(3), 337–349. DOI: 10.51903/jtie.v3i3.204

Talla, R. R. (2022). Integrating blockchain and ai to enhance supply chain transparency in energy sectors. *Asia Pacific Journal of Energy and Environment*, *9*(2), 109–118. DOI: 10.18034/apjee.v9i2.782

Ucar, A., Karakose, M., & Kırımça, N. (2024). Artificial intelligence for predictive maintenance applications: Key components, trustworthiness, and future trends. *Applied Sciences (Basel, Switzerland)*, *14*(2), 898. DOI: 10.3390/app14020898

Chapter 4
Revolutionizing Supply Chains in Indian Industries With AI, IoT, Blockchain, and Big Data Analytics:
Enhancing Visibility, Agility, and Resilience

P. Aranganathan
http://orcid.org/0000-0002-4132-5704
Hallmark Business School, India

S. Manikandan
http://orcid.org/0000-0002-1815-410X
Gnanam School of Business, India

R. V. Suresh
Hallmark Business School, India

B. Elamurugan
http://orcid.org/0000-0002-9747-1727
SRM Valliammai Engineering College, India

R. Sivarethinamohan
http://orcid.org/0000-0003-1918-8931
Symbiosis Centre for Management Studies, India

M. Kathiravan
The Oxford College of Engineering, India

ABSTRACT

Through the establishment of a global supply chain, the current economy has been based, leading to unimpeded flow of products and services across borders-relatively isolated from erratic markets, geopolitics, environmental concerns, and variations

DOI: 10.4018/979-8-2600-1855-2.ch004

from the consumer's end. It will be driven now by supply chain management with the advent of an era of new technologies like artificial intelligence, the Internet of Things (IoT), Blockchain and Big Data, which increase responsiveness, flexibility, and transparency. 'Big Data' enhances decisions, 'Blockchain' raises trust and transparency, 'IoT' enables real-time tracking and 'AI' would advance the capability to predict demand and manage inventory. Anything said thus far gets underlined by the synergies of the technologies themselves and is embedded within vast potentials that are yet opposed by high costs, skills gaps, and data security issues. To stay on top of the fast-moving economic landscape, companies in India will need strong, efficient supply chains and a platform that assists them to become global leaders.

1. INTRODUCTION

In the era of high technological advancement and fluctuating market dynamics, supply chains have curves from simple procurement and distribution networks to very interconnected, complex systems that demand visibility, agility, and resilience. The transition of supply chains is no longer an option but, any firm has to be able to achieve distinctive competitive advantage, improved operational efficiency, and great customer experience. Over the recent years, there have been disruptions such as those caused by pandemics and geopolitical tensions showing that old systems are far from ideal, emphasizing the necessity to have electronics-driven solutions.

The strategic process of completely reengineering networks to match company goals with demand in the wider economy is known as supply chain transformation. The deeper understanding of this procedure is not just about embracing emerging technologies but requires reconsideration of formed strategies, employment of organizational structure, and building up talent to leverage in things like Artificial Intelligence (AI), Internet of Things (IoT), Blockchain, Big Data Analytics, among others. This is changing everything in supply chain management and giving excellent real-time tracking, predicting insights, and validating secure transactions through creating collaborative and sustainable environments.

With the likes of "Make in India," the Production Linked Incentive (PLI) scheme, or even the National Logistics Policy, India is aspiring to develop as a center for manufacturing globally and within the supply chain. The country faces numerous challenges despite its progress: inefficiency and various disruptions in the supply chains, to name only a few. With the latest technology, Indian industries could have a unique opportunity to overcome such challenges of modern supply chains and upgrade to lean and agile structures and resilient systems poised to face uncertain changes in an ever-evolving global landscape.

It set out how AI, IoT, Blockchain, and Big Data Analytics are revolutionizing supply chains in India in this chapter through the introduction of new visibility systems been creating real-time tracking, increasing agility, enabling quick responses to disruptions, and building resilience in a robust business continuity planning system for meeting unforeseen challenges. More importantly, this is underlined by examples of case studies from different industries such as manufacturing, agriculture, pharmaceuticals, and e-commerce, used to explain all the benefits, challenges, and future trends in adopting those technologies.

That is quite complex, especially in industries that are considering the adoption of new and modern technologies in their supply chains. Nonetheless, this insight is equally concerned with taking productive elements on how systems can be made not only efficient and secure but also consonant with an economic vision for India. Visibility, agility, and resilience provide the frame and outline of the potential of an integrated approach to AI predicting scenarios, IoT generating real-time data, Blockchain ensuring trust, and Big Data Analytics translating it into clear advice. This suite of technologies, acting in concert, has the key to revolutionizing Supply Chains and making India a big player in the global Supply Chain Ecosystem.

2. SUPPLY CHAIN TRANSFORMATION

A fundamental and all-encompassing undertaking, supply chain transformation aims at ensuring survival through the reorganization and modernization of business supply chains (Christopher, 2016). It should begin with pursuing the raw material through the whole chain to transform it into a final product and deliver it to the ultimate consumer, all in close accordance with the major business strategy. The urgency for organizations to initiate supply chain transformation has been exacerbated by the simultaneous global disruptions through which companies must respond to existing challenges and exploit new opportunities.

2.1 Purpose of Supply Chain Transformation

Supply chain transformation goals may vary from organization to organization, but they all pursue one objective: aligning supply chain operations with the broader business goals (Hugos, 2018). For several companies, this involves real-time data and advancements to help make better decisions and responsiveness.

Key Drivers of Transformation Include:

1. Operational alignment - link Supply Chain Strategy with Business strategy.

2. Technology adoption - Embracing technologies like Artificial Intelligence (AI), the Internet of Things (IoT), Blockchain, and Big Data for pragmatic smart, effective processes (Ivanov et al., 2019).
3. Sustainable Development - Here, sustainability within the network ranges from how products are sourced to how they are ultimately distributed (Seuring & Müller, 2008).

2.2 Common Goals of Supply Chain Transformation

1. Improved Efficiency: Organizations improve their operations by identifying bottlenecks and utilizing fixed, installed equipment to eliminate manual, error-prone tasks and replace them with automated, accurate processes. This improves efficiency, thus reducing unnecessary operational delays for more productivity (Chopra & Meindl, 2021).
2. Cost Reduction: With time, automation and advanced technology will reduce Kosten for processing current operations. Financial savings will be made through less spillage of materials and the redirection of human resources toward strategic, high-value tasks (Hugos, 2018).
3. Increased transparency in the supply chain is related to the improvement in transparency externally and internally in terms of partners. It is evident in the transparency in cost modeling, data integration, data governance efficiency, and usage in many ways for organizations embracing digital supply chains to obtain more business insights for decision-making from an enhanced interconnected data accuracy that is required to work for everyone (Christopher, 2016).
4. Enhanced end-to-end transformation will provide firms with the following advantages: faster delivery of the products to the end customers, improvement in the quality of a product to a higher extent, and maintenance of the highest levels in the availability of materials within the company (Ivanov et al., 2019).
5. Greater agility: In the contemporary scenario and context in which a supply chain would be exactly changed while under pressure due to the uniqueness that surrounds its transition at any given critical time, a modernized setup can be easily adjusted to shocks and changes in demand. Therefore, an enabler is the use of advanced analytics that uses real-time data so that resources are appropriately modified to respond within time, thus making them resilient.
6. intense collaboration: In today's scenario, the one nucleus of a common economy through which all fibers bind the company with its suppliers across the globe. Common data and tools allow such symbiosis dialogue of opposing content, by securing comprehensive enhancement of the end-to-end value chain (Hugos, 2018).

7. Sustainability: Environmental considerations relating to the green transformation of supply chains have recently become an inherent part of the strategy. Organizations no longer see analytics only as an opportunity to become more effective, but also as a means to change behaviors that reduce environmental impacts at every step from sourcing to final distribution (Seuring & Muller, 2008).

2.3 Key Components of Supply Chain Transformation

1. Strategy: To begin the transformation of the supply chain in a structured, flexible, and scalable way it is necessary to clarify what kind of strategy one wants, how it links to goals, and is tailored to meet the challenges looming in the future (Christopher, 2016)
2. Technology: Among the numerous facets of the Supply Chain transformation technology is shaping and putting itself in the best possible manner. High-tech tools such as Supply Chain Management software, IoT devices, AI-assisting decision-making machines, and robotics will continue to bring more rapidity, accuracy, and safety (Ivanov et al., 2019).
3. Data Analytics: Data analysis is a must-employ activity that will enable the capture and examination of data-structured and unstructured. Data-derived insights help to fuel businesses in getting better at their supply chain operations, better at predicting, and better at visibility of the way forward and downward activities. (Chopra & Meindl, 2021).

2.4 Challenges in Supply Chain Transformation

Businesses that are engaging in supply chain transformation should encounter certain challenges:

- Apathy inside the Organization: One of those challenges is individuals or stakeholders who push against using new tech and other approaches (Hugos, 2018).
- Integration Problems: The integration of modern, advanced technologies with the technology that currently exists can indeed be considerably complicated and time-consuming.
- Budgetary and Resource Restrictions: The first investment necessary for the radical transformation of technologies and processes may be significant.

3. KEY CONCEPTS AND DEFINITIONS

Supply Chain Visibility (SCV): Supply chain visibility (SCV) refers to the ability to monitor and track components, sub-assemblies, and final products moving in the supply chain. Point-of-use data allows real-time visibility and traceable information flow throughout the supply chain so the monitoring and traceability of assets and resources will impact operational efficiency and safety. Barratt and Oke (2007) defined SCV as the level of sharing critical and mutually beneficial information across the supply chain partners. This element always allows people to keep a watch on their stock, delivery tracking, and general supply chain actions. SCV increases efficiency by solving problems like depleted stocks, addressing bottlenecks, ensuring regulatory compliance, and improving deliveries. Both internal operations and external partners, networks are the main focal points, with the external networks being more challenging (Barriball et al., 2020; Finkenstadt & Handfield, 2021).,

SCV, in contrast, aids in reducing risk exposure, in addition to being a useful tool for preparing for and surviving risks, as shown by the risk assessments prepared by Messina et al. (2023) and Apeji & Sunmola, (2023). When SCV is practiced, stakeholders can share their data, which in turn eradicates the unknown, pushing them toward proactive strategies, especially in light of problems (Kamble et al., 2020; Qader et al., 2022).

Supply Chain Agility (SCA): These describe supply chain agility as the ability of a company to adjust to changes perceived in the market, customer demands, or due to disruption to firm up supply chains. Supply chain agility is related to quick detection and reaction to changes in the environment caused by strategic moves and organization architecture recasting as stated by Weber and Tarba (2014). For him, agility includes preparation for the event, managing the inventory as envisaged, and effective collaboration between departments. Agile supply chains help businesses keep pace with market shifts, overcome disturbances, and be competitive. Thus, they invest in relevant technology and infrastructure and deliberately create analytics to increase agility and increase customer satisfaction.

Supply chain resilience (SCR): Capacity to anticipate and adapt or recover from disruptions in natural or man-made phenomena. The ultimate objectives of SCR are aimed at continuity, generation of less-stopped operations, or long-term management within the organization. Core in this context are the terms flexibility, contingency planning, and also visibility. In addition to those, technologies including AI, ML, blockchain, and digital twins boost resiliency even further. Through these technologies, connections are made in real-time, and insights are generated according to your requirements and even optimized for decision-making (Phan et al., 2023; Qader et al., 2022). One's capability to manage, adapt, or thrive despite uncertainties is described as resilience (Agarwal et al., 2022). It defines the ability of supply chains to develop disruptive tolerance but achieve evolution to the desired levels of sustainability (Sarkar et al., 2022).

4. EMERGING TECHNOLOGIES AND THEIR ROLE

Emerging technologies are revolutionizing supply chains in profound ways:

1. Artificial Intelligence (AI): Enhances predictive analytics and decision-making.
2. Internet of Things (IoT): Enables real-time tracking of goods and assets.
3. Blockchain: Improves transparency and trust by creating immutable records.
4. Big Data Analytics: Provides insights into consumer behavior, demand forecasting, and inventory management

Figure 1. Emerging Technologies in SCM

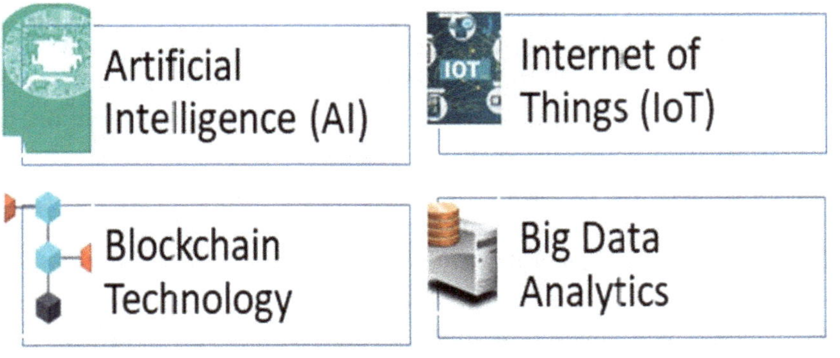

Source: Created by Authors

4.1 AI's Transformative Impact on Supply Chain Management

AI shapes the supply chain by executing data science in dealing with the complications of the supply chain, forecasting trends, and implementing tasks on time. This helps for better planning, production, logistics, and decision-making, significantly making the process of supply chains more efficient (Gharbaoui et al., 2024; Toorajipour et al., 2021). AI adoption has been boosted and intensified due to the impact of the COVID-19 pandemic, rolling out tools like generative AI and chatbots to smoothen out the processes. Machine learning (ML) improves demand management with market predictions and workflow optimization; it's a popular application for AI. This article provides a vision for the realization of the inevitable link between the Internet of Things (IoT) and artificial intelligence (AI) in inventory management and automation with real-time data collection. AI is used to empower total supply chain visibility, stakeholder collaboration, and fulfillment of sustainability objectives. The adoption of AI has made companies capable of accommodating dynamic procurement strategies that reverse potential disruptions in any supply chain while improving the resilience of the processes. AI continues its intervention in the supply chain in evolving market demand with high visibility and efficiency giving assurance in the sustainability and resilience of dynamic global settings (Singh et al., 2023).

4.1.1 Benefits of AI in Supply Chains: Enhancing Visibility, Agility, and Resilience

AI-driven supply chains enhance visibility, agility, and resilience, improving key organizational processes and ensuring long-term success.

Visibility: Organizations can access data, both historical and real-time, through leveraging AI, and thus further enhance decisions, identify problems early, and avert bottlenecks in advance, but keep the operations transparent (Shahzadi et al., 2024). One can track inventory in real-time, follow-on supply/demand listing, and resource utilization. This allows for the prediction and transparency of operations in organizations (Nsisong Louis Eyo-Udo, 2024).

Agile: AI models will forecast demand, inventory, and optimal routing to make the company more flexible (Dash et al., 2019). They fit into market changes quickly and operating simulations can further demonstrate where AI can augment operational efficiency and visualize disruptions in the operations that call for corrective actions (Shen et al., 2024). Automation and machine learning will better optimize business processes across production and logistics, which in turn ensures adaptability and flexibility (Ellaturu & Rajalakshmi, 2024).

Resilient: AI strengthens resilience by addressing risks associated with the supply chain in terms of suppliers and other natural disaster risks and external factors such as market volatility. Otherwise, AI facilitates decision-making using predictive analytics and needs to response in due time (Baryannis et al., 2018). It monitors vulnerabilities and enhances risk management through the optimization of locations, minimization of waste, and following rules (Awasthi, 2024; Shahzadi et al., 2024).

AI changes the face of supply by adding transparency, reaction time, and flexibility, so that decisions in an organization are data-driven, making them competitive and sustainable in dynamic.

Figure 2. Benefits of AI in SCM

Source: Created by Authors

4.1.2 Challenges of AI in Supply Chain

While AI is significant in improving efficiency in the chain supply, as it ensures agileness, it is also subject to problems in the stages of its implementation. It is not necessarily the technology factor of artificial intelligence that complicates its integration into the company, but many data protection and ethical concerns are particularly relevant to provision areas, such as logistics planning, where human know-how is irreplaceable (Joel et al., 2024; Boute and Udenio, 2021).

One of the major problems encountered is that training manpower highly consumes time and also involves still greater costs, in addition to massive capital outlays for AI software and machine-learning models (Kosasih et al., 2023). The inefficacy of AIs typically comes from the non-consolidated and interconnected data it relies on, solid walls built up between departments, and multiple systems that clog up the flows (Nsisong, 2024; Joel et al., 2024).

The usage of the existing AI applications is hampered by legacy issues, such as updated costs and timely incorporation issues (Kosasih et al., 2023). Further, businesses often confront the severe challenge of attracting and retaining talented professionals specifically in AI, which is not correlated per supply following demand for such pieces of knowledge in these two fields and supply chain (Patalas-Maliszewska et al., 2024).

Executables are the most important, clear transformation strategy that specifically directs AI activities toward achieving goals for companies, which would ultimately prevent money, resources, and problems among stakeholders. Overcoming the barriers attending an IT budget together with commitment will guarantee the success of the whole operation (Singh et al., 2023).

Investing in education, integrated systems, and talent acquisition is allowing organizations to reduce their exposure to these challenges by unlocking the transformative power of AI in logistics management.

Table 1. Risk Management Table

Risk	Description	Solution/Action
Inaccuracy of Data	The AI system relies on large datasets from multiple sources. Random data collection may introduce inaccuracies or biases.	Implement human review processes to ensure data quality, fairness, and unbiased decision-making, while enhancing explainability.
Overreliance on AI	AI is often misunderstood as a replacement for human intelligence. However, it should complement human capabilities, not replace them, particularly in supply chain risk management.	Maintain a balance by involving skilled human experts to oversee and manage supply chains, ensuring operations continue smoothly in case of AI failure.
Security and Privacy Vulnerabilities	Collecting extensive customer data for AI models increase risks of surveillance, hacking, and cyberattacks.	Establish robust data protection measures, prioritize consumer privacy, and provide clear assurances regarding data usage and security.

Source: Created by Authors

4.2 Internet of Things (IoT) in Supply Chains

"IoT is typically a network that connects every physical item to the virtual world of a device or things which are connected to the internet with the help of sensors, software, and technology for collecting, sharing, or analyzing data" (Gubbi et al. 2013). The domains that are executed across IoT include smart houses, healthcare, industrial automation, and agriculture, and also transform life through automated and/or cooperative operations. Its incorporation into the supply chain has changed all kinds of operations of production, transportation, storage, and delivery. Thanks to faster, real-time data collection and analysis, IoT helps increase efficiency, reduce costs, and improve customer satisfaction. This chapter talks about applications, benefits, and also a real-life application of IoT provided for point-of-use in supply chain management (Banaee et al. 2013).

4.2.1 Benefits of IoT in Supply Chain Management

Greater visibility is brought about through the integration of IoT in supply chain management, and this is normally associated with dramatic transformations in operations. Visibility, responsiveness, and resilience are all seen as consequences of embracing the different elements of IoT technologies in supply management.

Visibility: It is all about real-time updates and tags on goods by an IoT sensor and GPS to certify their location, condition of deployment, and where they are found. This exercise is more about observing products while being transported, such as pharmaceuticals, and how such conditions would maintain them as temperature or humidity. It is done to make the decisions easier and to solve problems before they occur. (Udeh et al., 2024)

Agility: In general, IoT enhanced agility in the supply chain by automating inventory control, optimizing space, and then supporting improved fleet operations with predictive analytics. The pace at which the supply chain responds to changes in demand and operational disruptions following IoT-oriented unmanned and autonomous vehicles or drones limits the occurrences of late shipments, and fuel waste, and increases efficiency at large (Winardi et al., 2024).

Resilience: IoT helps increase resilience in the supply chain via ongoing optimization and monitoring. With IoT, it is possible to predict equipment maintenance, early disruptions, and quick recovery from unexpected events. In this way, businesses can easily face these challenges, ensure continuity, and be able to fulfill their promises to their customers.

The supply chain developed through IoT maintains a link between visibility, agility, and resilience, which means businesses are better placed to survive the rapid successions of the endeavoring market.

4.2.2 Applications of IoT in Supply Chain

Currently, Indian supply chains have been transformed through the Internet of Things (IoT), which provides high visibility, agility, and resilience. Through the integration of sensors, devices, and analytics, IoT ensures the real-time data of inventories, shipments, and assets. Technologies such as RFID and GPS trackers make it even more transparent, helping to cut down on delay since perishables and high-end products arrive right on time, due to location and conditions tracked in conjunction with route optimization (Ben-Daya et al., 2019). It is amazing how IoT contributes towards agility by leveraging automation and predictive evaluation that monitor environmental conditions to provide dynamic route optimization (Al-Samad et al., 2024). The IoT enables predictive preparedness for disruptions, helping industries prepare for gaps and bottlenecks, and ensuring continued operation and reduced downtime (Seow, 2023).

Industrial Applications- Cases

Amazon: Amazon integrated more than 520,000 robots into its Kiva Systems, having bought it in 2012. They sport two main robotic systems, Proteus and Cardinal. In sum, Proteus is a robot that autonomously moves GoCarts and reduces heavy lifting, while Cardinal optimizes package sorting AI-driven computer vision. These technological advancements not only ensure better safeguarding but also increase the overall efficiency of the work process. So even though these systems are in place, Amazon intended to create over a million jobs to ensure automation is integrated with human labor, making it a healthy and productive work environment.

Walmart: Walmart has integrated many technological aspects towards the development of IoT-enabled smart shelves, AI-powered barcode readers, and real-time inventory tracking to ensure proper inventory management. Walmart has initiated the replenishment of product stocks to avoid breaks in the stock and to minimize errors while merchandising. These technologies are designed to have a decreased system error rate and maintain a sufficient amount of inventory stock.

DHL: DHL implemented IoT-enables RFID tags and GPS in every shipment it delivers. RFID enables exact monitoring of the location where each parcel is stored and is ready for release in real-time, alongside the condition of shipment. The GPS feature of the system tells exactly where a shipment is delivered. These technologies combined ensure there is good control of shipment at any time from origin to destination, thus preventing delays and alerting teams to route deviations or temperature deviations.

Maersk: The "Remote Container Management" (RCM) service, Maersk's IoT and GPS-based tracking system, combines both sensors into monitoring containers in real-time. It uses these sensors to check cargo conditions such as temperature and humidity to route optimize, avoid delays, and deliver goods on time and safely to customers.

4.3 Blockchain Technology in Supply Chains

Technological development has proven to be transforming both transparency and efficiency of supply chain management along with gaining trust, mainly with the help of its decentralized or immutable nature of trust. It has become so important that it offers a real-time view of supply chain movements and thus is of special relevance to food, pharmaceuticals, and luxury goods businesses, where supply chain integrity is in high demand.

Moreover, blockchain enhances accountability and enables authenticity checking of all stakeholders, hence speeding up the process of addressing discrepancies, and reducing fraud in trade. This saves companies money and time because accurately kept stock levels allow proper demand forecasting and, in turn, result in less waste in terms of inventory. Automation of payments and shipment approvals in addition brings benefits by reducing the time spent by smart contracts on in-between tasks because it is something that speeds up the process for better reaction to change (Wang et al., 2019).

Slowly, this market is going to escalate in size, with nearly $3,153.7 million in revenues by the end of 2028 and a compound annual growth rate (CAGR) of 51.3% (PRNewswire, 2022). However, high implementation costs are not its only barrier. Because most of the companies have already invested much of their existing dollars in legacy systems, blockchain can be a hard sell. Still significant though, workforce automation can streamline operations.

4.3.1 Prominent Use Cases of Blockchain in Supply Chain Management

Blockchain technology revolutionizes the supply chain, making it streamlined, trusted, and efficient to ensure traceability and transparency, smart contracts, inventory management, and compliance through immutable, decentralized ledgers.

Traceability: Blockchain provides a simpler recall chain, quality claims, and consumer confidence through secure tagging of every product movement from beginning to end destination (Laaper, 2017).

Transparency: decentralized ledgers ensure visibility, making for quick resolutions of problems in any operation.

Among others, Smart Contracts: Bringing in self-executing contracts or smart contracts will automate, payments and adherence to legal duties and contracts. This will save astronomical amounts in administrative costs while achieving great efficiency (Giovanni, 2020).

Inventory Management: Combining blockchain and IoT makes real-time management of inventories possible, with reduced surplus and stock-out. In the case of Vendor Managed Inventory (VMI), blockchain increases efficiency in modern scenarios (Bellany et al., 2024).

Compliance: Among other things, at the same time makes records like certifications ironclad, such that within these records, the use of smart contracts could be done not only to secure the information but also automation of regulatory processes upon this information.

Blockchain, on the other hand, opens up new possibilities for supply chains, making them transparent, accountable, and resilient.

Figure 3. Transformative applications in SCM

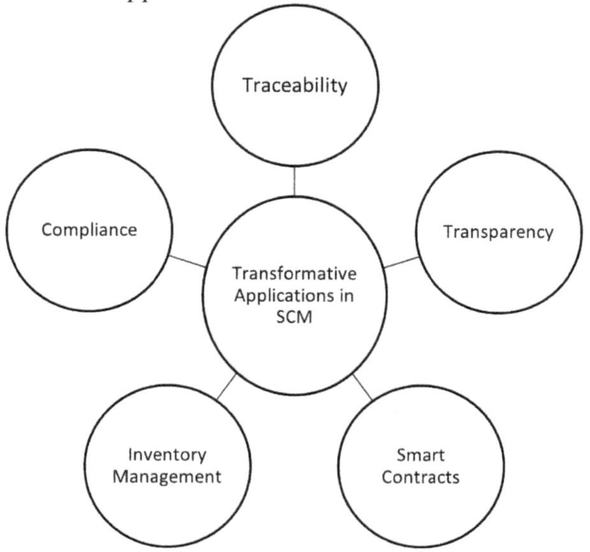

Source: Created by Authors

4.3.2 Blockchain Benefits in Supply Chain Management: Enhancing Visibility, Agility, and Resilience

With increased transparency, agility, and resilience, blockchain is disrupting supply chains as an indispensable transformation agent.

Promoting Trust Through Transparency: Because it is decentralized and transparent, blockchain inspires trust among different parties and optimizes operations.

Supply Chain Transparency: Supply chain stakeholders will truly be able to monitor operations through an immutable ledger that enables tracking goods in real time and having an accurate representation of these. Smart contracts will further automate certain processes such as payment settlements to help avoid delays and reduce all kinds of administrative burdens (Moosavi et al., 2021; Korepin et al., 2021).

Supply Chain Agility: In supply chains of the future, real-time data access will harmonize collaboration between producers, suppliers, and distributors, making them more amenable to dynamic upward changes or even disruptions. This is done with near-perfect collaboration with such web-based technologies as supply chain management and analytics in supporting inventory management and demand forecasting (Cole et al., 2019).

Building Resilience: Integrating an immutable audit trail in blockchain ensures that trust is established; reduces fraud; improves security; and even raises the level of some risks such as counterfeit products and other delays. This will strengthen the business against any disruptions (Korepin et al., 2021).

Blockchain has several capabilities making it a critical tool in advancing the supply chain management platform.

4.3.3 Challenges in Implementing Blockchain for Supply Chain Management

Blockchain makes supply chain transparency, flexibility, and resilience using different aspects. Also, because it requires large amounts of security, regulatory compliance, computerization, and physical security limit the higher speed in rendering transaction-generation processes more agile with solutions like sharding. Scalability is highly cumbersome in its requirements for computation as a challenge for architecture. As a result, transaction speed is limited and agility is lost. Regulatory challenges such as GDPR compromise the resilience of the blockchain and pose burdens to privacy protection and legal alignment with regulation.

(Korepin et al., 2021) Situations such as the lack of universally accepted and agreed-upon standards disturb the interoperability side of the chain; hence, no integration and no visibility can immediately happen without having universal standards industry-wide defined and apprehended according to the communication standard. Security issues include hacking and a couple of issues like hacking and the hashing of contracts. Risks like data breaches and other mistakes must be considered while devising a proactive framework for supply chain integrity rather than reacting passively (Azzi et al., 2019).

Strategies for Overcoming the Challenges

It is also very important to address these concerns to establish the potential of blockchain in this area to ameliorate supply chain transparency, flexibility, and resilience. Some of the ways by which institutions can counteract such challenges are as follows:

Scalability: Scalability conditions may be addressed in supply chains via sharding provided it breaks the blockchain down to smaller bundles, and uses layer two protocol to process transactions off-chain, and thereafter store them upon the blockchain. This will help increase both transaction speed and transaction capacity scaling along the expansion of the supply chain (Azzi et al., 2019).

Regulatory Compliance: The design of privacy-preserving technologies such as zero-knowledge proofs ensure compliance in the context of GDPR enforcement. Cooperation with regulatory authorities and the introduction of progressive designs will allow for meeting legal requirements without compromising the principles of transparency and data integrity (Korepin et al., 2021).

Interoperability: For this, industry cooperation is instrumental in setting standardized protocols for blockchain platforms. It aligns consensus mechanisms and ensures that smart contract languages are harmonized to enable collaboration and the flow of data communication within the supply chain partners to facilitate a seamless integration as well as enhanced transparency initiatives, as discussed also in the publication by Singh et al. (2022).

Security and Privacy: Security risks can be managed by investing in a robust cybersecurity framework and practicing regular audits as well as paying attention to the security of smart contract applications. Regularizing a close relationship with experts helps identify potential security holes early on to maintain the confidentiality and integrity of blockchain networks (Azzi et al., 2019).

4.3.4 Blockchain in SCM: Industry Applications

It makes clear the real-time tracking of progress being carried out, while it also makes the information record-mounted and increases the reach, while also improving collaboration, which is beneficial in eradicating barriers seen within various industries (Pournader et al., 2019).

Food and Agriculture: In conclusion, developers are smart to be careful with such high potentials regarding global food quality and protection. So that the IBM Food Trust platform can help companies find the histories of their products as quickly as possible and thus quickly discover the source of contamination, also promoting responsible practices (Pournader et al., 2019).

Healthcare: It also addresses the amid-tide scandal of counterfeit drugs that eventually sends a positive message on the use of medical supplies. For instance, Mediledger secures pharmaceutical movements such that it is possible to improve recall efficiency and trust (Korepin et al., 2021).

Retail: Walmart's Food Traceability Initiative reflects the reality further by proving an endeavor to increase visibility, security, and efficiency (Cole et al., 2019).

Automotive: Use cases are thriving in many sectors: in the automotive sphere, BMW includes cobalt in e-vehicle batteries (carried out by Moosavi in 2021), which promotes responsible sourcing, transparency, and sustainability.

For automation, security of data, and improved supply chain visibility, blockchain drives operational efficiency and establishes customer trust in all sectors.

4.4 Big Data Analytics in Supply Chains

Thinking big is key to big data analytics, which aims to maximize profits from data analytics, traditional methodologies, and management's vision for choices and tactics. Drawing on techniques such as data mining, machine learning, predictive analysis, and statistical analytics, processes information from many sources such as social media, sensors, and online transactions (Gandomi & Haider, 2015). Given the 5 Vs, namely, volume, velocity, variety, veracity, and value, Big Data is changing many sectors, including healthcare, operations, and engineering.

The global data space is rapidly expanding. Taylor (2023) reports 402.74 million terabytes generated daily, totaling 147 zettabytes annually, with projected values of 182 zottabytes by 2025 given the growing competition-related importance.

Figure 4. Amount of data created, consumed, and stored 2010-2023, with forecasts to 2028

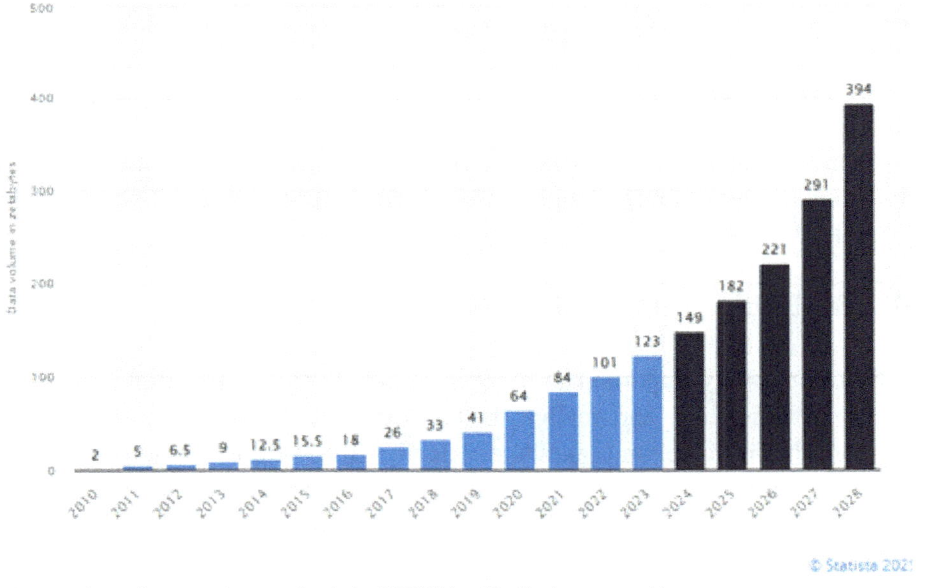

Source: https://www.statista.com/statistics/871513/worldwide-data-created/

Platforms like Hadoop and Spark support distributed computing for big data (Zikopoulos et al., 2012). In academia and business, Big Data Analytics transforms use cases into applications, such as performance tracking in education and customer segmentation in business (Chen et al., 2012). This technology is vital for organizations aiming to enhance efficiency, innovation, and customer experiences.

Table 2. Difference between traditional vs big data analytics

Aspect	Traditional Approach	Big Data Analytics
Data Volume	Handles small to medium datasets.	Processes massive datasets (petabytes or more).
Data Variety	Structured data (e.g., spreadsheets, databases).	Structured, semi-structured, and unstructured data.
Data Velocity	Batch processing with time delays.	Real-time or near-real-time data processing.
Analytical Techniques	Basic statistical methods and tools like SQL, Excel.	Advanced techniques like machine learning, AI, and NLP.
Scalability	Limited scalability, requiring costly infrastructure upgrades.	Highly scalable using distributed systems like Hadoop and Spark.
Data Integration	Manual integration of data sources.	Seamless integration from diverse sources (e.g., APIs, data lakes).
Insights and Applications	Descriptive analytics ("what happened").	Predictive and prescriptive analytics ("what will/should happen").
Cost and Infrastructure	Relies on expensive proprietary systems.	Often uses cost-effective open-source tools.
Decision-Making Speed	Slower due to manual processing.	Faster with real-time analysis and automation.

Source: Created by Authors

The table-2 highlights how Big Data Analytics surpasses traditional approaches in handling modern data challenges, offering greater speed, scalability, and insight potential.

4.4.1 Big Data in Supply Chain Management

Big Data is very important in optimizing supply chain operations, improving operational efficiency, and making better decisions. It ensures value creation, finds out what is value, and takes it efficiently. Big Data powers evidence-based decisions usually on vast amounts of information harvested in supply chains that must be analyzed to reveal much improved organizational processes and decisions. Big Data enhances demand forecasting, reduces safety stock, and boosts supplier performance. Big Data enables performance improvement by analyzing customer behavior, market trends, and logistics (Wilkin et al., 2020).

4.4.2 Benefits of Big Data in SCM

Big Data provides a huge boost in visibility, speed, and responsiveness to supply chain management, providing it with efficiency, attractiveness, and the saving of costs on efficiency decisions.

Supply Chain Visibility: Big Data augments real-time tracking and insight into supply chain operations; hence better inventory management, supplier selection, and transportation routing would be possible. The problems that may slow down both improvement and operations are detected early and are therefore facilitated, ensuring delivery costs and times are reduced (Waller and Fawcett, 2013; Fosso Wamba et al., 2015).

Supply Chain Agility: Big Data creates agility through better demand planning. Predictive analytics integrates historical data, market trends, and external factors to reduce stockouts and overproduction risk. Consequently, production schedules can be reconfigured when market changes occur (Seyedan & Mafakheri, 2020).

Supply Chain Resilience: Big Data creates resilience through proactive data-driven risk management. Data help organizations to predict possible supply disruptions, for instance, the delay in supply and geopolitical risk, to take action and thus ensure continuity and a burning customer experience (Tenkorang & Helo, 2016).

Through visibility, agility, and resilience, big data has transformed efficiencies in firms, better decision-making, and increased satisfaction of general customer needs along the supply chains.

4.4.3 Key applications of Big Data in SCM

Big Data is changing supply chain management (SCM) through enhanced "visibility, agility, and resilience. Key applications around these areas include:

Visibility within SCM: Real-time tracking of shipper's events accessing Big Data (i.e., with IoT sensors, GPS) makes it possible for businesses to identify quickly the inventories in the worst possible conditions for performance tuning. Monitoring operations continuously can show bottlenecks more clearly, and then will be able to better resources to help alleviate problems (Waller & Fawcett, 2013).

Agility in Forecasting & Demand Planning: Integration of historical data; market trends and other variables including weather through big data has improved planning accuracy. This makes the whole planning cycle very quick because there is a quick understanding of sudden process changes, therefore capacities can be scheduled to yield an optimum production line result where needed (Choi, Wallace, & Wang, 2017).

Resilience in Risk Management: This supports the ability to track every vulnerability and the extent of its exploitation. It consists, simply put, of having an excellent view of negative impacts that can be created by one or a combination of those threats. It is about building from success by leveraging old solutions and crafting new approaches.

Customer Satisfaction and Sustainability: This allows for a supply chain to be in sync with whatever a supply network feels their preferences should be. For other companies, furthermore, it extends customer tastes and preferences because it uplifts services for people from more receiving end locations (McAfee & Brynjolfsson, 2012).

Big Data can also lead to economic flexibility, job growth, low costs, and sustainability within supply chains.

4.4.4 Future Trends in Big Data for SCM

AI, machine learning, real-time data processing, and blockchain will drive Big Data from Supply Chain Management (SCM). These factors enhance predictive capabilities, demand forecasting, inventory optimization, and demand for Best Practices to support the work system (Farooq & Yen, 2024). As much as cloud and edge computing allow almost instant actionable insights (Hugos, 2018) and blockchain improves transparency and traceability (Kshetri, 2018), IoT will enhance visibility (Borgia, 2014) and big data will provide support for sustainable efforts such as monitoring and mitigating carbon footprints (Cetindamar et al., 2020). Key trends include:

1. Artificial Intelligence and Machine Learning: The capability to improve the predictive analytics of demand forecasting to develop risk mitigation.
2. Blockchain Integration: An increase in transparency is set by the formation of unaltered data in supply chains.
3. Digital Twins: Supply chain processes that simulate the inefficiencies.
4. 5G and IoT: Enhanced data capacity in real-time supply chain monitoring.
5. Pointed toward Sustainability: Carrying sustainability momentum by way of tracking carbon emissions and efficient resource use.

These innovations will help in sound decisions, operations, and sustainability in SCM.

4.4.5 Challenges in Implementing Big Data in SCM

Big Data faces several barriers in SCM such as the size and complicatedness of data, data quality issues, and integration with legacy systems (Jeble et al. 2018). These become more complicated by changes in regulation and, above all, by the increasing risk of privacy and security associated with the use of data. It further appreciates a valid strategy, investment, and collaboration with other organizations to actualize transformational benefits to the company in adopting big data. This will result in more effective and efficient decisions and operations.

Data Integration: This process takes a lot of time, and hard work, and is pretty complex, as it is collected from multiple sources and in multiple systems.

Accuracy and Quality of the Data: Wrong data can throw everything off in the wrong direction without wrong decisions but reduces the importance of Big Data analytics.

Very High Implementation Costs: High cost because of huge capital investment in Big Data Infrastructure, making it difficult for small and medium organizations.

Cyber Risks: Safety needs to be given first place for these data volumes, as large information may be used to attack them over the network.

Regulation Compliance: Every organization needs to modify its data regulations with respect of the law.

Skills Gap: It is a rarity to find anyone with top skills in data analytics and related fields as this is one of the prerequisites without the help of which no successful Big Data solution is going to be put into practice.

4.5 Challenges in Integrating Iot, Big Data, Data Analytics, And AI in Supply Chain Management

Combining IoT, Big Data, Data Analytics, and AI in Supply Chain Management (SCM) proposes significant potential changes but comes with many challenges that need to be addressed efficiently by the organizations.

1. Data Security and Privacy- Data security is among the most challenging exigencies to overcome with data privacy. The information reach produced out of IoT and Big Data systems is colossal, surrounding business partner details, pricing strategies, and customer records. Protection from data breaches includes robust security measures such as encryption and secure access controls. Complying with data privacy-related rules and regulations, like the GDPR, is imperative as it regards responsible data handling and trust among stakeholders building (Chowdhury & Quaddus, 2016).
2. Technical complexity- The integration of IoT and Big Data Analytics in SCM has its own set of technical complexities in terms of data being stored, processed, analyzed, and interpreted. Such effective handling requires the availability of advanced infrastructure and tools to alleviate the complexities. Experienced technology vendors could hasten implementation and improve operational efficiency (Abhulimen & Ejike, 2024).
3. Organizational Barriers: Organizational issues such as change resistance, non-skilled workers, and very high financial outlay will always deter the absorption

of high-end technology by companies. Training and development programs provide skills to employees for handling the technology. Moreover, culture to innovation and technological change are essential things to be carried on smooth integration (Nagurney et al., 2021).

4. Interoperability: Here, the real-life issue lies in standardization among devices, infrastructures, and communication processes that are part of the internet. This prevents the free interoperability of these systems. Standardized protocols are a remedy to addressing such challenges; in fact, adoption should also involve collaboration with those technology providers that adhere to the standards (Mathur, 2024).
5. Data Overload: The administration structure of cloud services is set in place to allow the processing of very large volumes of data, which can be so much that probably a potential lower limit must be defined at which point those systems will no longer capable of at least analyzing it anymore. Based on this, categorization, filtration, and compression are the best examples of effective data management strategies. Also, having the cloud's solution can ensure that data availability and manageability are always present (Jacobs & Chase, 2018).
6. Poor Data Quality and Integration Complexities: With AI and big data analytics, some of the problems faced by SCM include poor quality of data, the complexities of network build, and the requirement for a specialized skill set. Other issues entail data mining, visualization, and system integration. Hence, there ought to be a massive investment in trained personnel and focused data governance frameworks (Nasaruddin et al., 2017).
7. Ethical and Regulatory Concerns: AI raises significant ethical and regulatory challenges, including issues related to data storage, access rights, algorithmic bias, and the potential misuse of technology. Appropriate ethical and legal considerations are very important for effectively using AI in SCM functions. When ethics are not limited to a specific domain, they measure concerns broadly to meet all aspects concerning technology adoption (Chowdhury & Quaddus, 2016).
8. Scalability and Sustainability: In most cases, the cases are limited to expanding AI projects, making sure they can handle big data volumes and complexity whether they can handle increasing large volumes of data and complexity or heightened performance against the backdrop of environmental concerns, which include reducing the carbon footprint of IO technologies (Jacobs & Chase, 2018).

4.5.1 Strategies to Address Integration Challenges

Strategic Planning and Pilot Projects: Global corporate priorities and problem areas that AI-data analytics might drive will be placed in the first step. This core half of inbound logic is to be adopted for enabling the understanding of most of such concepts that can further make the knowledge conveyed in practice, resonate well with experience. POCs that offer low complexity with measurable high ROI, should become pilot projects which prove the approval of other project stakeholders (Jones et al., 2014).

Integration across functions: The creation of diverse teams at the executive level to comprise development experts, data miners, IT gurus, and business personnel is expected to trigger the collaborative creation of AI solutions aground with organizational goals (Wodeck, 2019).

Develop Upskilling and Training: Developing employee training is very important to equip the workforce with the requisite abilities for working effectively with artificial intelligence and related technology.

Agile and iterative approach: Continuous changes can be brought into effect via a very involving feedback collection mechanism of performance, display controls, and alterations in real-world rollouts. That effort forms part of the technological size better area profits (Druehl et al. 2018).

Collaborative Partnership: Partnering with technology vendors, research institutes, and industry colleagues brings in best practices, knowledge, and resources.

The technical, organizational, ethical, and sustainability concerns must all be tackled with an integrated approach, paving the way for organizations to realize the full potential of IoT, Big Data, Data Analytics, and AI in enhancing both efficiency and resilience in SCM, allowing for greater competitiveness.

4.6 Future Trends and Opportunities of Technologies in SCM

Technological development transforms supply chain management and helps to enable entirely autonomic, intelligent, and sustainable operations. These AI-driven self-learning systems are continuously optimizing in real time to become agile and resilient. Though IoT technology helps make better decisions with greater transparency, AI must be integrated with other modern technologies, such as the Internet of Things (IoT) and blockchain. Enriched views of data made possible by IoT sensors allow resolving any possible misunderstanding that arises. Blockchains, on the other hand, allow data to be available in near real-time, thus enhancing trust and credibility.

AI supports sustainability-related optimization in reducing energy usage emissions and waste. The very backbone of this lies in supply chains and is formulated by McKinsey. AI and machine learning shall further enhance predictive analytics to aid the determination of precise requirements for demand forecasting and stockkeeping.

Generative AI (Gen AI) is a hotbed termed SCM technology, with a 41% increase in CEO's planning investment by 2024 (KPMG). Gen AI big data analyses are done to improve procurement, category management, and strategic sourcing to improve decision-making in spend planning, demand analysis, and supplier risk management.

However, these technologies call for attention to data ethics, compliance, and errors in AI. Accenture suggests an end-to-end approach with physical and process operations and all possible data operations as well to maximize business processes. The idea should be to drive high ROI while promoting sustainable growth.

CONCLUSION

In the future, AI is said to drive the success of autonomous supply chain management increasingly giving businesses the tools to establish more resilient, efficient, and adaptive operations. The areas of human-made processes that AI-driven self-learning would significantly transform are forecasting demand, autonomous warehouses, and transportation. Such will position an autonomous supply chain to be the key determining factor for organizations that seek to remain relevant in a market that is growing very fast and constantly changing globally. Big data analytics, combined with technologies including IoT and blockchain, improves vital technique developments, including decision-making as well as strategies. IoT further enables real-time tracking and insights from data, while blockchain also ensures total transparency and safety in transactions, making total procurement integrity.

In addition, their applications in fields such as advanced technologies, machine learning, data mining, and predictive analysis can further boost operational efficiencies across industry sectors like healthcare, finance, and education besides supply chain management and manufacturing. The concept of Big Data in the end is to receive maximum benefits from existing resources. Despite the extent of its capabilities, challenges such as data integration, quality issues, and implementation costs continue to be influential when Big Data solutions are brought into the company. However, in light of the technology's progress, Big Data will continue being put to use in corporate and economic innovation, competitive advantage, and sustainability.

Future research would require exploring other impacts of AI, IoT, cryptocurrency, and other innovative technologies to enhance supply chain sustainability, perhaps concentrating on bridging data integration and security. Equally as fierce as important will be the investigations on how generative AI and quantum computing (QC) will shape the future of supply chain innovation.

REFERENCES

Abhulimen, A., & Ejike, O. (2024). Solving supply chain management issues with AI and Big Data analytics for future operational efficiency. Computer Science & IT Research Journal. https://doi.org/.DOI: 10.51594/csitrj.v5i8.1396

Addo-Tenkorang, R., & Helo, P. (2016). Big data applications in operations/supply-chain management: A literature review. *Computers & Industrial Engineering*, *101*, 528–543. DOI: 10.1016/j.cie.2016.09.023

Al-Samad, K., Sufian, M. A., Haque, S., Faruq, O., Hossain, M. A., Talukder, T., & Shayed, A. U. (2024). Leveraging IoT for Enhanced Supply Chain Management in Manufacturing. AIJMR-Advanced International Journal of Multidisciplinary Research, 2(5).

Apeji, U. D., & Sunmola, F. T. (2023). Sustainable supply chain visibility assessment and proposals for improvements using fuzzy logic. *Journal of Modelling in Management*, *18*(3), 701–726. DOI: 10.1108/JM2-08-2021-0181

Awasthi, S. (2024). Artificial Intelligence in Supply Chain Management. Journal of Student Research. https://doi.org/.DOI: 10.47611/jsrhs.v13i1.5996

Azzi, R., Kilany, R., & Sokhn, M. (2019). The power of a blockchain-based supply chain. *Computers & Industrial Engineering*, *135*, 582–592. DOI: 10.1016/j.cie.2019.06.042

Banaee, H., Ahmed, M. U., & Loutfi, A. (2013). Data mining for wearable sensors in health monitoring systems: A review of recent trends and challenges. *Sensors (Basel)*, *13*(12), 17472–17500. DOI: 10.3390/s131217472 PMID: 24351646

Barratt, M., & Oke, A. (2007). Antecedents of supply chain visibility in retail supply chains: A resource-based theory perspective. *Journal of Operations Management*, *25*(6), 1217–1233. DOI: 10.1016/j.jom.2007.01.003

Barriball, E., George, K., Marcos, I., & Radtke, P. (2020). Jump-starting resilient and reimagined operations: COVID-19 has created an imperative for companies to reconfigure their operations, and an opportunity to transform them. McKinsey & Company, May 2020. https://www.mckinsey.com/business-functions/operations/our-insights/jump-starting-resilientand-reimagined-operations

Baryannis, G., Validi, S., Dani, S., & Antoniou, G. (2018). Supply chain risk management and artificial intelligence: State of the art and future research directions. *International Journal of Production Research*, *57*(7), 2179–2202. DOI: 10.1080/00207543.2018.1530476

Bellany, K., Dhiba, Y., & Loulid, A. (2024). Blockchain and the new vendor-managed inventory: proposal of a conceptual model based on innovation in inter-organisational Supply Chain Management Practices. 2024 IEEE 15th International Colloquium on Logistics and Supply Chain Management (LOGISTIQUA), 1-8. https://doi.org/ DOI: 10.1109/LOGISTIQUA61063.2024.10571530

Ben-Daya, M., Hassini, E., & Bahroun, Z. (2019). Internet of things and supply chain management: A literature review. *International Journal of Production Research, 57*(15-16), 4719–4742. DOI: 10.1080/00207543.2017.1402140

Borgia, E. (2014). The Internet of Things Vision: Key Features, Applications, and Open Issues. Computer Communications.

Boute, R., & Udenio, M. (2021). AI in Logistics and Supply Chain Management. PROD: Empirical (Supply) (Topic). https://doi.org/.DOI: 10.2139/ssrn.3862541

Cetindamar, D., Shdifat, B., & Erfani, S. (2020). Assessing big data analytics capability and sustainability in supply chains.

Chen, H., Chiang, R. H., & Storey, V. C. (2012). Business intelligence and analytics: From big data to big impact. *Management Information Systems Quarterly, 36*(4), 1165–1188. DOI: 10.2307/41703503

Choi, T. M., Wallace, S. W., & Wang, Y. (2017). Big data analytics in operations management. *Production and Operations Management, 27*(10), 1868–1881. DOI: 10.1111/poms.12838 PMID: 26766385

Chowdhury, M. M. H., & Quaddus, M. (2016). Supply chain readiness, response and recovery for resilience. *Supply Chain Management, 21*(6), 709–731. DOI: 10.1108/SCM-12-2015-0463

Christopher, M. (2016). Logistics and Supply Chain Management: Logistics & Supply Chain Management. Pearson UK.

Chopra, S., & Meindl, P. (2021). Supply Chain Management STRATEGY, PLANNING, AND OPERATION (5th ed.). Pearson.

Cole, R., Stevenson, M., & Aitken, J. (2019). Blockchain technology: Implications for operations and supply chain management. *Supply Chain Management, 24*(4), 469–483. Advance online publication. DOI: 10.1108/SCM-09-2018-0309

Dash, R., McMurtrey, M., Rebman, C., & Kar, U. (2019). Application of Artificial Intelligence in Automation of Supply Chain Management. Journal of Strategic Innovation and Sustainability. https://doi.org/.DOI: 10.33423/jsis.v14i3.2105

Druehl, J. C., & Hsuan, J. (2018). *Technological Innovations: Impacts on Supply Chains. Burgess, The Executive Guide to Artificial Intelligence*. Springer International Publishing., DOI: 10.1007/978-3-319-63820-1

Ellaturu, V., & Rajalakshmi, L. (2024). Ai-Driven Solutions for Supply Chain Management. *Journal of Informatics Education and Research*. https://doi.org/.DOI: 10.52783/jier.v4i2.849

Farooq, M., & Yen, Y. Y. (2024). Artificial Intelligence in Supply Chain Management: A Comprehensive Review and Framework for Resilience and Sustainability.

Finkenstadt, D. J., & Handfield, R. (2021). Blurry vision: Supply chain visibility for personal protective equipment during COVID-19. *Journal of Purchasing and Supply Management*, *27*(3), 100689. DOI: 10.1016/j.pursup.2021.100689

Fosso Wamba, S., & Akter, S. (2015). Big data analytics for supply chain management: A literature review and research agenda. In Enterprise and Organizational Modeling and Simulation: 11th International Workshop, EOMAS 2015, Held at CAiSE 2015, Stockholm, Sweden, June 8-9, 2015, Selected Papers 11 (pp. 61-72). Springer International Publishing. DOI: 10.1007/978-3-319-24626-0_5

Gandomi, A., & Haider, M. (2015). Beyond the hype: Big data concepts, methods, and analytics. *International Journal of Information Management*, *35*(2), 137–144. DOI: 10.1016/j.ijinfomgt.2014.10.007

Gharbaoui, O., Boukhari, H., & Mazouz, Y. (2024). Analyzing the evolution of artificial intelligence (AI) in supply chain management: a bibliometric analysis. *2024 International Conference on Circuit, Systems and Communication (ICCSC)*, 1-7. https://doi.org/DOI: 10.1109/ICCSC62074.2024.10617358

Giovanni, P. (2020). Blockchain and smart contracts in supply chain management: A game theoretic model. *International Journal of Production Economics*, *228*, 107855. DOI: 10.1016/j.ijpe.2020.107855

Gubbi, J., Buyya, R., Marusic, S., & Palaniswami, M. (2013). Internet of Things (IoT): A vision, architectural elements, and future directions. *Future Generation Computer Systems*, *29*(7), 1645–1660. DOI: 10.1016/j.future.2013.01.010

Hugos, M. H. (2018). *Essentials of Supply Chain Management*. Wiley. DOI: 10.1002/9781119464495

Ivanov, D., Dolgui, A., & Sokolov, B. (2019). The impact of digital technology and Industry 4.0 on the ripple effect and supply chain risk analytics. *International Journal of Production Research*, *57*(3), 829–846. DOI: 10.1080/00207543.2018.1488086

Jacobs, R., & Chase, R. (2018). *Operations and Supply Chain Management* (15th ed.). The McGraw-Hill Education.

Jeble, A., et al. (2018). Big Data Analytics in Supply Chain Management. International Journal of Advanced Operations Management.

Joel, O. S., Oyewole, A. T., Odunaiya, O. G., & Soyombo, O. T. Leveraging artificial intelligence for enhanced supply chain optimization: A comprehensive review of current practices and future potentials, International Journal of Management & Entrepreneurship Research P-ISSN: 2664-3588, E-ISSN: 2664-3596 Volume 6, Issue 3, P.No.707-721, March 2024 DOI: DOI: 10.51594/ijmer.v6i3.882

Kamble, S. S., Gunasekaran, A., & Sharma, R. (2020). Modeling the blockchain enabled traceability in agriculture supply chain. *International Journal of Information Management*, *52*, 101967. DOI: 10.1016/j.ijinfomgt.2019.05.023

Korepin, V., Dzenzeliuk, N., Seryshev, R., & Rogulin, R. (2021). Improving supply chain reliability with blockchain technology. *Maritime Economics & Logistics*. Advance online publication. DOI: 10.1057/s41278-021-00197-4

Kosasih, E., Papadakis, E., Baryannis, G., & Brintrup, A. (2023). A review of explainable artificial intelligence in supply chain management using neurosymbolic approaches. *International Journal of Production Research*, *62*(4), 1510–1540. DOI: 10.1080/00207543.2023.2281663

Kshetri, N. (2018). Blockchain's roles in meeting key supply chain management objectives. *International Journal of Information Management*, *39*, 80–89. DOI: 10.1016/j.ijinfomgt.2017.12.005

Laaper, S. F. (2017). Using blockchain to drive supply chain innovation. London, UK: Deloitte.

. Mathur, T. (2024). Reviewing Optimization Techniques in Supply Chains: AI and Blockchain Perspectives. INTERANTIONAL JOURNAL OF SCIENTIFIC RESEARCH IN ENGINEERING AND MANAGEMENT. .DOI: 10.55041/IJSREM35739

McAfee, A., & Brynjolfsson, E. (2012). Big data: The management revolution. *Harvard Business Review*, *90*(10), 60–68. PMID: 23074865

Messina, D., Soares, A. L., Barros, A. C., & Zimmermann, R. (2023). How visible is your supply chain? A model for supply chain visibility assessment. In Supply Chain Forum [). Taylor & Francis.]. *International Journal (Toronto, Ont.)*, *24*(4), 462–474.

Moosavi, J., Naeni, L., Fathollahi-Fard, A., & Fiore, U. (2021). Blockchain in supply chain management: a review, bibliometric, and network analysis. Environmental Science and Pollution Research, 1 - 15. https://doi.org/.DOI: 10.1007/s11356-021-13094-3

Nagurney, A., Zhang, D. and Zhang, D. (2021). Artificial intelligence and supply chain management: A comprehensive literature review and research agenda. Journal of Business Research. Journal of Business Research, 130, pp.392–402., pp. 392–402.

Nasaruddin, F., Gani, A., Karim, A., Hashem, I., Siddiqa, A., & Yaqoob, I. (2017). Big IoT Data Analytics: Architecture, Opportunities, and Open Research Challenges. *IEEE Access : Practical Innovations, Open Solutions*, *5*, 5247–5261. DOI: 10.1109/ACCESS.2017.2689040

Nsisong Louis Eyo-Udo. (2024). Leveraging artificial intelligence for enhanced supply chain optimization. *Open Access Research Journal of Multidisciplinary Studies*. https://doi.org/.DOI: 10.53022/oarjms.2024.7.2.0044

Patalas-Maliszewska, J., Szmołda, M., & Łosyk, H. (2024). Integrating Artificial Intelligence into the Supply Chain in Order to Enhance Sustainable Production—A Systematic Literature Review. *Sustainability (Basel)*, *16*(16), 7110. Advance online publication. DOI: 10.3390/su16167110

Phan, V. D. V., Huang, Y. F., Hoang, T. T., & Do, M. H. (2023). Evaluating barriers to supply chain resilience in vietnamese SMEs: The fuzzy VIKOR approach. *Systems*, *11*(3), 121. DOI: 10.3390/systems11030121

Pournader, M., Shi, Y., Seuring, S., & Koh, S. (2019). Blockchain applications in supply chains, transport and logistics: A systematic review of the literature. *International Journal of Production Research*, *58*(7), 2063–2081. DOI: 10.1080/00207543.2019.1650976

Qader, G., Junaid, M., Abbas, Q., & Mubarik, M. S. (2022). Industry 4.0 enables supply chain resilience and supply chain performance. *Technological Forecasting and Social Change*, *185*, 122026. DOI: 10.1016/j.techfore.2022.122026

Seow, R. (2023). Entrenching Supply Chain Resilience Beyond Boundaries: A Dynamic Framework in Post-Covid Landscape. [JTOM]. *Journal of Technology and Operations Management*, *18*(2), 20–48. DOI: 10.32890/jtom2023.18.2.3

Seuring, S., & Muller, M. (2008). From a literature review to a conceptual framework for sustainable supply chain management. *Journal of Cleaner Production*, *16*(15), 1699–1710. DOI: 10.1016/j.jclepro.2008.04.020

Seyedan, M., & Mafakheri, F. (2020). Predictive big data analytics for supply chain demand forecasting: Methods, applications, and research opportunities. *Journal of Big Data*, *7*(1), 53. Advance online publication. DOI: 10.1186/s40537-020-00329-2

Shahzadi, G., Jia, F., Chen, L., & John, A. (2024). AI adoption in supply chain management: A systematic literature review. *Journal of Manufacturing Technology Management*, *35*(6), 1125–1150. Advance online publication. DOI: 10.1108/JMTM-09-2023-0431

Shen, R., Zhou, F., Ye, X., Zhong, L., & Feng, S. (2024). Research on the application of artificial intelligence technology in supply chain management. *E3S Web of Conferences*. https://doi.org/.DOI: 10.1051/e3sconf/202456503017

Singh, C., Thakkar, R., & Warraich, J. (2022). Blockchain in Supply Chain Management. European Journal of Engineering and Technology Research. https://doi.org/.DOI: 10.24018/ejeng.2022.7.5.2888

Singh, R., Modgil, S., & Shore, A. (2023). Building artificial intelligence enabled resilient supply chain: A multi-method approach. *Journal of Enterprise Information Management*, *37*(2), 414–436. DOI: 10.1108/JEIM-09-2022-0326

Taylor, P. (2023). Amount of data created, consumed, and stored 2010-2020, with forecasts to 2025. Statista. Available online: https://www. statista. com/statistics/871513/worldwide-data-created/(accessed on 24 October 2023).

Toorajipour, R., Sohrabpour, V., Nazarpour, A., Oghazi, P., & Fischl, M. (2021). Artificial intelligence in supply chain management: A systematic literature review. *Journal of Business Research*, *122*, 502–517. Advance online publication. DOI: 10.1016/j.jbusres.2020.09.009

Udeh, E. O., Amajuoyi, P., Adeusi, K. B., & Scott, A. O. (2024). The role of IoT in boosting supply chain transparency and efficiency. *Magna Scientia Adv. Res. Rev.*, *12*(1), 178–197. DOI: 10.30574/msarr.2024.11.1.0081

Waller, M. A., & Fawcett, S. E. (2013). Data science, predictive analytics, and big data: A revolution that will transform supply chain design and management. *Journal of Business Logistics*, *34*(2), 77–84. DOI: 10.1111/jbl.12010

Weber, Y., & Tarba, S. Y. (2014). Strategic agility: A state-of-the-art introduction to the special section on strategic agility. *California Management Review*, *56*(3), 5–12. DOI: 10.1525/cmr.2014.56.3.5

Wilkin, C., Ferreira, A., Rotaru, K., & Gaerlan, L. R. (2020). Big data prioritization in SCM decision-making: Its role and performance implications. *International Journal of Accounting Information Systems*, *38*, 100470. DOI: 10.1016/j.accinf.2020.100470

Winardi, S., Wong, N. P., Halim, A., & Megawan, S. (2024). Enhancing Warehouse Inventory Management through IoT Tools for Monitoring Stock Items. In 2024 2nd International Conference on Technology Innovation and Its Applications (ICTIIA) (pp. 1-6). IEEE. DOI: 10.1109/ICTIIA61827.2024.10761815

Wodecki (2019). Influence of Artificial Intelligence on Activities and Competitiveness of an Organization, in Artificial Intelligence in Value Creation, Cham: Springer International Publishing, 2019, pp. 133–246. .DOI: 10.1007/978-3-319-91596-8_3

Zikopoulos, P., Eaton, C., deRoos, D., Detusch, T., & Lapis, G. (2012). *Understanding Big Data: Analytics for Enterprise Class Hadoop and Streaming Data (IBM.).* McGraw.

Chapter 5
Harnessing Emerging Technologies for Enhancing Supply Chain Resilience:
A New Perspective

G. Sridhar
http://orcid.org/0009-0004-2748-572X
The Gandhigram Rural Institute, India

H. Samuel Thavaraj
http://orcid.org/0009-0005-7541-4608
The Gandhigram Rural Institute, India

Seema Vinod
http://orcid.org/0009-0003-4558-7757
The Gandhigram Rural Institute, India

V. Monica Hepzibah Pushpabai
http://orcid.org/0009-0007-5493-8378
Anna Government College for Women, India

ABSTRACT

Supply chain resilience is critical in addressing disruptions that jeopardize business continuity, with traditional risk management strategies often falling short. AI techniques,Bayesian networks, are particularly highlighted for their potential, though the growth phase of resilience remains insufficiently explored. Recent crises, including the pandemic and geopolitical dealings like the Russian assault of Ukraine, must

DOI: 10.4018/979-8-2600-1855-2.ch005

accelerate the adoption of digital tools, encouraging a shift from lean strategies to "just-in-case" approaches. These developments stress on proactive digital capabilities to mitigate risks and manage uncertainties. Despite their promise, challenges such as security risks,interoperability issues, and limited digital maturity constrain the full utilization of disruptive technologies. This study synthesizes to offer a comprehensive perspective on how emerging technologies transform supply chain risk management. It concludes by underscoring the need for further exploration of the growth phase and optimization of digital technologies to achieve sustained resilience.

INTRODUCTION

In todays organized and dynamic commercial environment, supply chains face unprecedented exposure to disruptions fluctuating from usual disasters and pandemics to geopolitical tensions and cyberattacks. These disturbances have highlighted the implication of SCRs as a cornerstone of organisational sustainability and competitiveness. Traditional risk management approaches, often reactive and linear, are no longer adequate to address the growing complexity and interdependencies within global supply chains. As a result, businesses are looking for advanced solutions to not only mitigate risks but also enhance their capability to familiarize and recover in uncertainty. Emerging skills, including AI, blockchain, and the IoT, are at the forefront of these solutions, offering transformative potential for strengthening SCRs. These expertises allow actual data integration, analytical analysis, and seamless communication throughout the supply chain, enhancing critical stages such as readiness, response, and recovery. AI-powered models like Bayesian networks provide advanced decision-making capabilities, while blockchain ensures transparency and traceability. It enables end on perceptibility, enabling organisations to detect disruptions early and act swiftly. Together, these technologies are redefining traditional paradigms of SCM by development greater quickness and robustness. Current worldwide events, such as the pandemic conflicts, have further underlined the pressing need for technological integration in resource shackle actions. These disruptions have exposed vulnerabilities in lean supply chain models, prompting a shift toward strategies that prioritise flexibility and preparedness over cost efficiency. However, the adoption of these technologies, including concerns of safety, interoperability, and digital maturity.

Addressing these barriers requires a multifaceted method involving share in digital infrastructure, fostering digital literacy, and establishing standardised frameworks that promote technological compatibility and cybersecurity. The adoption of AI-driven predictive analytics improves SCR by improving mandate forecasting, risk assessment, and decision-making. Machine learning systems analyse vast extents of data to classify designs and forecast disruptions before they occur, enabling organisations to implement proactive mitigation strategies. Blockchain technology enhances transparency and traceability by securely recording transactions risks and inefficiencies. Additionally, IoT-enabled devices facilitate real-time monitoring of goods in transit, improving visibility and allowing for immediate response to potential disruptions. While these technologies significantly enhance resilience, their implementation requires substantial investment, training, and a shift in organisational culture. Beyond technological advancements, supply chain resilience depends on organisational agility and adaptive capabilities. Agile supply chains can quickly adjust to changing market conditions and disruptions, maintaining service levels and operational efficiency. This requires a shift from linear, cost-driven models to dynamic, responsive frameworks that integrate risk management into strategic planning.

Organisations must cultivate a resilience-oriented mindset, where flexibility and adaptability become core components of supply chain management. Employee training, cross-functional collaboration, and scenario-based planning contribute to an organisation's aptitude to react effectively to disruptions. Government guidelines and monitoring outlines play a important part in determining supply chain resilience strategies. Regulatory requirements for data security, trade compliance, and sustainability influence how organisations structure their supply chains. Governments can support businesses by providing incentives for digital transformation, investing in infrastructure development, and facilitating knowledge-sharing initiatives. Public-private partnerships foster innovation and create a supportive ecosystem for resilience-building initiatives. Organisations that had already invested in digital transformation and resilience-building measures were better equipped to navigate the crisis. The pandemic accelerated the adoption of digital technologies, compelling businesses to rethink traditional supply chain models and prioritise resilience over cost efficiency. Future research should focus on quantifying the impact of digital resilience strategies and exploring sector-specific resilience models.

Comprehensive frameworks that integrate advanced technologies across all phases of supply chain resilience are increasingly necessary. Models such as the AI-SCRes framework can systematically incorporate technological innovations into resilience strategies. Future research should prioritise empirical studies assessing the real-world impact of these technologies and their applications across different supply chain contexts. Additionally, cross-industry collaboration and policy support are essential for fostering innovation and adoption. Research should also explore the role of supply chain resilience in sustainability, as resilient supply chains are more adaptable to regulatory changes and environmental challenges. The future of supply chain resilience depends on continuous innovation and collaboration among businesses, policymakers, and technology providers. Organisations must proactively integrate digital technologies while addressing existing barriers. Strategies combining technological advancements with organisational agility, workforce development, and regulatory alignment are crucial for building robust and adaptive supply chains. Moreover, addressing the underexplored growth phase of resilience will be key to long-term competitiveness in an increasingly volatile global environment. By tackling these challenges and fostering collaboration, organisations can develop comprehensive resilience strategies that ensure operational sustainability and competitiveness. The integration of emerging technologies offers immense potential to enhance resilience, allowing businesses to transition from reactive risk management to proactive strategies. The findings of this study provide a foundation for future research and practice, emphasising the importance of continuous innovation and collaboration in building resilient and adaptive supply chains. As global challenges persist, supply chain resilience will remain a key determinant of long-term success and sustainability.

OBJECTIVES

Sustainable Supply Chain Management (SSCM) plays a crucial role in balancing ecological, fiscal, and social priorities, especially in emerging economies. These economies face distinct challenges such as rapid industrialization, limited infrastructure, and socio-economic disparities. However, they also present significant opportunities for sustainable growth through rising consumer awareness and technological advancements. This study identifies actionable strategies to address resource constraints, reduce waste, and enhance efficiency. It explores the potential of digitalization and circular economy principles to drive innovation and foster long-term sustainability. Furthermore, it emphasizes the importance of leadership, cross-sector partnerships, and capacity-building initiatives. These strategies promote resilience, inclusive development, and collaboration across industries. By adopting these approaches, emerging economies can enhance their competitiveness while supporting global sustainability goals. Ultimately, the study offers valuable insights into creating supply chains that align economic, environmental, and social imperatives for sustainable progress. Sustainable Supply Chain Management (SSCM) plays a crucial role in balancing ecological, fiscal, and social priorities, particularly in emerging economies where rapid industrialization and socio-economic disparities present both challenges and opportunities.

These economies are undergoing transformative shifts, and the need for sustainability in supply chain operations has never been more pronounced. By integrating environmental considerations, ethical labor practices, and economic efficiency, SSCM helps organizations navigate complex global markets while ensuring long-term viability. The adoption of sustainable practices in supply chains is not merely a compliance requirement but a strategic necessity that contributes to resilience, innovation, and competitiveness. Emerging economies often struggle with limited infrastructure, regulatory inconsistencies, and financial constraints that hinder the implementation of sustainable supply chain practices. However, these same economies possess immense potential for sustainable growth, driven by increasing consumer awareness, technological advancements, and governmental initiatives aimed at fostering sustainability. Businesses in these regions must adopt innovative strategies that optimize resource utilization, reduce waste, and enhance overall efficiency. One of the key drivers of SSCM is digitalization, which enables real-time monitoring, predictive analytics, and improved decision-making. Through artificial intelligence, blockchain, and the Internet of Things, supply chains can become more transparent, responsive, and accountable. These technologies help businesses track sustainability metrics, ensure compliance with environmental regulations, and mitigate risks associated with supply chain disruptions. Circular economy principles play a pivotal role in enhancing SSCM by promoting resource efficiency, waste reduction, and product lifecycle extension. Instead of the traditional linear model of production and consumption, circular supply chains focus on reusing, recycling, and remanufacturing materials to minimize environmental impact. This approach not only reduces dependency on finite resources but also generates economic benefits by creating new business opportunities and cost-saving mechanisms. Companies adopting circular economy principles gain a competitive edge by meeting the growing consumer demand for sustainable products while reducing operational costs associated with resource depletion and waste management. Leadership and cross-sector partnerships are essential for advancing SSCM initiatives. Effective leadership fosters a culture of sustainability within organizations, ensuring that sustainability goals are embedded in corporate strategies.

Leaders who prioritize sustainability encourage innovation, enhance stakeholder engagement, and drive organizational change. Cross-sector collaborations between businesses, governments, non-governmental organizations, and academia facilitate knowledge exchange, capacity-building initiatives, and the development of industry-wide sustainability standards. These partnerships play a crucial role in addressing systemic challenges, such as supply chain fragmentation, resource scarcity, and policy enforcement. Capacity-building initiatives enhance the ability of businesses and supply chain partners to adopt sustainable practices. Training programs, workshops, and skill development initiatives equip stakeholders with the knowledge and tools necessary to implement SSCM effectively. Education and awareness campaigns help suppliers, manufacturers, and consumers understand the benefits of sustainable supply chains and encourage proactive participation. Governments and industry associations must work together to create incentive structures that reward businesses for adopting sustainable practices, thereby fostering a business environment that prioritizes long-term sustainability over short-term gains. Resilience is a critical component of SSCM, especially in the face of economic uncertainties, climate change, and geopolitical tensions.

Businesses that integrate sustainability into their supply chains build resilience by diversifying supplier networks, reducing dependency on volatile resources, and investing in adaptive technologies. Flexible supply chain models that incorporate digitalization, automation, and local sourcing enable organizations to respond effectively to disruptions while maintaining sustainability commitments. By fostering resilience, companies can navigate challenges more effectively and sustain growth even in dynamic market conditions. Inclusive development is another important aspect of SSCM, ensuring that supply chain benefits are equitably distributed across stakeholders, including small and medium enterprises (SMEs), workers, and local communities. Ethical sourcing, fair trade practices, and social responsibility initiatives contribute to social sustainability by improving labor conditions, promoting gender equality, and supporting economic empowerment. Businesses that prioritize inclusivity in their supply chains enhance their reputations, build stronger stakeholder relationships, and contribute to broader societal well-being. Collaboration across industries is essential for scaling SSCM initiatives and achieving collective sustainability goals. Industry-wide collaborations foster innovation, enable resource-sharing, and drive the development of standardized sustainability metrics. Collaborative efforts between competitors, suppliers, and regulatory bodies create a unified approach to sustainability, ensuring that best practices are widely adopted and continuously improved.

These collaborations facilitate the pooling of resources for large-scale sustainability projects, such as renewable energy adoption, sustainable packaging solutions, and carbon footprint reduction initiatives. By adopting a holistic approach to SSCM, emerging economies can enhance their competitiveness while contributing to global sustainability efforts. Sustainable supply chains create value not only for businesses but also for society and the environment. Companies that integrate sustainability into their supply chain strategies experience improved brand reputation, increased consumer trust, and enhanced investor confidence. Consumers are increasingly making purchasing decisions based on sustainability considerations, and businesses that fail to adapt risk losing market relevance. Government policies and regulations play a fundamental role in driving SSCM adoption. Regulatory frameworks that enforce environmental standards, promote corporate social responsibility, and incentivize sustainable practices encourage businesses to integrate sustainability into their supply chain operations. Governments must work collaboratively with industry stakeholders to develop policies that strike a balance between sustainability objectives and economic growth. Public-private partnerships can accelerate the implementation of sustainable supply chain initiatives by leveraging resources, expertise, and technology.

The transition towards SSCM requires a paradigm shift in business operations, moving from short-term profit maximization to long-term value creation. Companies that embrace sustainability as a core business principle achieve operational efficiencies, reduce costs associated with environmental fines and resource wastage, and enhance innovation capabilities. Sustainable supply chains not only mitigate risks but also create opportunities for differentiation and market leadership. Investment in research and development (R&D) is crucial for advancing SSCM. Businesses that allocate resources to sustainability-focused R&D drive innovation in eco-friendly materials, energy-efficient technologies, and waste reduction solutions. Collaboration between academic institutions and industry players fosters knowledge-sharing and the development of cutting-edge sustainability solutions. Companies that invest in sustainability-oriented R&D position themselves as pioneers in their respective industries, gaining a competitive advantage in an increasingly sustainability-conscious market. Financial incentives and funding mechanisms are essential for supporting businesses in their sustainability transitions. Access to green financing, sustainability-linked loans, and impact investment opportunities enable businesses to implement SSCM initiatives without compromising financial stability. Governments and financial institutions should collaborate to create funding programs that incentivize businesses to adopt sustainable practices while ensuring economic feasibility.

Financial support mechanisms can accelerate the adoption of renewable energy, sustainable logistics, and carbon-neutral manufacturing processes. Stakeholder engagement is fundamental to the success of SSCM. Transparent communication with stakeholders, including investors, employees, consumers, and suppliers, builds trust and fosters accountability. Businesses that actively engage stakeholders in sustainability initiatives create a culture of shared responsibility and collective action. Sustainability reporting, third-party certifications, and corporate sustainability disclosures enhance transparency and demonstrate a company's commitment to sustainable practices. Consumer behavior plays a pivotal role in shaping the demand for sustainable products and services. Companies that educate consumers on the environmental and social impacts of their purchasing decisions contribute to a more sustainable marketplace. Marketing strategies that highlight sustainability attributes, eco-labeling, and green certifications influence consumer preferences and drive demand for responsibly sourced products. Businesses that align their supply chain strategies with consumer sustainability expectations gain a competitive edge and strengthen brand loyalty. Global supply chains are interconnected, and sustainability challenges require collaborative solutions.

International cooperation, knowledge-sharing platforms, and cross-border partnerships facilitate the exchange of best practices and the development of harmonized sustainability standards. Organizations such as the United Nations, World Trade Organization, and sustainability-focused industry consortia play a vital role in fostering global sustainability efforts. Businesses that actively participate in international sustainability initiatives contribute to a collective movement towards a more sustainable and equitable global economy. The future of SSCM lies in continuous innovation, commitment, and collective action. As environmental and social challenges intensify, businesses must proactively integrate sustainability into their supply chain operations. The adoption of emerging technologies, adherence to sustainability principles, and engagement in industry collaborations will drive the evolution of sustainable supply chains. Companies that prioritize SSCM will be better positioned to navigate regulatory changes, consumer expectations, and market dynamics. By embedding sustainability into supply chain strategies, businesses can create long-term value, enhance resilience, and contribute to global sustainability goals. The transformation towards sustainable supply chains requires a multi-stakeholder approach, involving governments, businesses, consumers, and civil society. As the global economy continues to evolve, SSCM will remain a fundamental driver of responsible business practices, economic stability, and environmental preservation. By embracing sustainable supply chain management, businesses can shape a future where economic growth and sustainability go hand in hand, fostering a more resilient and equitable world.

REVIEW OF LITERATURE

Modern supply chains operate in an increasingly unstable global environment, where disruptions arising from pandemics, geopolitical tensions, natural disasters, and cyber threats have become more frequent and severe. These challenges highlight the inadequacies of traditional risk management strategies, which often depend on reactive measures and static approaches that fail to address the dynamic complexities of contemporary supply networks. As supply chains grow more interconnected and reliant on global operations, the need for a proactive, flexible, and technology-driven resilience framework has become imperative for ensuring business continuity and long-term competitiveness. The evolving landscape of supply chain management demands a shift from conventional risk mitigation practices to resilience-focused strategies that enhance adaptability and responsiveness. Companies are increasingly recognizing the importance of integrating advanced technologies such as artificial intelligence, blockchain, and the Internet of Things to improve supply chain visibility, streamline communication, and enable predictive analytics. Artificial intelligence facilitates real-time data analysis, allowing organizations to anticipate potential disruptions and develop strategic responses before issues escalate. Blockchain technology ensures transparency and security by providing immutable records of transactions, thereby reducing the risk of fraud and improving trust among supply chain stakeholders. The Internet of Things enhances end-to-end monitoring by enabling real-time tracking of goods and assets, improving operational efficiency and decision-making. Despite the promise of emerging technologies, their integration into supply chain operations presents significant challenges. Many organizations face barriers such as digital immaturity, interoperability issues, cybersecurity risks, and resistance to technological adoption. Smaller enterprises and businesses operating in developing economies often struggle with the financial and infrastructural investments required for digital transformation. Addressing these challenges necessitates a comprehensive approach that includes investment in digital literacy programs, policy support for technological innovation, and the establishment of standardized frameworks that facilitate seamless data exchange across supply chain networks. Cross-industry collaborations and public-private partnerships also play a crucial role in accelerating the adoption of resilient supply chain practices by fostering knowledge-sharing and resource pooling. The disruptions caused by recent global crises, such as the COVID-19 pandemic and geopolitical conflicts, have further underscored the urgency of strengthening supply chain resilience.

The vulnerabilities exposed by these events have compelled organizations to rethink their operational strategies and adopt more robust, risk-averse models. Many companies are transitioning from lean, cost-driven supply chain structures to more flexible, demand-driven frameworks that prioritize redundancy, diversification, and contingency planning (Kassa et al., 2023; Zhao et al., 2023). The shift from "just-in-time" to "just-in-case" inventory strategies exemplifies this transition, ensuring that businesses can absorb shocks without compromising service levels. Moving forward, organizations must integrate resilience into the core of their supply chain strategies, leveraging technological advancements and innovative risk management approaches. Future research should focus on quantifying the long-term impact of digital resilience initiatives, developing industry-specific resilience models, and identifying best practices for scalable implementation. By addressing existing gaps and proactively adapting to evolving challenges, businesses can build supply chains that are not only efficient but also resilient, ensuring sustained success in an increasingly volatile global marketplace.

As organizations struggle to adapt to these challenges, the cascading effects of minor disruptions amplify across industries, magnifying their impact on global operations and economies. Supply chain vulnerabilities are no longer isolated to specific regions or sectors but have far-reaching consequences that can destabilize entire markets. The reliance on interconnected networks means that even minor inefficiencies or bottlenecks can trigger significant disruptions, affecting production cycles, inventory levels, and distribution channels. This interdependency underscores the need for a holistic approach to supply chain resilience, where companies not only anticipate risks but also cultivate agility to respond dynamically. To achieve this, businesses must invest in predictive analytics, scenario planning, and digital transformation initiatives that enhance visibility and decision-making capabilities. Supply chain leaders must embrace collaboration with technology providers, industry peers, and policymakers to create ecosystems that support seamless data sharing and real-time risk assessment. Moreover, organizations should focus on workforce training and digital literacy programs to equip employees with the necessary skills to navigate the complexities of modern supply chains effectively. Governments and regulatory bodies also play a crucial role in strengthening supply chain resilience by fostering supportive policies, investing in infrastructure, and promoting public-private partnerships. Incentivizing innovation and research in resilient supply chain models can further drive the development of standardized frameworks that facilitate adaptability across diverse industries. As businesses strive to build more robust supply chains, resilience must be embedded into corporate strategies, ensuring long-term sustainability and the ability to withstand future disruptions (Belhadi et al., 2024; Shoomal et al., 2024).

Supply chain resilience (SCRes) has consequently emerged as a vital focus area, redefining risk management paradigms to incorporate proactive strategies that emphasize agility, adaptability, and visibility. Traditional risk management approaches, which rely heavily on reactive measures, have proven insufficient in addressing the complexities of modern global supply chains. In an era where disruptions can stem from pandemics, geopolitical conflicts, cyber threats, and climate change, businesses must transition from static, contingency-based models to dynamic frameworks that integrate predictive analytics and real-time decision-making. The integration of emerging technologies such as artificial intelligence (AI), blockchain, and the Internet of Things (IoT) has become instrumental in strengthening SCRes. AI-driven predictive analytics enable organizations to anticipate potential disruptions, optimize demand forecasting, and enhance supply chain visibility.

Blockchain ensures transparency, security, and trust among stakeholders by creating immutable transaction records, mitigating risks related to fraud and counterfeiting. IoT-enabled devices facilitate real-time monitoring of supply chain operations, allowing companies to identify inefficiencies, track shipments, and respond swiftly to emerging threats. These technologies collectively empower businesses to move beyond reactive approaches, fostering a proactive culture of resilience that enhances operational continuity. Despite the potential of these technological advancements, challenges remain in achieving widespread adoption. Many organizations, particularly small and medium enterprises (SMEs), face financial and technical barriers that prevent them from leveraging cutting-edge solutions effectively. Addressing these challenges requires strategic investments in digital infrastructure, workforce upskilling, and policy frameworks that promote technological standardization and cybersecurity. Cross-industry collaboration and public-private partnerships will be essential in driving the adoption of resilient supply chain strategies, ensuring that businesses can collectively withstand and recover from disruptions (Colehower, 2023; Naz et al., 2022). These proactive strategies enable organisations to anticipate disruptions, respond efficiently, and recover swiftly, minimising operational downtime and economic loss (Agarwal et al., 2024; Rha, 2020).

Research highlights the growing acceptance of advanced digital expertise, such as artificial intelligence (AI), blockchain, and the Internet of Things (IoT), which play a key role in strengthening supply chain resilience (SCRes) by providing real-time monitoring, predictive analytics, and enhanced communication across supply chain systems. These technologies have revolutionized traditional risk management approaches, enabling businesses to transition from reactive strategies to proactive resilience-building measures. AI-driven predictive models allow organizations to anticipate potential disruptions, optimize inventory management, and improve demand forecasting, reducing the impact of supply chain shocks. Blockchain enhances transparency, security, and trust among supply chain stakeholders by ensuring immutable and verifiable transaction records, mitigating risks associated with fraud, counterfeiting, and data manipulation. IoT facilitates end-to-end visibility by connecting smart devices, allowing businesses to track shipments, monitor environmental conditions, and detect operational inefficiencies in real time. The integration of these digital tools has become imperative in addressing the increasing complexity of global supply chains.

The COVID-19 pandemic, geopolitical conflicts, and cybersecurity threats have exposed vulnerabilities in traditional supply chain models, emphasizing the need for agility, adaptability, and data-driven decision-making. Companies that have invested in digital transformation are better equipped to navigate uncertainties and maintain operational continuity in the face of disruptions. However, challenges such as digital immaturity, high implementation costs, interoperability issues, and data privacy concerns remain significant barriers to widespread adoption, particularly for small and medium enterprises (SMEs) and businesses in developing economies. Overcoming these challenges requires a multifaceted approach, including investments in digital infrastructure, workforce upskilling, regulatory support, and cross-industry collaboration. Governments and industry leaders must work together to establish standardized frameworks that promote technological compatibility, cybersecurity, and ethical data usage. Additionally, fostering a culture of digital literacy and innovation will be crucial in enabling businesses to leverage emerging technologies effectively. As supply chain disruptions continue to grow in frequency and severity, integrating AI, blockchain, and IoT into supply chain resilience strategies is no longer a competitive advantage but a necessity. Future research should focus on empirical assessments of digital resilience initiatives, industry-specific case studies, and the development of scalable frameworks to ensure the seamless adoption of advanced technologies. By addressing existing gaps and proactively leveraging digital solutions, organizations can build supply chains that are not only efficient but also resilient, ensuring long-term sustainability and competitiveness in an increasingly volatile global market (Liu et al., 2023; Zamani et al., 2023).

AI has been particularly instrumental in modeling complex risk scenarios, enhancing decision-making processes, and improving responsiveness during crises. Through machine learning algorithms and predictive analytics, AI enables organizations to identify potential disruptions before they occur, allowing for proactive risk mitigation strategies. Bayesian networks and deep learning models help businesses assess the probability of various risk events and simulate their potential impacts, thereby improving preparedness and response capabilities. During crises, AI-driven automation plays a critical role in optimizing supply chain operations. For instance, AI enhances demand forecasting accuracy by analyzing historical sales data, market trends, and external factors such as weather patterns or geopolitical developments. AI-powered robotic process automation (RPA) streamlines logistics and procurement processes by automating repetitive tasks, increasing efficiency, and reducing human errors. One of the most significant contributions of AI to supply chain resilience is its ability to improve supply chain visibility. By integrating AI with the Internet of Things (IoT), businesses can monitor real-time data from interconnected devices, tracking shipments, monitoring environmental conditions, and identifying potential bottlenecks. This end-to-end visibility enhances agility, allowing organizations to swiftly adapt to changing circumstances and minimize disruptions. Despite its transformative potential, AI adoption in supply chain resilience faces challenges such as high implementation costs, the need for skilled professionals, data privacy concerns, and interoperability issues with existing systems. Overcoming these barriers requires strategic investments in AI infrastructure, workforce training, and regulatory support to ensure ethical and secure data usage (Kassa et al., 2023; Zhao et al., 2023).

Blockchain technology, with its secure and transparent data-sharing capabilities, fosters trust and collaboration among stakeholders, while IoT enables continuous monitoring and data collection across supply chain nodes. By leveraging blockchain, organizations can create tamper-proof, decentralized ledgers that record every transaction in the supply chain, ensuring authenticity and traceability. This transparency reduces the risk of fraud, counterfeiting, and data manipulation, thereby strengthening stakeholder confidence. Smart contracts, a key feature of blockchain, automate and enforce agreements without intermediaries, streamlining procurement, payments, and compliance processes. The integration of blockchain with supply chain management enhances operational efficiency by reducing delays, improving documentation accuracy, and minimizing disputes. For instance, blockchain can verify the origin and quality of raw materials in industries such as pharmaceuticals and food supply chains, ensuring compliance with safety regulations. Additionally, real-time visibility into inventory movements prevents bottlenecks, optimizing supply chain performance. IoT, when combined with blockchain, further strengthens supply chain resilience by enabling continuous monitoring through interconnected devices. Sensors embedded in shipments, warehouses, and production facilities collect real-time data on location, temperature, humidity, and other environmental factors, ensuring quality control and compliance. This data is securely stored on the blockchain, preventing unauthorized alterations and providing a reliable audit trail.

Despite its potential, the widespread adoption of blockchain and IoT in supply chain resilience faces challenges such as high implementation costs, technological complexity, and interoperability issues. Additionally, concerns regarding data privacy and regulatory compliance must be addressed to ensure seamless integration. Overcoming these barriers requires industry-wide collaboration, investment in digital infrastructure, and the development of standardized frameworks. Future research should explore scalable blockchain solutions tailored to diverse supply chain contexts and assess the long-term impact of IoT-driven monitoring on operational efficiency and risk mitigation. By embracing these technologies, organizations can build agile, transparent, and resilient supply chains capable of withstanding disruptions and maintaining competitiveness in an evolving global landscape (Z. Yang et al., 2024; Zamani et al., 2023). However, challenges such as digital immaturity, interoperability issues, and security concerns persist, necessitating further research and investment to entirely realise the potential of these tools (Birkel et al., 2023; Shoomal et al., 2024). By integrating these technologies into supply chain operations, businesses can shift from reactive risk management to robust resilience strategies, ensuring continuity and competitiveness in an era of increasing uncertainty (Belhadi et al., 2024; Colehower, 2023). Future research should prioritise cross-industry collaboration and empirical studies to address existing gaps, particularly the underexplored growth phase of SCRes, and develop comprehensive frameworks for sustainable supply chain management (Kassa et al., 2023; Z. Yang et al., 2024).

Emerging technologies, including artificial intelligence (AI), blockchain, and the Internet of Things (IoT), are transforming supply chain resilience (SCRes) by addressing the limitations of traditional systems and providing innovative solutions to modern challenges. These tools assist actual data assimilation, predictive analytics, and decentralised communication, all of which are critical for ornamental stream sequence elasticity, perceptibility, and receptiveness (Shoomal et al., 2024; Zamani et al., 2023). AI-driven algorithms, for example, are capable of modelling complex risk scenarios and enabling advanced decision-making under uncertain conditions (Kassa et al., 2023; Z. Yang et al., 2024). Blockchain technology enhances data security and transparency, fostering faith and collaboration among supply chain investors by confirming tamper-proof and auditable records (Belhadi et al., 2024; Zhao et al., 2023). Simultaneously, IoT facilitates continuous monitoring of supply chain nodes through interconnected sensors and devices, providing actionable insights into real-time operational conditions (Naz et al., 2022; Zamani et al., 2023).

These technological capabilities collectively strengthen critical SCRes phases, such as readiness, response, and recovery, allowing businesses to mitigate risks, adapt rapidly, and reduce downtime during disruptions (Agarwal et al., 2024; Birkel et al., 2023). However, despite the evident benefits, significant gaps persist in understanding how these technologies can be leveraged to support the growth phase of SCRes, which focuses on long-term organisational adaptability and competitive advantage (Colehower, 2023; Liu et al., 2023). Barriers such as technological interoperability issues, digital immaturity, and security concerns further impede the widespread adoption of these tools, highlighting the need for targeted research and investment to optimise their potential (Rha, 2020; Shoomal et al., 2024). Addressing these challenges and fully integrating AI, blockchain, and IoT into supply chain strategies could unlock new opportunities for enhancing resilience and achieving sustainable organisational growth (Z. Yang et al., 2024; Zamani et al., 2023). The COVID-19 epidemic uncovered important exposures in overall supply chains, compelling organisations to rapidly adopt digital tools to mitigate risks and address the unprecedented challenges it presented (Naz et al., 2022; Rha, 2020). Digitalisation emerged as a critical enabler for businesses, facilitating a strategic shift from reactive "just-in-time" models focused on efficiency and cost minimisation to more proactive "just-in-case" approaches that prioritise flexibility and resilience (Colehower, 2023). This shift underscores the importance of technological integration in managing uncertainty and maintaining continuity in times of crisis. Investigation by (Agarwal et al., 2024; Liu et al., 2023) highlights the transformative role of AI-driven techniques, such as Bayesian networks, which enhance real-time decision-making by analysing complex risk scenarios and predicting disruptions.

These technologies allow businesses to anticipate challenges and streamline recovery efforts, significantly reducing downtime and related expenses (Yang, 2020; Zhao et al., 2023). Despite their potential, barriers such as limited digital maturity, fragmented data systems, and issues of technological interoperability persist, impeding widespread adoption of these advancements (Birkel et al., 2023; Shoomal et al., 2024). These tasks are particularly pronounced in smaller organisations and developing economies, where resources and expertise may be insufficient to fully implement advanced digital solutions (Naz et al., 2022; Zamani et al., 2023). Overcoming these obstacles requires collaborative efforts among stakeholders to enhance technological compatibility, improve digital infrastructure, and foster skills development within supply chain networks (Belhadi et al., 2024; Colehower, 2023). By addressing these challenges, organisations can bind the occupied probable of digital tools to form tough supply chains capable of thriving in an increasingly uncertain global environment. The integration of emerging technologies into supply chain resilience (SCRes) frameworks has been explored through theoretical lenses such as active abilities philosophy and organisational information processing philosophy, which provide valuable visions into leveraging these technologies to enhance adaptability and decision-making (Belhadi et al., 2024; Rha, 2020) Dynamic capabilities theory focuses on an organisation's skill to wisdom, grab, and convert in reply to disruptions, while organisational information processing theory emphasises efficient data flow and decision-making, both of which are strengthened by digital tools like AI, blockchain, and IoT (Liu et al., 2023; Yang, 2020). These skills enhance critical resilience capabilities absorptive, response, and recovery by enabling predictive analytics, real-time data integration, and automated workflows, improving supply chain performance across financial, ecofriendly, and societal dimensions (Shoomal et al., 2024; Zamani et al., 2023). For example, blockchain ensures secure collaboration among stakeholders, IoT facilitates actual monitoring, and AI drives data-driven executive, as demonstrated in the AI-SCRes framework proposed by (Kassa et al., 2023). However, challenges like interoperability, security issues, and resource constraints hinder widespread adoption, necessitating systematic approaches to discourse these barriers (Belhadi et al., 2024; Naz et al., 2022). Strategic alignment, policy support, and cross-industry collaboration are essential to optimise the integration of these technologies, enabling organisations to build resilient supply chains capable of navigating complex and volatile global environments (Shoomal et al., 2024; Z. Yang et al., 2024).

Despite the transformative probable of digitalisation in enhancing supply fetter resilience (SCRes), numerous challenges hinder its optimal implementation. Key issues include data security, standardisation, and the scalability of digital tools, which create significant barriers for organisations attempting to leverage advanced technologies effectively (Birkel et al., 2023; Shoomal et al., 2024). Blockchain technology, for example, is highly effective in improving data transparency and ensuring secure transactions, but its adoption demands substantial financial investment and coordinated collaboration among diverse supply chain stakeholders, complicating its widespread implementation (Belhadi et al., 2024; Zamani et al., 2023). Similarly, while the Internet of Things (IoT) enhances actual monitoring and operational visibility, concerns about interoperability, data privacy, and energy efficiency often limit its application, particularly in fragmented supply chain ecosystems (Naz et al., 2022; Shoomal et al., 2024). The absence of standardisation in facts formats and communication protocols further exacerbates these challenges, creating inefficiencies in the assimilation of digital expertise across global stream chains (Liu et al., 2023; Z. Yang et al., 2024). Additionally, digital maturity varies widely across industries and regions, with smaller organisations and developing economies frequently struggling to adopt these technologies due to resource constraints and limited expertise (Colehower, 2023; Zamani et al., 2023). Lecture to these barriers requires a concerted effort to foster digital knowledge, promote cross-industry collaborations, and establish regulatory frameworks that support data standardisation and cybersecurity (Belhadi et al., 2024; Birkel et al., 2023).

Strategic partnerships and investments in digital infrastructure are critical to overcoming these obstacles, enabling organisations to fully capitalise on the benefits of technologies like blockchain, IoT, and AI for SCRes (Rha, 2020; Shoomal et al., 2024). By addressing these challenges, organisations can unlock the potential of digitalisation to shape robust, resistant stream chains capable of navigating increasingly volatile global environments (Z. Yang et al., 2024; Zhao et al., 2023). Bibliometric analyses and methodical appraisals have highlighted significant trends in the connection of supply chain resilience (SCRes) and emerging technologies. Readings such as those by (Z. Yang et al., 2024; Zamani et al., 2023) have mapped key thematic clusters linking technologies like AI and IoT to resilience phases, including readiness, response, and recovery. While these phases have garnered considerable research attention, the growth phase a critical component for long-term resilience and adaptability remains notably underexplored (Chaudhary et al., n.d.; Shoomal et al., 2024).

This gap in understanding limits businesses' ability to leverage digital tools effectively for sustained resilience in dynamic market conditions. Addressing this deficiency requires focused research to develop comprehensive frameworks encompassing all SCRes phases, including the often-overlooked growth phase. In conclusion, while emerging technologies present transformative opportunities for SCRes, their successful integration into supply chain management is a complex undertaking that necessitates strategic planning, cross-industry collaboration, and empirical studies. Overcoming barriers such as digital immaturity, technological interoperability, and limited adoption will be key to unlocking their full potential. By synthesising existing insights and give a lecture these gaps, upcoming research can development the development of robust strategies that enhance SCRes, enabling businesses to navigate uncertainties effectively and achieve sustainable operational success (Rha, 2020; Shoomal et al., 2024; Z. Yang et al., 2024; Zamani et al., 2023). Emerging technologies hold immense potential to revolutionize supply chain resilience (SCRes), but their integration into supply chain management is a multifaceted process that demands careful strategic planning and collaboration among stakeholders. As global supply chains become increasingly complex and vulnerable to disruptions, businesses must adopt innovative approaches that go beyond traditional risk management. SCRes has evolved into a strategic imperative, incorporating proactive measures that emphasize agility, adaptability, and visibility to ensure long-term sustainability and competitiveness. This review synthesizes insights from existing studies to highlight critical opportunities for advancing research and practical applications in the field, particularly in addressing gaps such as the underexplored growth phase of SCRes, which is vital for fostering long-term adaptability and competitive advantage. One of the primary drivers of supply chain resilience is the integration of advanced digital technologies, including artificial intelligence (AI), blockchain, and the Internet of Things (IoT). These technologies play a pivotal role in strengthening SCRes by enabling real-time monitoring, predictive analytics, and seamless communication across supply chain networks. AI-driven models, such as Bayesian networks and machine learning algorithms, enhance decision-making by identifying potential risks and optimizing responses before disruptions escalate. Blockchain technology, with its decentralized and immutable ledger system, fosters trust and transparency by securely recording transactions and ensuring data integrity. IoT, through interconnected sensors and devices, facilitates continuous tracking of goods and assets, improving visibility and responsiveness.

Despite the transformative potential of these technologies, significant challenges remain that hinder their widespread adoption. Digital immaturity, interoperability issues, and resistance to technological adoption are among the key barriers that organizations must overcome to fully leverage the benefits of AI, blockchain, and IoT. Many companies, particularly small and medium-sized enterprises (SMEs), struggle with the high costs of digital transformation, lack of technical expertise, and concerns over data security. Additionally, fragmented data systems and a lack of standardized frameworks complicate integration efforts, limiting the effectiveness of these technologies in enhancing SCRes.

Addressing these challenges requires a multi-faceted approach that encompasses both technological and organizational strategies. Investments in digital infrastructure, workforce training, and policy frameworks are essential to bridge the digital divide and enable seamless technology adoption. Organizations must prioritize digital literacy initiatives to equip employees with the necessary skills to leverage AI, blockchain, and IoT effectively. Furthermore, cross-industry collaborations and strategic partnerships can facilitate knowledge sharing and drive innovation, enabling businesses to develop more resilient supply chain models. Governments and regulatory bodies also have a crucial role to play by creating supportive policies that encourage digital adoption and ensure data privacy and security compliance.

The underexplored growth phase of SCRes presents a significant opportunity for future research and development. While much attention has been given to the readiness, response, and recovery phases of SCRes, the growth phase remains inadequately addressed in existing literature. This phase focuses on long-term resilience-building strategies that enable organizations to continuously adapt to evolving challenges and maintain a competitive edge. Developing comprehensive frameworks that integrate emerging technologies across all SCRes phases can provide a structured approach to resilience enhancement, ensuring that businesses are well-equipped to navigate uncertainties and disruptions. Empirical research is critical in assessing the real-world impact of digital technologies on SCRes. Studies that evaluate the effectiveness of AI-driven risk assessment models, blockchain-enabled supply chain transparency, and IoT-based monitoring systems can provide valuable insights into best practices and implementation strategies. Additionally, sector-specific research can help identify tailored solutions for different industries, recognizing that supply chain dynamics vary across sectors such as manufacturing, healthcare, retail, and logistics. By generating evidence-based findings, researchers can guide policymakers and industry leaders in making informed decisions about technology investments and resilience-building initiatives.

Collaboration between academia, industry, and government entities is essential to drive innovation and accelerate the adoption of digital solutions for SCRes. Public-private partnerships can facilitate the development of standardized frameworks, interoperability protocols, and regulatory guidelines that promote seamless integration of emerging technologies. Moreover, collaborative research initiatives can foster interdisciplinary approaches, combining expertise in supply chain management, data science, cybersecurity, and business strategy to develop holistic resilience solutions. The evolution of SCRes must also consider sustainability and ethical considerations. As businesses embrace digital transformation, they must ensure that resilience strategies align with environmental, social, and governance (ESG) principles. Sustainable supply chain practices, such as circular economy models, carbon footprint reduction, and ethical sourcing, should be integrated into resilience frameworks to create long-term value for businesses and society. The responsible use of AI and blockchain must also be prioritized, addressing concerns related to algorithmic bias, data privacy, and ethical decision-making.

FINDINGS OF THE STUDY

The review of literature highlights the growing openness of overall supply chains to disruptions caused by pandemics, geopolitical tensions, natural disasters, and cyber threats, highlighting the inadequacy of traditional reactive risk management strategies. These challenges have driven a paradigm shift towards supply chain resilience, which emphasises proactive approaches that incorporate agility, adaptability, and visibility to anticipate and mitigate risks. Advanced technologies such as artificial intelligence, blockchain, and the Internet of Things have arisen as pivotal in strengthening supply chain resilience, enabling immediate data integration, predictive analytics, and decentralised communication through supply chain links. However, significant gaps persist in addressing the underexplored growth phase of supply chain resilience, critical for fostering long-term organisational adaptability and success. The study identifies artificial intelligence's transformative role in modelling complex risk scenarios and enhancing decision-making processes. AI-driven tools, such as Bayesian networks, improve the accuracy and efficiency of readiness, response, and recovery phases, while blockchain fosters secure and transparent data sharing, building trust among stakeholders. The Internet of Things enhances supply chain monitoring through interconnected devices, providing actionable insights into operational performance. Despite these benefits, barriers such as digital immaturity, interoperability issues, and data isolation concerns limit the extensive acceptance of these technologies, particularly in smaller organisations and developing regions with limited resources and expertise. Emerging technologies hold immense potential to revolutionise supply chain resilience, but their integration into supply chain management is a multifaceted process that demands careful strategic planning and collaboration among stakeholders.

The increasing complexity and volatility of global supply chains necessitate resilience strategies that go beyond traditional reactive risk management. Supply chain disruptions caused by pandemics, geopolitical tensions, natural disasters, and cyber threats have demonstrated the inadequacy of conventional approaches. In response, advanced technologies such as artificial intelligence, blockchain, and the Internet of Things have emerged as transformative tools that enhance visibility, flexibility, and responsiveness. These technologies offer significant advantages by enabling real-time monitoring, predictive analytics, and secure data sharing, which contribute to the readiness, response, and recovery phases of supply chain resilience. However, the growth phase of supply chain resilience, which focuses on fostering long-term organisational adaptability and competitiveness, remains underexplored, representing a critical area for future research. Despite the potential benefits of emerging technologies, significant barriers continue to hinder their widespread adoption and integration. Digital immaturity, interoperability challenges, data privacy concerns, and resource constraints pose substantial obstacles, particularly for smaller organisations and developing economies.

Overcoming these barriers requires a multifaceted approach that includes investment in digital infrastructure, fostering digital literacy, and establishing standardised frameworks that promote technological compatibility and cybersecurity. The success of these efforts depends on coordinated actions among various stakeholders, including businesses, governments, and technology providers. Cross-sector partnerships and public-private collaborations are essential for building resilient supply chains that can withstand disruptions and ensure operational continuity. The adoption of AI-driven predictive analytics has been instrumental in enhancing supply chain resilience by improving demand forecasting, risk assessment, and decision-making. Machine learning algorithms analyse vast amounts of data to identify patterns and predict disruptions before they occur, allowing organisations to implement proactive mitigation strategies. Blockchain technology contributes to transparency and traceability by securely recording transactions across the supply chain, reducing risks associated with fraud, counterfeiting, and inefficiencies. Additionally, IoT-enabled devices facilitate real-time monitoring of goods in transit, improving visibility and enabling immediate responses to potential disruptions. While these technologies offer significant advantages, their successful implementation requires substantial investment, employee training, and a cultural shift within organisations to embrace digital transformation.

Supply chain resilience is not solely dependent on technological advancements but also on organisational agility and adaptive capabilities. Agile supply chains can quickly adjust to changing market conditions and disruptions while maintaining service levels and operational efficiency. This shift requires organisations to move away from traditional cost-driven models towards dynamic, responsive frameworks that integrate risk management into strategic planning. A resilience-oriented mindset, characterised by flexibility and adaptability, must be embedded within organisational culture. Employee training, cross-functional collaboration, and scenario-based planning play crucial roles in enhancing an organisation's ability to respond effectively to disruptions. Furthermore, leadership commitment to resilience strategies is essential for driving long-term success. Government policies and regulatory frameworks significantly influence supply chain resilience strategies. Regulatory requirements for data security, trade compliance, and sustainability shape how organisations design and manage their supply chains. Governments can support businesses by providing incentives for digital transformation, investing in infrastructure development, and facilitating knowledge-sharing initiatives. Public-private partnerships play a crucial role in fostering innovation and creating an enabling environment for resilience-building initiatives. By aligning policy measures with technological advancements, governments can help organisations overcome barriers to digital integration and strengthen their overall resilience. The COVID-19 pandemic exposed vulnerabilities in global supply chains, highlighting the need for more resilient systems capable of withstanding prolonged disruptions. Organisations that had already invested in digital transformation and resilience-building measures were better equipped to navigate the crisis. The pandemic accelerated the adoption of digital technologies, compelling businesses to rethink traditional supply chain models and prioritise resilience over cost efficiency. Lessons from the pandemic underscore the importance of proactive risk management and digital readiness in ensuring supply chain continuity. Future research should focus on quantifying the impact of digital resilience strategies and exploring sector-specific resilience models to enhance preparedness for future disruptions. The need for comprehensive frameworks that integrate advanced technologies across all phases of supply chain resilience has become increasingly evident. Developing models such as the AI-SCRes framework can help organisations systematically incorporate technological innovations into their resilience strategies. Future research should prioritise empirical studies to assess the real-world impact of these technologies and explore their application in diverse supply chain contexts. Additionally, fostering cross-industry collaboration and policy support is essential for creating an ecosystem that facilitates innovation and adoption. Research should also investigate the role of supply chain resilience in achieving sustainability goals, as resilient supply chains are inherently more adaptable to regulatory changes and environmental challenges.

The future of supply chain resilience depends on continuous innovation and collaboration among businesses, policymakers, and technology providers. Organisations must take a proactive approach to digital integration, investing in emerging technologies while simultaneously addressing existing barriers. Strategies that combine technological advancements with organisational agility, workforce development, and regulatory alignment will be essential for building robust and adaptive supply chains. Moreover, addressing the underexplored growth phase of supply chain resilience will be crucial for fostering long-term competitiveness and adaptability in an increasingly volatile global environment. By tackling these challenges and leveraging collaborative approaches, organisations can develop comprehensive resilience strategies that ensure operational sustainability and competitiveness. The integration of emerging technologies into supply chain management offers immense potential to enhance resilience, enabling organisations to navigate uncertainties and sustain a competitive advantage. Addressing existing gaps and overcoming technological barriers will allow businesses to transition from reactive risk management to proactive resilience strategies. The findings of this study provide a foundation for future research and practice, highlighting the importance of continuous innovation and collaboration in building resilient and adaptive supply chains. As businesses and economies continue to face complex challenges, supply chain resilience will remain a key determinant of long-term success and sustainability. Further findings reveal that while readiness and response phases of supply chain resilience have received substantial attention, the growth phase remains inadequately addressed in existing research. This limits businesses' ability to leverage digital tools for sustained resilience and competitive advantage. Bibliometric analyses and systematic reviews highlight the need for comprehensive frameworks, such as the AI-SCRes framework, which integrates advanced technologies across all supply chain resilience phases to maximise their impact. The study concludes that overcoming barriers such as technological incompatibility, security concerns, and fragmented data systems requires cross-industry collaboration, strategic partnerships, and investment in digital infrastructure. Future research should focus on empirical studies to assess real-world impacts, promote digital literacy, and develop standardised frameworks. Addressing these gaps will enable organisations to unlock the full potential of emerging technologies, ensuring robust and sustainable supply chains capable of thriving in volatile global environments.

Corporate social responsibility initiatives, sustainability certifications, and eco-labeling programs help build consumer trust and differentiate brands in competitive markets. Educating consumers about sustainable choices, promoting responsible consumption, and encouraging behavioral changes contribute to the success of sustainable supply chain management initiatives. Businesses must proactively communicate their sustainability efforts, engage in stakeholder dialogue, and align their strategies with consumer expectations to achieve long-term success. The future of sustainable supply chain management lies in continuous innovation, collaboration, and commitment to sustainability principles. As global challenges such as climate change, resource scarcity, and social inequalities persist, businesses must adopt forward-thinking strategies to enhance supply chain resilience and sustainability. Investing in research and development, embracing circular economy principles, and leveraging emerging technologies will drive the next phase of sustainable supply chain management evolution. Collaboration among governments, industry leaders, academia, and non-governmental organizations is essential to address systemic challenges and create a sustainable and inclusive global supply chain ecosystem. Despite its transformative potential, sustainable supply chain management requires sustained commitment and proactive measures to overcome existing barriers. Companies must integrate sustainability into their core business strategies, align their supply chain practices with global sustainability goals, and continuously innovate to stay ahead of evolving challenges. By fostering collaboration, regulatory support, and technological innovation, sustainable supply chain management can serve as a powerful tool for achieving long-term sustainability and resilience in global supply chains. As businesses, governments, and consumers collectively embrace sustainability, it will continue to shape the future of responsible and ethical supply chain management, driving positive environmental, social, and economic outcomes.

CONCLUSION

The findings of this study emphasize the critical importance of supply chain resilience in addressing the increasing complexity and volatility of global supply chains. Traditional risk management strategies, which often rely on reactive measures, have proven insufficient in mitigating the cascading effects of disruptions caused by pandemics, geopolitical tensions, natural disasters, and cyber threats. Consequently, supply chain resilience has emerged as a strategic imperative, with advanced technologies such as artificial intelligence, blockchain, and the Internet of Things playing a transformative role in enhancing visibility, flexibility, and responsiveness. These technologies offer significant potential to improve key resilience phases readiness, response, and recovery by enabling real-time monitoring, predictive analytics, and secure data sharing. However, the growth phase of supply chain resilience, which focuses on fostering long-term organizational adaptability and competitiveness, remains underexplored, representing a critical area for future research. Despite the promise of emerging technologies, significant barriers continue to impede their full integration into supply chain management. Issues such as digital immaturity, interoperability challenges, data privacy concerns, and resource constraints are particularly pronounced in smaller organizations and developing economies. Addressing these barriers requires a multifaceted approach, including investment in digital infrastructure, fostering digital literacy, and establishing standardized frameworks that promote technological compatibility and cybersecurity. The need for strategic planning and collaboration among stakeholders is paramount, as successful implementation depends on coordinated efforts to align technological advancements with organizational goals. Cross-sector partnerships and public-private collaborations play a crucial role in building resilient supply chains by sharing expertise, resources, and risk mitigation strategies. The adoption of AI-driven predictive analytics enhances supply chain resilience by improving demand forecasting, risk assessment, and decision-making.

Machine learning algorithms analyze vast amounts of data to identify patterns and predict disruptions before they occur, enabling organizations to implement proactive mitigation strategies. Blockchain technology enhances transparency and traceability by securely recording transactions across the supply chain, reducing the risks of fraud, counterfeiting, and inefficiencies. Additionally, IoT-enabled devices facilitate real-time monitoring of goods in transit, improving visibility and allowing for immediate response to potential disruptions. While these technologies significantly enhance resilience, their implementation requires substantial investment, training, and a shift in organizational culture. Supply chain resilience is not solely dependent on technological advancements but also on organizational agility and adaptive capabilities. Agile supply chains can quickly adjust to changing market conditions and disruptions, maintaining service levels and operational efficiency. This requires a shift from linear, cost-driven models to dynamic, responsive frameworks that integrate risk management into strategic planning. Organizations must cultivate a resilience-oriented mindset, where flexibility and adaptability become core components of supply chain management. Employee training, cross-functional collaboration, and scenario-based planning contribute to an organization's ability to respond effectively to disruptions. Government policies and regulatory frameworks play a significant role in shaping supply chain resilience strategies. Regulatory requirements for data security, trade compliance, and sustainability influence how organizations structure their supply chains. Governments can support businesses by providing incentives for digital transformation, investing in infrastructure development, and facilitating knowledge-sharing initiatives (WTO, 2020). Public-private partnerships foster innovation and create a supportive ecosystem for resilience-building initiatives.

The COVID-19 pandemic underscored the vulnerabilities of global supply chains, highlighting the need for resilient systems capable of withstanding prolonged disruptions. Organizations that had already invested in digital transformation and resilience-building measures were better equipped to navigate the crisis. The pandemic accelerated the adoption of digital technologies, compelling businesses to rethink traditional supply chain models and prioritize resilience over cost efficiency. Future research should focus on quantifying the impact of digital resilience strategies and exploring sector-specific resilience models. This study highlights the importance of developing comprehensive frameworks, such as the AI-SCRes framework, to integrate advanced technologies across all phases of supply chain resilience. Future research should prioritize empirical studies to assess the real-world impact of these technologies and explore their application in diverse supply chain contexts.

Additionally, cross-industry collaboration and policy support are essential to create an ecosystem that facilitates innovation and adoption. Research should also explore the role of supply chain resilience in achieving sustainability goals, as resilient supply chains are inherently more adaptable to regulatory changes and environmental challenges. The study underscores the transformative potential of Sustainable Supply Chain Management (SSCM) as a comprehensive context to address ecological, communal, and financial challenges in supply chains. By integrating practices such as green procurement, energy efficiency, ethical labour standards, and resource optimisation, SSCM demonstrates its capacity to balance profitability with sustainability. Over the past two decades, SSCM has gained significant momentum, with research and practice focusing on themes such as innovation, disruption management, circular economy principles, and environmental sustainability. These efforts have been instrumental in reshaping supply chain strategies, making sustainability a core business objective rather than a supplementary concern. One of the most significant results of the reading is SSCM's ability to positively impact environmental performance. The adoption of green technologies, closed-loop supply chains, and energy-efficient production processes has proven effective in mitigating environmental degradation, especially in rapidly industrialising regions. In addition to environmental benefits, SSCM plays a crucial role in enhancing social sustainability.

By addressing issues such as labour rights, workplace safety, and equitable benefit distribution, SSCM fosters more inclusive and ethical supply chains. Strategies such as virtuous finding, rational skill certifications, and corporate social responsibility (CSR) initiatives have been shown to improve both employee satisfaction and overall supply chain performance. Collaborative networks and strong leadership are critical enablers in this process, especially in regions where socio-economic inequalities are deeply entrenched. However, achieving social sustainability requires a cultural shift within organisations, robust policy frameworks, and active engagement with local communities to ensure that the benefits of sustainable practices are equitably distributed. The role of advanced technologies in SSCM cannot be overstated. Innovations such as blockchain, artificial intelligence (AI), and the Internet of Things (IoT) have revolutionised supply chain management by enhancing visibility, enabling actual observing, and improving executive. Blockchain ensures transparency and accountability in procurement processes, while AI-driven analytics facilitate predictive maintenance and risk management. IoT applications, including sensor-based monitoring, optimise resource allocation and minimise waste. Despite their transformative potential, these technologies face adoption barriers such as high implementation costs, data privacy concerns, and interoperability challenges. Collaborative efforts among governments, technology providers, and industry leaders are essential to make these technologies accessible and scalable, mainly for small and medium-sized enterprises in developing marketplaces. SSCM has proven to be a transformative approach to building sustainable and resilient supply chains, but significant challenges remain, particularly in emerging economies. Overcoming these challenges requires a multifaceted approach, including targeted policies, cross-sector collaboration, and continuous innovation. By addressing barriers such as institutional voids, socio-economic disparities, and technological adoption hurdles, SSCM can become a cornerstone for achieving global sustainability goals. Upcoming study and training must attention on empirical trainings, collaborative strategies, and long-term commitments to ensure that SSCM continues to evolve and deliver sustainable value across environmental, social, and economic dimensions. As industries and economies transition toward sustainability, SSCM offers a pathway to align development with the imperatives of environmental stewardship and social equity. In conclusion, the integration of emerging technologies into supply chain management offers immense potential to enhance resilience, enabling organizations to navigate uncertainties and sustain competitive advantage. By addressing existing gaps and overcoming barriers, businesses can transition from reactive risk management to robust resilience strategies, ensuring sustainable operations in an increasingly volatile global environment. The findings of this study provide a foundation for future research and practice, underscoring the need for continuous innovation and collaboration to build resilient and adaptive supply chains. As businesses and economies continue to face complex challenges, supply chain resilience will remain a key determinant of long-term success and sustainability.

REFERENCES

. Agarwal, P., Malhotra, S. K., & Swami, S. (2024). The role of smart technologies in managing supply chain post pandemic: An exploratory scientific procedures and rationales for systematic literature review. *Journal of Science and Technology Policy Management.*

Belhadi, A., Kamble, S., Subramanian, N., Singh, R. K., & Venkatesh, M. (2024). Digital capabilities to manage agri-food supply chain uncertainties and build supply chain resilience during compounding geopolitical disruptions. *International Journal of Operations & Production Management, 44*(11), 1914–1950. DOI: 10.1108/IJOPM-11-2022-0737

Birkel, H., Hohenstein, N.-O., & Hähner, S. (2023). How have digital technologies facilitated supply chain resilience in the COVID-19 pandemic? An exploratory case study. *Computers & Industrial Engineering, 183*, 109538. DOI: 10.1016/j.cie.2023.109538

. Chaudhary, S., Chotia, V., Islam, N., Alghafes, R., & KALISZ, D. (n.d.). Building Supply Chain Resilience Through Disruptions: The Role of Digital Technologies, Social Capital, and Ambidexterity. *Social Capital, and Ambidexterity.*

Colehower, J. (2023). Using Technology to Improve Supply-Chain Resilience. *Harvard Business Review.*

Kassa, A., Kitaw, D., Stache, U., Beshah, B., & Degefu, G. (2023). Artificial intelligence techniques for enhancing supply chain resilience: A systematic literature review, holistic framework, and future research. *Computers & Industrial Engineering, 186*, 109714. DOI: 10.1016/j.cie.2023.109714

Liu, W., He, Y., Dong, J., & Cao, Y. (2023). Disruptive technologies for advancing supply chain resilience. *Frontiers of Engineering Management, 10*(2), 360–366. DOI: 10.1007/s42524-023-0257-1

Naz, F., Kumar, A., Majumdar, A., & Agrawal, R. (2022). Is artificial intelligence an enabler of supply chain resiliency post COVID-19? An exploratory state-of-the-art review for future research. *Operations Management Research : Advancing Practice Through Research, 15*(1), 378–398. DOI: 10.1007/s12063-021-00208-w

Rha, J. S. (2020). Trends of research on supply chain resilience: A systematic review using network analysis. *Sustainability (Basel), 12*(11), 4343. DOI: 10.3390/su12114343

Shoomal, A., Jahanbakht, M., Componation, P. J., & Ozay, D. (2024). Enhancing supply chain resilience and efficiency through internet of things integration: Challenges and opportunities. *Internet of Things : Engineering Cyber Physical Human Systems*, *27*, 101324. DOI: 10.1016/j.iot.2024.101324

Yang, C.-C. (2020). The effectiveness analysis of the practices in five quality management stages for SMEs. *Total Quality Management & Business Excellence*, *31*(9–10), 955–977. DOI: 10.1080/14783363.2018.1456010

Yang, Z., Guo, X., Sun, J., Zhang, Y., & Wang, Y. (2024). What Does Not Kill You Makes You Stronger: Supply Chain Resilience and Corporate Sustainability Through Emerging IT Capability. *IEEE Transactions on Engineering Management*, *71*, 10507–10521. DOI: 10.1109/TEM.2022.3209613

Zamani, E. D., Smyth, C., Gupta, S., & Dennehy, D. (2023). Artificial intelligence and big data analytics for supply chain resilience: A systematic literature review. *Annals of Operations Research*, *327*(2), 605–632. DOI: 10.1007/s10479-022-04983-y PMID: 36212520

Zhao, X., Xu, Y., Vasa, L., & Shahzad, U. (2023). Entrepreneurial ecosystem and urban innovation: Contextual findings in the lens of sustainable development from China. *Technological Forecasting and Social Change*, *191*, 122526. DOI: 10.1016/j.techfore.2023.122526

Chapter 6
Sustainable Supply Chain Practices in Emerging Agricultural Entrepreneurship: A Study With Reference to Tamil Nadu

Priyanka K.
http://orcid.org/0009-0005-0704-2363
Alagappa University, India

Gurupandi M.
Alagappa Univesity, India

ABSTRACT

Sustainable supply chain practices are crucial for enhancing the economic resilience, environmental conservation, and social equity of agricultural entrepreneurship. This study examines key determinants, challenges, and impacts of sustainability in agricultural supply chains, particularly in Tamil Nadu. Findings indicate that resource efficiency, waste management, and green logistics significantly contribute to long-term profitability and resilience. However, financial constraints, inadequate infrastructure, and policy inconsistencies hinder widespread adoption. Empirical analysis using regression modeling and factor analysis highlights the role of fintech and digital solutions in improving sustainability practices. Addressing these barriers through targeted policy interventions, financial support mechanisms, and capacity-building initiatives can enable agricultural entrepreneurship to drive sustainable development, ensuring food security and rural economic growth.

DOI: 10.4018/979-8-2600-1855-2.ch006

INTRODUCTION

Agricultural entrepreneurship plays a vital role in economic development, especially in developing economies, where the agricultural sector contributes significantly to employment and GDP. However, traditional agricultural practices often exert substantial pressure on environmental resources, leading to deforestation, soil degradation, water scarcity, and greenhouse gas emissions. In response to these challenges, sustainable supply chain practices have emerged as a strategic approach to balancing economic growth with environmental conservation and social responsibility.

Sustainability in agricultural supply chains involves adopting practices that minimize environmental impact, improve resource efficiency, and enhance social equity. These include reducing carbon footprints, adopting renewable energy sources, minimizing waste generation, and promoting ethical labour practices. Despite the evident benefits, developing economies face considerable challenges in implementing sustainable supply chain practices. These challenges include inadequate infrastructure, financial constraints, lack of regulatory support, and limited awareness among agricultural entrepreneurs.

This study aims to explore the sustainable supply chain practices adopted by agricultural entrepreneurs, analyse the challenges they encounter, and evaluate the economic, environmental, and social impacts of these practices. Additionally, the research seeks to propose strategies to improve sustainability in agricultural supply chains, thereby contributing to broader sustainable development goals. Sustainable supply chain practices have become a crucial aspect of agricultural entrepreneurship, particularly in developing economies. With increasing global demand for food security, environmental conservation, and economic stability, sustainable supply chains in agriculture ensure that products are produced, processed, and distributed in a manner that minimizes environmental impact while maximizing social and economic benefits. In developing economies, where agriculture remains a dominant source of employment and livelihood, integrating sustainability into supply chains can enhance productivity, improve market access, and foster rural entrepreneurship(FAO, 2020).

Agricultural entrepreneurs in developing countries face multiple challenges, including inefficient supply chain logistics, post-harvest losses, limited access to technology, and financial constraints. Sustainable supply chain practices, such as organic farming, resource-efficient logistics, blockchain-based traceability, and eco-friendly packaging, can help overcome these barriers (Bank, 2019). These practices not only enhance business profitability but also contribute to climate resilience and rural development. Moreover, the adoption of digital platforms and financial technology (fintech) solutions has created new opportunities for small and medium-sized agricultural enterprises (SMEs) to integrate into global supply networks (UNDP, 2021).

This study aims to analyze the impact of sustainable supply chain practices on emerging agricultural entrepreneurship in developing economies. It explores the challenges entrepreneurs face in implementing sustainability-driven supply chains and identifies the role of technology, policy interventions, and financial support in enhancing supply chain efficiency. By examining real-world case studies and empirical data, this research provides insights into best practices that can enable agricultural entrepreneurs to thrive in competitive markets while ensuring long-term sustainability. This study highlights the important of resource efficiency in ensuring agricultural sustainability. It discusses strategies such as precision farming, optimized input usage, and reducing post-harvest losses to enhance productivity while minimizing environmental impacts.

Agriculture plays a critical role in economic development, food security, and rural employment. However, traditional agricultural supply chains have contributed to environmental degradation, inefficient resource use, and social inequalities. The need for sustainable supply chain practices has become imperative to address these challenges. Sustainability in agricultural supply chains involves integrating eco-friendly practices such as renewable energy adoption, waste reduction, and ethical labour management. Despite the potential benefits, agricultural entrepreneurs, especially in developing economies, face several obstacles in adopting these practices. This study examines the determinants, challenges, and impacts of sustainable supply chain practices among agricultural entrepreneurs in Tamil Nadu, a region known for its agrarian economy.

LITERATURE REVIEW

Concept of sustainable supply chain in agriculture refer to the integration of environmentally friendly, socially responsible, and economically viable practices throughout the supply chain. (Carter, C. R., & Rogers, 2008). Define SSCM as the strategic coordination of traditional supply chain management with sustainability objectives, ensuring long-term profitability while reducing negative environmental and social impacts. Studies by (Dubey, R., 2017) highlight the importance of circular economy principles in agricultural supply chains, emphasizing resource efficiency, waste reduction, and sustainable sourcing. Similarly, (Rao, P., & Holt, 2005)suggest that sustainable supply chain practices improve operational efficiency and enhance competitive advantage in agribusiness. Research by (Govindan et al., 2014) identifies key determinants of sustainable supply chain practices in agriculture, including financial resources, technological advancements, regulatory policies, and stakeholder collaboration. Financial investments in sustainable technologies, such as precision agriculture and renewable energy solutions, have been shown to enhance resource efficiency and reduce environmental impact (Moktadir, M. A., et al., 2018). Moreover, stakeholder engagement, including government support, consumer awareness, and supplier collaboration, plays a crucial role in fostering sustainability in agricultural supply chains (Seuring, S., & Müller, 2008). Studies indicate that regulatory frameworks and policy incentives significantly influence the adoption of sustainable practices (Pagell & Wu, 2009). Developing economies face unique challenges in adopting sustainable supply chain practices. According to (Van Hoek, 2001), limited infrastructure, inadequate financial resources, and weak regulatory enforcement hinder the implementation of sustainable practices in agriculture. Additionally, small-scale agricultural entrepreneurs often lack access to advanced technologies and knowledge required for sustainable supply chain management (Singh, R. K., et al., 2021). change among traditional farmers. Research by (Kannan, D et al., 2014) suggests that overcoming these barriers requires a multi-stakeholder approach, including government interventions, private sector investments, and capacity-building initiatives. Empirical studies highlight the positive impacts of sustainable supply chain practices on economic, environmental, and social dimensions. Sustainable practices such as green logistics, waste management, and resource efficiency contribute to cost savings and long-term profitability in agribusiness (Luthra, S et al., 2016). Environmental benefits include reduced carbon emissions, improved soil health, and water conservation, which enhance ecological balance (Touboulic, A et al., 2015). Socially, sustainable supply chain practices promote fair labor conditions, improve rural livelihoods, and support community development. Studies by (Elkington, 1997). emphasize the triple bottom line approach, which integrates economic prosperity, environmental stewardship, and social well-being as key pillars of sustainability.

Sustainable agricultural practices have been widely recognized as essential for ensuring long-term food security and environmental conservation. According to (Kumar 2020), adopting sustainable supply chain efficiency in agriculture can reduce environmental degradation while improving resource utilization. Additionally, the role of financial technology in agricultural entrepreneurship has been emphasized by (Sharma and Patel 2021), who highlight how fintech solutions facilitate credit access, enhance digital transactions, and enable market expansion for agri-entrepreneurs. However, one of the major challenges to sustainability in agricultural supply chains is the lack of adequate infrastructure, as reported by (Singh 2019), who points out that poor transportation and storage facilities contribute to post-harvest losses and inefficiencies in rural supply networks.

Financial constraints also play a crucial role in hindering sustainable practices. (Das 2020) explains that small-scale farmers often struggle to access the necessary funds for investing in renewable energy solutions and eco-friendly agricultural methods, further limiting their ability to implement sustainability-driven supply chains. Moreover, the integration of advanced digital technologies, such as blockchain and artificial intelligence, is emerging as a game-changer in the agricultural sector. (Chatterjee and Bose 2021) discuss how digital transformation through AI-driven supply chain management and blockchain-based traceability enhances transparency and efficiency in agricultural trade.

Policy frameworks and government interventions are also critical in driving sustainability in agricultural entrepreneurship. (Iyer 2019) argues that weak regulatory support and a lack of policy incentives discourage small farmers from adopting sustainable agricultural models. Additionally, (Menon 2020) highlights the importance of training and capacity-building programs in equipping agricultural entrepreneurs with knowledge on sustainable supply chain management. Strengthening educational initiatives and skill development programs can enable farmers to adopt best practices effectively.

The transition to renewable energy sources in agriculture is another key factor in achieving sustainability. (Banerjee 2021) underscores the need for increased adoption of solar-powered irrigation, biofuels, and other green energy solutions to reduce dependence on fossil fuels and lower greenhouse gas emissions. From a financial perspective, (Prasad 2020) suggests that governments and financial institutions should introduce low-interest loans, subsidies, and investment schemes tailored specifically for sustainable agri-startups. The social impact of sustainable agriculture also remains significant, as (Kapoor 2020) discusses how fair labor practices, gender-inclusive policies, and ethical sourcing contribute to improved livelihoods and economic stability in rural communities.

Existing research highlights the importance of sustainability in agricultural supply chains. Sustainable supply chain practices in agricultural entrepreneurship focus on improving efficiency reducing environmental impact, and enhancing economic viability. Emerging economies, particularly in developing regions, face unique challenges such as inadequate infrastructure, financial constraints, and climate risks. However, technological advancements and policy initiatives are transforming agriculture supply chains by promoting sustainability. Studies shows that integrating renewable energy, precision farming and organic inputs reduces carbon emissions and enhances long-term sustainability. Farmers and agribusiness adopting circular economy principles such as waste to energy conversion can improve resource efficiency (Gadanakis, 2024).

In the current global scenario, sustainable supply chain management (SSCM) has become a crucial factor for ensuring the long-term viability of agriculture entrepreneurship, particularly in developing economics

The global shift towards sustainability has necessitated the adoption of sustainable supply chain practices in various sectors, including agriculture. Agricultural entrepreneurship, particularly in developing economics, plays a vital role in ensuring food security, poverty alleviation, and economic growth. However, the sectors face significant challenges such as limited access to resources, poor infrastructure, and climate change vulnerabilities. This paper investigates how sustainable supply chain management (SSCM) can address these challenges, promoting resilience and sustainability in agriculture entrepreneurship.

Sustainable supply chain in agriculture is importance for ensuring long-term food security, protecting the environment, promoting social equity and maintaining consumer trust, impact of agricultural production throughout the entire supply chain ethical labour standards, and economic viability for farmers and communities involved.

Theoretical Framework

The literature that discusses the evolution of sustainability in the field of agricultural entrepreneurship supply chain research is the main topic of this section. As a starting point for comprehending the entire picture, we seek to identify the present research mainstream. Additionally, we emphasize key points covered in the literature on an agricultural supply chain that is sustainable.

Figure 1.

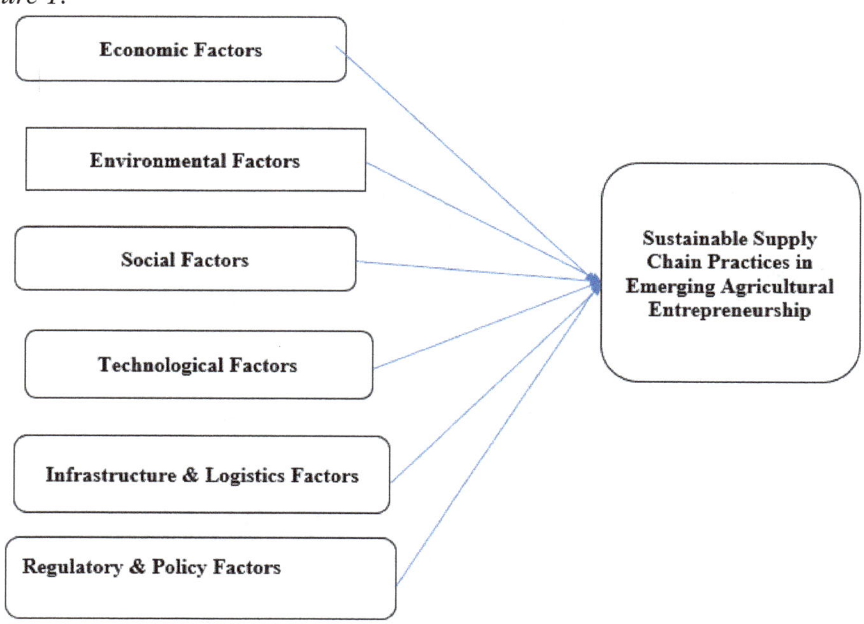

Challenges in Sustainable Supply Chain Management

Limited access to credit and funding options. Financial constraints prevent small-scale entrepreneurs from investing in sustainable technologies (Smith et al., 2019). Limited access to credit and funding remains a significant challenge for entrepreneurs, particularly for women and small business owners. Various studies highlight that financial institutions often perceive startups as high-risk investments, leading to stringent loan requirements, high-interest rates, and collateral demands that many entrepreneurs struggle to meet. Research by (Giglio, 2020) categorizes these barriers into supply-side constraints imposed by financial institutions, demand-side limitations due to financial illiteracy, enterprise-related challenges such as lack of credit history, and socio-cultural restrictions, especially for women entrepreneurs.

Access to credit is a persistent challenge for small-scale agricultural entrepreneurs. Many smallholders are financially excluded due to strict collateral requirements, high interest rates, and inadequate financial literacy (Sarma & Pais, 2011; Dev, 2006). Studies emphasize that financial inclusion is a key enabler of agricultural development, yet formal credit institutions often perceive agricultural lending as risky, leading to restrictive credit policies (Stiglitz & Weiss, 1981). The lack of tailored financial products for small-scale farmers exacerbates the problem, limiting investments in productivity and sustainability (Geron, Llanto, & Badiola, 2016). Consumer demand for sustainable agricultural products is growing, but smallholder farmers struggle to meet market expectations due to high certification costs and complex compliance requirements. Research suggests that limited knowledge about sustainability standards and fluctuating market trends make it difficult for farmers to capitalize on eco-conscious consumer behavior (OECD, 2021). Additionally, price volatility and lack of stable contracts create uncertainty, making sustainable farming financially risky (Céu & Gaspar, 2024). Climate change disrupts agricultural supply chains by increasing droughts, floods, and unpredictable weather patterns. Céu and Gaspar (2024) highlight that climate risks affect credit access, as lenders perceive farming as an unstable investment. Moreover, climate adaptation strategies such as drought-resistant crops and efficient irrigation systems require significant capital, which many smallholders lack. Policymakers and financial institutions must integrate climate resilience measures into agricultural credit policies to mitigate risks (Céu & Gaspar, 2024). Sustainable supply chains must prioritize labor rights, yet small-scale farmers often struggle to maintain ethical labor practices due to financial constraints. Studies indicate that poor working conditions, low wages, and lack of social protections are prevalent in agriculture, especially in developing economies (Sandhu & Hussain, 2020). Supply chain pressure to minimize costs often leads to labor exploitation, underscoring the need for stronger policies and enforcement of fair trade certifications (OECD, 2021). The adoption of sustainable farming practices is hindered by inadequate training and technical knowledge. Geron et al. (2016) argue that government and private-sector collaborations in capacity-building programs and farmer cooperatives can improve knowledge transfer. Additionally, integrating digital literacy programs can enhance farmers' ability to adopt modern, technology-driven sustainability solutions (Geron, Llanto, & Badiola, 2016). While technologies like blockchain, AI, and IoT improve efficiency and traceability, their adoption is low due to high costs and lack of awareness. Research suggests that smart farming solutions can enhance resource management and reduce environmental impact, but they require government subsidies and private-sector investment for widespread adoption (OECD, 2021). International sustainability certifications, such as organic and fair trade, enable farmers to access premium markets. However, compliance is often expensive and time-consuming. Studies highlight that subsidized certification programs, cooperative-led initiatives, and policy interventions can improve smallholder participation in certified supply chains (Sandhu & Hussain, 2020). Agricultural markets are highly volatile, with frequent price fluctuations affecting farmers' profitability. Research suggests that price stabilization mechanisms, such as contract farming and government-backed market interventions, can help reduce risks for small-scale producers. However, the lack of financial safety nets leaves farmers vulnerable to sudden market downturns (Geron et al., 2016). Frequent changes in subsidy structures, environmental regulations, and trade policies create uncertainty in the agricultural sector. Research emphasizes the need for long-term, stable policy frameworks that support sustainable supply chains. Governments should prioritize regulatory consistency to encourage investment in sustainable farming (OECD, 2021). Poor infrastructure, including inadequate storage facilities and weak transportation networks, leads to high post-harvest losses. Céu and Gaspar (2024) emphasize that investments in cold storage, processing units, and rural transportation systems are necessary for improving market connectivity and reducing waste. Without these investments, supply chain inefficiencies continue to hinder sustainability efforts (Céu & Gaspar, 2024).

Research Gap

While existing literature provides valuable insight into sustainable supply chain practices in agriculture, there are number of gaps not addressed. First, a majority of research is conducted in development economics whose infrastructure and finance are well established, and as such there is la lack of research on the special challenges agricultural entrepreneurs encounter in developing economics. Second, few empirical studies exist on the effect of sustainable supply chain practices on the economic resilience of small and medium agricultural businesses. Third, previous studies mostly cover single sustainability aspects but do not offer a comprehensive approach encompassing economic environmental and social sustainability in agricultural supply chain. Additionally, although prior studies have investigated sustainability practices by small-scale agriculture entrepreneurs. Fillings these gaps will offer a better understanding of how sustainable supply chain practices can be effectively adopted in developing economies.

Research Problem

The implementation of sustainable supply chain practices in agricultural entrepreneurship faces significant financial constraints, particularly in developing economies. Many small-scale farmers and agripreneurs struggle to access credit and funding to invest in sustainable technologies such as renewable energy, smart irrigation systems, and eco-friendly packaging. According to Das and Banerjee (2020), financial institutions often perceive agricultural startups as high-risk investments, leading to stringent loan requirements and limited financial support. Additionally, government subsidies and incentives are often insufficient or poorly structured, making it difficult for entrepreneurs to transition to sustainable farming methods (Patel et al., 2021). Without proper financial backing, the adoption of sustainable practices remains a challenge, hindering economic resilience and environmental conservation efforts.

Another critical challenge in sustainable agricultural supply chains is infrastructure inadequacy, which contributes to inefficiencies in production, transportation, and storage. Poor road networks, lack of cold storage facilities, and limited access to efficient logistics increase post-harvest losses and reduce profitability for farmers (Singh, 2019). The World Bank (2019) highlights that infrastructure deficits in rural supply chains are a major barrier to sustainability, preventing farmers from accessing markets efficiently. Moreover, inadequate logistics often lead to increased carbon footprints due to inefficient transportation methods. Investment in rural infrastructure, including improved storage and transportation systems, is crucial for enhancing the sustainability of agricultural supply chains (Chatterjee & Bose, 2021).

Research Question

1. What are the key sustainable supply chain practices adopted by agricultural entrepreneurs in developing economic?
2. What are the challenges agriculture entrepreneurs face in implementing sustainable supply chain practices?

RESEARCH METHODOLOGY

This study employs a quantitative research approach to analyze sustainable supply chain practices in emerging agricultural entrepreneurship, focusing on Tamil Nadu. A stratified random sampling technique is used to ensure diverse representation. The sample consists of 250 agricultural entrepreneurs, categorized based on factors such as business experience, educational background, and income levels. In the present research, Primary Data: Collected through a structured questionnaire targeting 250 agricultural entrepreneurs in Tamil Nadu. In the research, secondary data is also collected Books, newspapers, Periodicals, Seminars and Discussions, Articles, Journals, and Websites. To find a solution for the objectives of the study appropriate statistical tools socio economic sustainable agriculture entrepreneurs in Tami Nadu., and Frequency analysis for demographic profiling a profile of the respondents and their activities. Chi-Square Test used to examine the association between categorical variables such as Age, Education, challenges agriculture entrepreneurs face in implementing sustainable supply chain practices. ANOVA used to check if the adoption of sustainable supply chain practices by agricultural entrepreneurs in developing economies significant based on the business experience and Exploratory factors Analysis used to key factors influence challenges agriculture entrepreneurs face in implementing sustainable supply chain practices.

Hypothesis

H_{01}: There is no significant adoption of sustainable supply chain practices by agricultural entrepreneurs in developing economies.

H_{02}: There is no significant impact of challenges on the implementation of sustainable supply chain practices in agricultural entrepreneurship.

Table 1. Socio Economic Profile

Demographic profile	Parameters	Frequency	Percentage
Age	Below 25 years	22	8.8
	25-30 years	46	18.4
	30-35 years	83	33.2
	Above 35 years	99	39.6
	Total	**250**	**100**

continued on following page

Table 1. Continued

Demographic profile	Parameters	Frequency	Percentage
Gender	Male	158	63.2
	Female	92	36.8
	Total	**250**	**100**
Educational Background	SSLC	23	9.2
	HSC	42	16.8
	Graduate	83	33.2
	Any other	102	40.8
	Total	**250**	**100**
Marital Status	Married	118	47.2
	Unmarried	94	37.6
	Widowed	22	8.8
	Divorce	16	6.4
	Total	**250**	**100**
Monthly Income	Below 30,000	15	6
	30000-50000	48	19.2
	50000-70000	75	30
	Above 70000	112	48.8
	Total	**250**	**100**
Business Experiences	Below 2 years	8	3.2
	3-5 years	16	6.4
	6-8years	98	39.2
	Above 9 years	128	51.2
	Total	**250**	**100**

The socio-economic profile of the respondents provides valuable insights into the demographic and economic characteristics of agricultural entrepreneurs. The age distribution indicates that the majority of respondents (39.6%) are above 35 years, followed by those in the 30-35 years age group (33.2%). This suggests that most agricultural entrepreneurs are middle-aged, likely possessing substantial experience in the field.

In terms of gender, the majority of the respondents are male (63.2%), while females account for 36.8%. This signifies a gender disparity in agricultural entrepreneurship, which may reflect traditional societal norms and challenges faced by women in entering the sector.

The educational background of the respondents shows that a significant proportion (40.8%) have educational qualifications beyond graduation, while 33.2% are graduates. Meanwhile, 16.8% have completed higher secondary education (HSC), and 9.2% have completed SSLC. This indicates that most agricultural entrepreneurs have received formal education, which could contribute to their understanding and adoption of sustainable business practices.

Regarding marital status, nearly half of the respondents (47.2%) are married, while 37.6% are unmarried. A smaller percentage of respondents are widowed (8.8%) or divorced (6.4%). This distribution suggests that family responsibilities might influence entrepreneurial decisions and financial stability.

The analysis of monthly income reveals that the largest proportion of respondents (48.8%) earn above 70,000, followed by 30% in the 50,000- 70,000 income bracket. Meanwhile, 19.2% of respondents earn between 30,000- 50,000, and only 6% earn below 30,000. This indicates that a significant portion of agricultural entrepreneurs generate substantial income, which may facilitate investments in sustainable agricultural practices.

Finally, business experience is a critical factor, with more than half (51.2%) of respondents having over nine years of entrepreneurial experience. Another 39.2% have 6-8 years of experience, while a smaller proportion (6.4%) have 3-5 years of experience, and only 3.2% have less than two years of experience. This suggests that most entrepreneurs in the sample have a well-established presence in the industry, potentially enabling them to implement sustainable supply chain practices effectively.

Overall, the socio-economic profile highlights the predominance of experienced, educated, and financially stable entrepreneurs, with a notable gender gap and varying levels of business experience. These factors could have significant implications for the adoption of sustainable supply chain practices in agricultural entrepreneurship.

ANOVA Test

The Anova test is conducted to find the significance of the responses with the questionnaire we used data analysis and a data collection. Here is the analysis of the responses, performed using SPSS.

H_{01}: There is no significant adoption of sustainable supply chain practices across business experience

ANOVA Test

The Anova test is conducted to find the significance of the responses with the questionnaire we used data analysis and a data collection. Here is the analysis of the responses, performed using SPSS.

Table 2. ANOVA

ANOVA						
Variables		**Sum of Squares**	**Df**	**Mean Square**	**F**	**Sig.**
Availability of credit, subsidies, and government support.	Between Groups	1.962	2	.981	.719	**.489**
	Within Groups	173.307	248	1.365		
	Total	**175.269**	**249**			
Long-term profitability of sustainable practices.	Between Groups	2.445	2	1.223	.830	**.438**
	Within Groups	187.124	248	1.473		
	Total	**189.569**	**249**			
Adoption of eco-friendly irrigation and soil preservation.	Between Groups	2.269	2	1.134	3.972	**0.004**
	Within Groups	123.801	248	.975		
	Total	**126.069**	**249**			
Capacity-building initiatives for farmers.	Between Groups	12.146	2	6.073	4.295	**.016**
	Within Groups	179.585	248	1.414		
	Total	**191.731**	**249**			
Demand driven by sustainability-conscious consumers.	Between Groups	1.962	2	.981	.719	**.489**
	Within Groups	173.307	248	1.365		
	Total	**175.269**	**249**			
Investments in rural infrastructure and development.	Between Groups	2.445	2	1.223	.830	**.438**
	Within Groups	187.124	248	1.473		
	Total	**189.569**	**249**			
Adoption of sustainable packaging	Between Groups	5.329	2	2.664	2.114	**.125**
	Within Groups	160.064	248	1.260		
	Total	**165.392**	**249**			
Reducing waste and improving efficiency.	Between Groups	3.440	2	1.720	5.188	**0.002**
	Within Groups	176.529	248	1.390		
	Total	**179.969**	**249**			
Supportive regulations for sustainable agriculture.	Between Groups	2.022	2	1.011	.873	**.420**
	Within Groups	147.055	248	1.158		
	Total	**149.077**	**249**			
Adherence to organic, fair trade, and other certifications.	Between Groups	.605	2	.302	4.501	**0.004**
	Within Groups	153.426	248	1.208		
	Total	**154.031**	**249**			

The ANOVA (Analysis of Variance) results provide insights into whether there are significant differences in perceptions regarding various sustainable supply chain practices among different groups. The analysis examines multiple sustainability-related factors, with the key findings summarized below: Availability of Credit, Subsidies, and Government Support

The ANOVA test yielded an F-value of 0.719 and a p-value of 0.489, indicating no significant differences among groups regarding the availability of financial support for sustainability. This suggests that respondents have a similar perception of financial accessibility, regardless of their demographic or business characteristics. Long-Term Profitability of Sustainable Practices

The F-value of 0.830 and p-value of 0.438 suggest that there is no statistically significant variation in how respondents view the profitability of sustainable practices in the long run. This implies that entrepreneurs, regardless of their background, may share a common perspective on the economic feasibility of sustainability initiatives. Adoption of Eco-Friendly Irrigation and Soil Preservation A significant difference was observed with an F-value of 3.972 and a p-value of 0.004. This indicates that different groups perceive eco-friendly irrigation and soil preservation differently, possibly due to variations in access to sustainable farming resources or knowledge of best practices. Capacity-Building Initiatives for Farmers

The ANOVA test showed an F-value of 4.295 and a p-value of 0.016, indicating a statistically significant difference in perceptions regarding the effectiveness of capacity-building programs. This suggests that some groups, such as those with more experience or higher education levels, may view training and knowledge-sharing initiatives differently than others. Demand Driven by Sustainability-Conscious Consumers With an F-value of 0.719 and a p-value of 0.489, the results indicate no significant variation in how respondents perceive consumer demand for sustainable products. This suggests a general agreement that sustainability awareness among consumers is influencing market demand at a consistent level. Investments in Rural Infrastructure and Development The F-value of 0.830 and p-value of 0.438 suggest no significant differences in opinions on investments in rural infrastructure. This implies that respondents have similar views on the role of infrastructure in supporting sustainable agricultural supply chains. Adoption of Sustainable Packaging

The ANOVA results for sustainable packaging show an F-value of 2.114 and a p-value of 0.125, indicating no significant differences among groups. This suggests a shared understanding of the importance of sustainable packaging, though differences might exist that are not statistically significant. Reducing Waste and Improving Efficiency

A highly significant difference was found, with an F-value of 5.188 and a p-value of 0.002. This indicates that respondents hold varying opinions on the importance of waste reduction and efficiency improvements in sustainable supply chains. Factors such as financial capability, awareness levels, and operational scale might contribute to these differences. Supportive Regulations for Sustainable Agriculture With an F-value of 0.873 and a p-value of 0.420, the results indicate no statistically significant differences in perceptions regarding government policies and regulations. This suggests that respondents generally agree on the role of regulations in promoting sustainability. Adherence to Organic, Fair Trade, and Other Certifications A significant variation was observed, with an F-value of 4.501 and a p-value of 0.004. This suggests that different groups have distinct perceptions regarding the importance and impact of certifications like organic and fair trade. Factors such as education, market exposure, and business scale may influence these differences.

H_{02}: There is no significant impact of challenges on the implementation of sustainable supply chain practices in agricultural entrepreneurship.

Table 3. Chi-Square Test

Chi-Square Test				
Problems	**Chi-Square Test**	**Value**	**Df**	**Sig**
Age * Limited access to credit and funding options for small-scale agriculture entrepreneurs	Pearson Chi-Square	5.624[a]	7	.584
	Likelihood Ratio	6.072	7	.531
	N of Valid Cases	250		
	a. 4 cell (25.0%) have expected count less than 5. The minimum expected count is .49.			
Age * Influence of consumer preferences for sustainable products on business viability	Pearson Chi-Square	6.651[a]	6	.354
	Likelihood Ratio	7.056	6	.316
	N of Valid Cases	250		
	a.2 cells (14.3%) have expected count less than 5. The minimum expected count is 3.44			
Age * Impact of changing climate conditions on sustainable supply chain operation	Pearson Chi-Square	5.017[a]	6	.542
	Likelihood Ratio	5.269	6	.510
	N of Valid Cases	250		
	a.2 cells (14.3%) have expected count less than 5. The minimum expected count is 2.95			
Age * Fair wages, safe working conditions, and social well -being of agriculture worker	Pearson Chi-Square	3.277[a]	7	.858
	Likelihood Ratio	3.669	7	.871
	N of Valid Cases	250		
	a.2 cells (12.5%) have expected count less than 5. The minimum expected count is .49.			
Age* Lack Training farmer and supply chain stakeholder on sustainable benefits	Pearson Chi-Square	4.061[a]	7	.773
	Likelihood Ratio	4.128	7	.756
	N of Valid Cases	250		
	a.2 cells (12.5%) have expected count less than 5. The minimum expected count is .49.			

continued on following page

Table 3. Continued

Chi-Square Test				
Problems	**Chi-Square Test**	**Value**	**Df**	**Sig**
Age * Lack of Awareness of smart farming technologies	Pearson Chi-Square	6.123[a]	7	.525
	Likelihood Ratio	6.880	7	.441
	N of Valid Cases	250		
	a.6 cells (37.5%) have expected count less than 5. The minimum expected count is .49.			
Age * Impact of international and domestic sustainable certifications on market access	Pearson Chi-Square	2.721[a]	7	.910
	Likelihood Ratio	2.741	7	.908
	N of Valid Cases	250		
	a.7 cells (43.8%) have expected count less than 5. The minimum expected count is .98.			
Age * Lack of stable markets for sustainable agriculture products	Pearson Chi-Square	3.765[a]	7	.642
	Likelihood Ratio	3.896	7	.573
	N of Valid Cases	250		
	a.4 cells (40.0%) have expected count less than 5. The minimum expected count is 2.95.			
Age * Inconsistent government policies affecting agribusiness sustainability	Pearson Chi-Square	4.145[a]	7	.763
	Likelihood Ratio	4.543	7	.715
	N of Valid Cases	250		
	a.2 cells (20.0%) have expected count less than 5. The minimum expected count is 1.97.			
Age * Lack of proper agriculture infrastructure for storage and distribution	Pearson Chi-Square	6.424[a]	7	.491
	Likelihood Ratio	6.890	7	.440
	N of Valid Cases	250		
	a.2 cells (12.5.0%) have expected count less than 5. The minimum expected count is .49.			
Education * Limited access to credit and funding options for small-scale agriculture entrepreneurs	Pearson Chi-Square	7.087[a]	7	.420
	Likelihood Ratio	7.564	7	.373
	N of Valid Cases	250		
	a.2 cells (14.3%) have expected count less than 5. The minimum expected count is 3.42.			

continued on following page

Table 3. Continued

Chi-Square Test				
Problems	**Chi-Square Test**	**Value**	**Df**	**Sig**
Education * Influence of consumer preferences for sustainable products on business viability	Pearson Chi-Square	8.230[a]	6	.222
	Likelihood Ratio	8.323	6	.215
	N of Valid Cases	250		
	a. 2ells (14.3%) have expected count less than 5. The minimum expected count is 3.42			
Education * Impact of changing climate conditions on sustainable supply chain operation	Pearson Chi-Square	4.826[a]	6	.566
	Likelihood Ratio	4.905	6	.556
	N of Valid Cases	250		
	a.2 cells (14.3%) have expected count less than 5. The minimum expected count is2.93.			
Education * Fair wages, safe working conditions, and social well -being of agriculture worker	Pearson Chi-Square	5.003[a]	6	.660
	Likelihood Ratio	5.417	6	.609
	N of Valid Cases	250		
	a.2 cells (12.5%) have expected count less than 5. The minimum expected count is .49.			
Education* Lack Training farmer and supply chain stakeholder on sustainable benefits	Pearson Chi-Square	3.945[a]	7	.786
	Likelihood Ratio	4.125	7	.756
	N of Valid Cases	130		
	a.6 cells (37.5.0%) have expected count less than 5. The minimum expected count is 1.46.			
Education * Lack of Awareness of smart farming technologies	Pearson Chi-Square	5.783[a]	7	.565
	Likelihood Ratio	6.416	7	.492
	N of Valid Cases	250		
	a.6 cells (37.5%) have expected count less than 5. The minimum expected count is .49.			
Education * Impact of international and domestic sustainable certifications on market access	Pearson Chi-Square	7.769[a]	7	.353
	Likelihood Ratio	9.339	7	.229
	N of Valid Cases	250		
	a.7 cells (43.8%) have expected count less than 5. The minimum expected count is .98.			

continued on following page

Table 3. Continued

Chi-Square Test				
Problems	**Chi-Square Test**	**Value**	**Df**	**Sig**
Education * Lack of stable markets for sustainable agriculture products	Pearson Chi-Square	4.145	7	0.763
	Likelihood Ratio	4.543	7	0.716
	N of Valid Cases	250		
	a.4 cells (12.5%) have expected count less than 5. The minimum expected count is .49.			
Education* Inconsistent government policies affecting agribusiness sustainability	Pearson Chi-Square	6.424[a]	7	.491
	Likelihood Ratio	6.890	7	.440
	N of Valid Cases	250		
	a.14 cells (56.0%) have expected count less than 5. The minimum expected count is .37.			
Education * Lack of proper agriculture infrastructure for storage and distribution	Pearson Chi-Square	5.783[a]	7	.565
	Likelihood Ratio	6.416	7	.492
	N of Valid Cases	250		
	a.15 cells (60.0%) have expected count less than 5. The minimum expected count is .37.			

The Chi-Square test results reveal that neither age nor education significantly influence perceptions of key agricultural sustainability challenges. Across all tested variables, the p-values are above 0.05, indicating no statistically significant association. Regardless of age, respondents share similar concerns about limited access to credit, consumer preferences for sustainable products, climate change impact on supply chains, fair wages, training deficiencies, lack of awareness of smart farming technologies, certification impact on market access, unstable markets, inconsistent government policies, and inadequate infrastructure. Similarly, education level does not significantly alter views on these issues, suggesting that agricultural sustainability challenges are universally recognized. This finding implies that policy interventions and support mechanisms should be designed to address these challenges broadly, ensuring that solutions are accessible and beneficial to all agricultural entrepreneurs, irrespective of demographic differences.

Table 4. Kaise-Mayer-Olkin Measure of sampling Adequacy

Kaise-Mayer-Olkin Measure of sampling Adequacy		**.765**
Bartiett's Test of sphericity	Approx. Chi-square	3216.406
	Df	45
	Sig.	.000

The Kaiser-Meyer-Olkin (KMO) Measure of Sampling Adequacy and Bartlett's Test of Sphericity are essential preliminary tests in factor analysis to determine the suitability of the dataset for extracting meaningful factors. In this study, the KMO value was found to be 0.765, indicating that the sample is adequate for factor analysis. The KMO statistic measures the proportion of variance among the variables that might be common variance. A value closer to 1.0 suggests that the dataset is highly suitable for factor analysis, while a value below 0.50 indicates that factor analysis may not be appropriate. Based on the accepted guidelines, where a KMO value above 0.70 is considered adequate, the result of 0.765 suggests that the data meets the minimum requirement for factor extraction. Furthermore, Bartlett's Test of Sphericity was conducted to examine whether the correlation matrix is an identity matrix, which would imply that the variables are unrelated and unsuitable for factor analysis. The test yielded a Chi-square value of 3216.406 with 45 degrees of freedom (df) and a significant p-value of 0.000. Since the significance value is less than 0.05, we reject the null hypothesis, confirming that there are sufficient correlations among the variables to proceed with factor analysis. This means that the dataset contains meaningful interrelationships that can be grouped into underlying factors. In conclusion, the combination of a KMO value of 0.765 and a statistically significant Bartlett's test result indicates that the data is appropriate for factor analysis. This allows for the identification of key latent variables that influence the adoption of sustainable supply chain practices in agricultural entrepreneurship. Moving forward, factor extraction techniques such as Principal Component Analysis (PCA) or Exploratory Factor Analysis (EFA) can be applied to uncover the most significant dimensions affecting sustainability in agricultural supply chains.

Table 5. Extraction Method: Principal Component Analysis.

Communalities	**Initial**	**Extraction**
Limited access to credit and funding options for small-scale agricultural entrepreneurs.	1.000	.862
Influence of consumer preferences for sustainable products on business viability.	1.000	.861
Impact of changing climate conditions on sustainable supply chain operations.	1.000	.927
Fair wages, safe working conditions, and social well-being of agricultural workers.	1.000	.833
Training farmers and supply chain stakeholders on sustainability benefits.	1.000	.827

Communalities	Initial	Extraction
Awareness of smart farming technologies	1.000	.784
Impact of international and domestic sustainability certifications on market access.	1.000	.829
Price fluctuations and lack of stable markets for sustainable agricultural products.	1.000	.728
Inconsistent government policies affecting agribusiness sustainability.	1.000	.564
Lack of proper agricultural infrastructure for storage and distribution.	1.000	.994

The Principal Component Analysis (PCA) communalities indicate how well each variable is explained by the extracted factors. High communalities suggest strong representation in the factor model. Key Influencing Factors: Variables like climate change impact (0.927) and infrastructure deficits (0.994) are critical, as they are almost entirely explained by the extracted components, highlighting their significance in sustainable supply chains. Financial and Market Constraints: Limited access to credit (0.862) and consumer demand for sustainable products (0.861) show that funding limitations and market preferences significantly affect sustainability adoption. Labour and Training Needs: Fair wages and safe working conditions (0.833) and training programs (0.827) emphasize the role of human capital in sustainable supply chain management. Regulatory and Market Stability Challenges: Variables like inconsistent policies (0.564) and price fluctuations (0.728) show moderate representation, suggesting external influences beyond supply chain control. Overall, the high communalities suggest that the extracted factors are highly effective in explaining the variance of most variables, confirming the appropriateness of factor analysis for this dataset. The results emphasize that financial constraints, infrastructure, climate conditions, labour issues, and market demand are key dimensions influencing sustainable supply chain practices in agricultural entrepreneurship. Moving forward, factor loading analysis will help determine how these variables group into underlying themes, which can provide valuable insights for policy recommendations and strategic planning in sustainable agriculture.

Table 6. Extraction Method: Principal Component Analysis

Total Variance Explained									
Component	Initial Eigenvalues			Extraction Sums of Squared Loadings			Rotation Sums of Squared Loadings		
	Total	% of Variance	Cumulative %	Total	% of Variance	Cumulative %	Total	% of Variance	Cumulative %
1	6.114	61.137	61.137	6.114	61.137	61.137	4.444	44.437	44.437
2	2.097	20.971	82.108	2.097	20.971	82.108	3.767	37.670	82.108
3	.540	5.405	87.513						
4	.371	3.708	91.220						
5	.249	2.493	93.713						

Total Variance Explained									
Component	Initial Eigenvalues			Extraction Sums of Squared Loadings			Rotation Sums of Squared Loadings		
	Total	% of Variance	Cumulative %	Total	% of Variance	Cumulative %	Total	% of Variance	Cumulative %
6	.212	2.119	95.832						
7	.166	1.663	97.495						
8	.146	1.464	98.959						
9	.098	.981	99.939						
10	.006	.061	100.000						

In this analysis, two principal components were extracted, as their eigenvalues are greater than 1.0 (a common criterion for factor selection in PCA). These two components together explain 82.108% of the total variance, indicating that the dataset can be effectively summarized using these two factors. Component 1 has an eigenvalue of 6.114, explaining 61.137% of the variance before rotation. This suggests that the first factor is highly influential and accounts for the majority of the variation in the dataset. After rotation, this component accounts for 44.437% of the variance, indicating that multiple factors contribute to the dataset's structure. Component 2 has an eigenvalue of 2.097, explaining an additional 20.971% of the variance, bringing the cumulative variance explained to 82.108%. After rotation, this component accounts for 37.670% of the variance, confirming its significance in the analysis. The high variance explained indicates that most of the information is retained in the extracted components, reducing data complexity while preserving meaningful insights. Moving forward, factor loadings can be examined to determine which variables are associated with each component, allowing for a deeper understanding of the key factors influencing sustainable supply chain practices in agricultural entrepreneurship.

Figure 2.

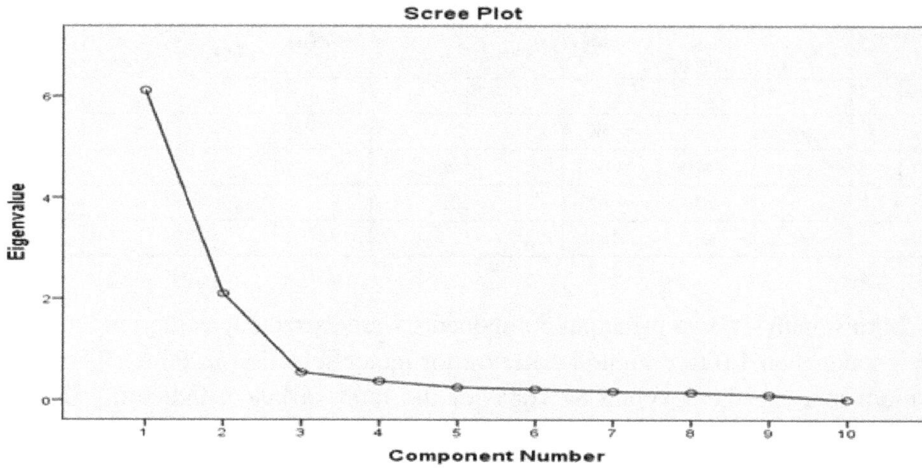

The Scree Plot visually represents the eigenvalues associated with each principal component, helping to determine the optimal number of components to retain in the analysis. The plot shows a steep decline in eigenvalues from the first to the second component, indicating that these two components capture most of the variance in the dataset. Beyond the second component, the eigenvalues begin to level off, forming an "elbow" point, which suggests that additional components contribute only marginally to explaining variance. This pattern aligns with the Kaiser Criterion, which recommends retaining components with eigenvalues greater than 1. In this case, the first two components account for a significant proportion of the variance, while the remaining components add minimal explanatory power. Therefore, the analysis should focus on these two principal components, as they provide the most meaningful insights while reducing dimensionality and complexity in the dataset.

DISCUSSION

The socio-economic profile of the respondents provides valuable insights into the demographic and economic characteristics of agricultural entrepreneurs. The age distribution indicates that the majority of respondents (39.6%) are above 35 years, followed by those in the 30-35 years age group (33.2%). This suggests that most agricultural entrepreneurs are middle-aged, likely possessing substantial experience in the field.

In terms of gender, the majority of the respondents are male (63.2%), while females account for 36.8%. This signifies a gender disparity in agricultural entrepreneurship, which may reflect traditional societal norms and challenges faced by women in entering the sector.

The educational background of the respondents shows that a significant proportion (40.8%) have educational qualifications beyond graduation, while 33.2% are graduates. Meanwhile, 16.8% have completed higher secondary education (HSC), and 9.2% have completed SSLC. This indicates that most agricultural entrepreneurs have received formal education, which could contribute to their understanding and adoption of sustainable business practices.

Regarding marital status, nearly half of the respondents (47.2%) are married, while 37.6% are unmarried. A smaller percentage of respondents are widowed (8.8%) or divorced (6.4%). This distribution suggests that family responsibilities might influence entrepreneurial decisions and financial stability.

The analysis of monthly income reveals that the largest proportion of respondents (48.8%) earn above 70,000, followed by 30% in the 50,000- 70,000 income bracket. Meanwhile, 19.2% of respondents earn between 30,000- 50,000, and only 6% earn below 30,000. This indicates that a significant portion of agricultural entrepreneurs generate substantial income, which may facilitate investments in sustainable agricultural practices.

Finally, business experience is a critical factor, with more than half (51.2%) of respondents having over nine years of entrepreneurial experience. Another 39.2% have 6-8 years of experience, while a smaller proportion (6.4%) have 3-5 years of experience, and only 3.2% have less than two years of experience. This suggests that most entrepreneurs in the sample have a well-established presence in the industry, potentially enabling them to implement sustainable supply chain practices effectively.

Overall, the socio-economic profile highlights the predominance of experienced, educated, and financially stable entrepreneurs, with a notable gender gap and varying levels of business experience. These factors could have significant implications for the adoption of sustainable supply chain practices in agricultural entrepreneurship.

The ANOVA analysis reveals both significant and non-significant variations in respondents' perceptions of sustainable supply chain practices: No Significant Differences in Financial and Market Factors: Availability of credit, government support ($p = 0.489$), and investments in rural infrastructure ($p = 0.438$) show no significant differences, indicating that respondents generally agree on financial constraints and infrastructure needs. Perceptions of long-term profitability of sustainable practices ($p = 0.438$) and consumer demand for sustainability ($p = 0.489$) are also consistent across groups. Significant Differences in Adoption of Sustainable Practices: Eco-friendly irrigation and soil preservation (p = 0.004) and capacity-building initiatives (p = 0.016) have significant variations, suggesting that access to resources and education impact sustainability adoption. Waste reduction and efficiency improvement (p = 0.002) also show significant differences, possibly due to financial and operational constraints among respondents. Certifications like organic and fair trade (p = 0.004) vary by education, market exposure, and business scale. Mixed Views on Regulatory Support and Packaging: Government policies and regulations (p = 0.420) show no significant differences, suggesting broad agreement on their role in sustainability. Sustainable packaging (p = 0.125) has some variation but is not statistically significant. The findings suggest that while financial and policy-related challenges are widely acknowledged, awareness, education, and access to resources significantly influence sustainability adoption. Addressing these disparities through targeted training, funding, and regulatory incentives can enhance sustainable supply chain integration in agriculture.

The Chi-Square test results reveal that neither age nor education significantly influence perceptions of key agricultural sustainability challenges. Across all tested variables, the p-values are above 0.05, indicating no statistically significant association. Regardless of age, respondents share similar concerns about limited access to credit, consumer preferences for sustainable products, climate change impact on supply chains, fair wages, training deficiencies, lack of awareness of smart farming technologies, certification impact on market access, unstable markets, inconsistent government policies, and inadequate infrastructure. Similarly, education level does not significantly alter views on these issues, suggesting that agricultural sustainability challenges are universally recognized. This finding implies that policy interventions and support mechanisms should be designed to address these challenges broadly, ensuring that solutions are accessible and beneficial to all agricultural entrepreneurs, irrespective of demographic differences.

The Principal Component Analysis (PCA) communalities indicate how well each variable is explained by the extracted factors. High communalities suggest strong representation in the factor model. Key Influencing Factors: Variables like climate change impact (0.927) and infrastructure deficits (0.994) are critical, as they are almost entirely explained by the extracted components, highlighting their significance in sustainable supply chains. Financial and Market Constraints: Limited access to credit (0.862) and consumer demand for sustainable products (0.861) show that funding limitations and market preferences significantly affect sustainability adoption. Labour and Training Needs: Fair wages and safe working conditions (0.833) and training programs (0.827) emphasize the role of human capital in sustainable supply chain management. Regulatory and Market Stability Challenges: Variables like inconsistent policies (0.564) and price fluctuations (0.728) show moderate representation, suggesting external influences beyond supply chain control. Overall, the high communalities suggest that the extracted factors are highly effective in explaining the variance of most variables, confirming the appropriateness of factor analysis for this dataset. The results emphasize that financial constraints, infrastructure, climate conditions, labour issues, and market demand are key dimensions influencing sustainable supply chain practices in agricultural entrepreneurship. Moving forward, factor loading analysis will help determine how these variables group into underlying themes, which can provide valuable insights for policy recommendations and strategic planning in sustainable agriculture. The transition toward sustainable supply chain practices in agricultural entrepreneurship is a complex but necessary process that requires coordinated efforts from entrepreneurs, policymakers, financial institutions, and technology providers. While economic, environmental, and social benefits are evident, overcoming challenges related to financing, infrastructure, policy support, and technological adoption is crucial for ensuring long-term sustainability in agriculture.

CONCLUSION

The study underscores the critical role of sustainable supply chain practices in enhancing the economic resilience, environmental conservation, and social equity of agricultural entrepreneurship. By integrating resource efficiency, waste management, green logistics, and ethical labour practices, entrepreneurs can achieve long-term profitability while minimizing negative environmental impacts. However, significant challenges persist, including limited access to credit, inadequate infrastructure, lack of awareness, and regulatory inconsistencies. Addressing these barriers requires a multi-stakeholder approach, including government incentives, financial support mechanisms, infrastructure development, and capacity-building initiatives. The integration of fintech and digital solutions further presents a promising pathway to improving supply chain efficiency and sustainability in agriculture. By fostering collaboration between policymakers, financial institutions, and agricultural entrepreneurs, sustainable supply chain practices can contribute to global efforts toward environmental and economic sustainability. Ultimately, overcoming these challenges will enable agricultural entrepreneurship to play a transformative role in achieving sustainable development goals, ensuring food security, and promoting rural economic growth.

LIMITATIONS AND FURTHER RESEARCH DIRECTIONS

This study provides valuable insights into sustainable supply chain practices in agricultural entrepreneurship; however, it has certain limitations that should be acknowledged. Firstly, the research is geographically limited to Tamil Nadu, which may restrict the applicability of findings to other regions with different economic, climatic, and policy conditions. Additionally, while a structured sampling method was used, a larger and more diverse sample could enhance the generalizability of the results, particularly by including a wider range of agricultural sectors and regions. Another limitation is the reliance on self-reported data through surveys and interviews, which may be subject to respondent bias, affecting the accuracy of the findings. Moreover, the study captures sustainability challenges and impacts at a specific point in time, but it does not account for long-term changes, requiring a longitudinal approach for better insights.

Further research can address these limitations by conducting comparative studies across different regions or countries to understand how sustainable supply chain practices vary in different economic and environmental contexts. Longitudinal studies tracking sustainability efforts over time would help evaluate the long-term impact of sustainability interventions and evolving policies. Another crucial area for future research is the integration of advanced digital technologies such as blockchain, IoT, and AI-driven analytics to improve transparency and efficiency in agricultural supply chains. Additionally, exploring the role of climate change policies, carbon footprint regulations, and international trade in shaping sustainable agricultural practices could provide a broader perspective. Research on consumer behavior and market trends related to sustainability-conscious purchasing decisions would further contribute to the understanding of demand-driven sustainability adoption. Finally, comparative policy analysis focusing on successful sustainability initiatives from different countries could offer actionable recommendations for policymakers in Tamil Nadu and other developing agricultural economies.

REFERENCES

. Banerjee, T. (2021). Renewable Energy Adoption in Agricultural Supply Chains. *UNEP Report.*

Bank., W. (2019). Enabling the Business of Agriculture 2019. World Bank Group, Washington D.C.

Carter, C. R., & Rogers, D. S. (2008). A framework of sustainable supply chain management. *International Journal of Physical Distribution & Logistics Management*, *38*(5), 360–387. DOI: 10.1108/09600030810882816

Céu, M. S., & Gaspar, R. M. (2024). *A Review on Climate Change, Credit Risk, and Agriculture*. Rural Sustainability Research. [DOI:10.2478/plua-2024-0004]

Chatterjee, S., & Bose, A. (2021). Digital Transformation in Agriculture: The Impact of Blockchain and AI. *World Economic Forum.*

Das, M. (2020). *Overcoming Financial Barriers in Sustainable Agriculture. Organisation for Economic Co-operation and Development*. OECD.

Dubey, R., Gunasekaran, A., Papadopoulos, T., Childe, S. J., Shibin, K. T., & Wamba, S. F. (2017). Sustainable supply chain management: Framework and further research directions. *Journal of Cleaner Production*, *142*, 1119–1130. DOI: 10.1016/j.jclepro.2016.03.117

Elkington, J. (1997). *Cannibals with Forks: The Triple Bottom Line of 21st Century Business*. Capstone Publishing.

Food and Agriculture Organization (FAO). (2020). [*Overcoming Water Challenges in Agriculture*. FAO, Rome. Retrieved from https://www.fao.org/publications]. *The State of Food and Agriculture*, *2020*, •••.

Gadanakis, Y. (2024). Advancing Farm Entrepreneurship and Agribusiness Management for Sustainable Agriculture. *Agriculture*, *14*(8), 1288. DOI: 10.3390/agriculture14081288

Geron, Llanto, & Badiola. (2016). *Financial Inclusion in Agricultural Credit: A Demand and Supply Perspective*. Philippine Journal of Public Policy

Giglio, F. (2020). Access to Credit and Women Entrepreneurs: A Systematic Literature Review. *European Research Studies Journal*, *23*(4), 312–335

Govindan, , Rajendran, S., Sarkis, J., & Murugesan, P. (2014). Multi criteria decision making approaches for green supplier evaluation and selection: A literature review. *Journal of Cleaner Production*, *98*, 66–83. DOI: 10.1016/j.jclepro.2013.06.046

Iyer, S. (2019). *Policy Interventions for Sustainable Agricultural Development. Food and Agriculture Organization*. FAO.

Kannan, D.. (2014). Role of stakeholder pressure and knowledge management in sustainable supply chain management: Empirical evidence from the Indian cement industry. *International Journal of Production Economics*, *171*, 160–172.

Kapoor, D. (2020). The Social Impact of Sustainable Agriculture on Rural Communities. *World Bank Report.*

Kumar, R. (2020). Sustainable Agricultural Practices and Supply Chain Efficiency. *Food and Agriculture Organization (FAO).*

Luthra, S.. (2016). Barriers to industrial symbiosis in Indian firms: A TISM approach. *Journal of Cleaner Production*, *148*, 141–157.

Menon, R. (2020). *The Need for Training and Capacity Building in Agri-Entrepreneurship. United Nations Environment Programme*. UNEP.

Moktadir, M. A., Rahman, T., Rahman, M. H., Ali, S. M., & Paul, S. K. (2018). Drivers to sustainable manufacturing practices and circular economy: A perspective of leather industries in Bangladesh. *Journal of Cleaner Production*, *174*, 1366–180. DOI: 10.1016/j.jclepro.2017.11.063

OECD. (2021). *Sustainable Agriculture and Market Access: Global Trends and Challenges*. Organization for Economic Co-operation and Development.

Pagell, M., & Wu, Z. (2009). Building a more complete theory of sustainable supply chain management using case studies of 10 exemplars. *The Journal of Supply Chain Management*, *45*(2), 37–56. DOI: 10.1111/j.1745-493X.2009.03162.x

Prasad, H. (2020). *Financial Strategies for Sustainable Agri-Startups. International Monetary Fund*. IMF.

Rao, P., & Holt, D. (2005). Do green supply chains lead to competitiveness and economic performance? *International Journal of Operations & Production Management*, *25*(9), 898–916. DOI: 10.1108/01443570510613956

Sandhu, N., & Hussain, Z. (2020). Labor Rights and Social Equity in Agricultural Supply Chains. *Journal of Agricultural Economics.*

Sarma, M., & Pais, J. (2011). *Financial Inclusion and Agricultural Credit Access.* World Bank Reports.

Seuring, S., & Müller, M. (2008). From a literature review to a conceptual framework for sustainable supply chain management. *Journal of Cleaner Production, 16*(5), 1699–1710. DOI: 10.1016/j.jclepro.2008.04.020

Sharma, V., & Patel, A. (2021). *The Role of Fintech in Enhancing Agri-Entrepreneurship. United Nations Development Programme.* UNDP.

Singh, P. (2019). Infrastructure Challenges in Rural Supply Chains. *World Bank Report.*

Singh, R. K.. (2021). Analysing the interaction of barriers in the adoption of sustainable supply chain management practices in MSMEs. *Journal of Cleaner Production,* •••, 281.

Stiglitz, J., & Weiss, A. (1981). Credit Rationing in Markets with Imperfect Information. *The American Economic Review.*

Touboulic, A., et al. (2015). Theories in sustainable supply chain management: A structured literature review. *International Journal of Physical Distribution & Logistics Management, 45*(1\2), 16–42.

UNDP. (2021). *Sustainable Agriculture and Food Security: Empowering Rural Communities.*

Van Hoek, R. (2001). The contribution of performance measurement to the expansion of third-party logistics alliances in the supply chain. *International Journal of Operations & Production Management, 21*(1), 15–29. DOI: 10.1108/01443570110358431

Chapter 7

Revamping Nutri -Cereal Supply Chain Values to Entice Digital Natives for Nutritional and Health Sustainability

A. Anisha
http://orcid.org/0009-0001-3830-6350
Alagappa University, India

K. Chandrasekar
Alagappa University, India

ABSTRACT

The growing influence of digital natives on food consumption patterns underscores the need for a sustainable, transparent, and technology-driven nutri-cereal supply chain. This study explores how blockchain, IoT, and AI-driven innovations enhance supply chain efficiency, traceability, and consumer engagement while promoting healthier dietary habits. The research highlights how digital interventions, ethical sourcing, and regenerative farming practices align with the sustainability preferences of digital-native consumers. By integrating digital tools and personalized nutrition platforms, the Nutri-cereal industry can foster trust and encourage informed decision-making. Findings suggest that leveraging digital engagement strategies, targeted marketing, and traceability solutions can transform the supply chain, benefiting consumers and smallholder farmers alike. The study emphasizes that adapting supply chain values to meet evolving consumer expectations is critical for achieving long-term nutritional and health sustainability.

DOI: 10.4018/979-8-2600-1855-2.ch007

1. INTRODUCTION

To address significant challenges such as nutritional and health sustainability, it is increasingly important to understand the evolving dynamics of global food chains. Having grown up in a society dominated by digital technology, digital natives represent a unique group that can significantly impact sustainable practices through their purchasing decisions. Their demands for ethical sourcing, environmental responsibility, and transparency are reshaping supply chain values and creating opportunities for innovation in promoting sustainable and healthier lifestyles. Blockchain technology and digital platforms have become effective tools for enhancing supply chain traceability and transparency, enabling digital natives to make informed decisions (Aung & Chang, 2021). Additionally, incorporating health-focused digital interventions into supply chains, such as applications for personalized nutrition, aligns with the tech-savvy and health-conscious preferences of this group (Chen et al., 2018; Chopra et al., 2022). Recent research highlights the growing awareness of the negative effects of food production on the environment and human health, leading to increased demand for locally sourced and plant-based products (Rothgerber, 2020). Targeted advertising and innovative supply chain models can encourage digital natives to adopt sustainable consumption habits, benefiting both their long-term health and the environment. Nutri-cereals, often referred to as superfoods due to their rich nutrient profiles and climate resilience, have emerged as essential components of sustainable diets.

Their supply chain presents an opportunity to promote sustainability and health while catering to the dietary needs of digital natives. It is vital to adapt supply chain values to meet the expectations of this tech-savvy group, who increasingly seek transparent, ethically sourced, and environmentally friendly food products. Consumer engagement, sustainability, and traceability are critical challenges for modern Nutri-cereal supply chains. Advances in digital technologies such as blockchain and the Internet of Things (IoT) have enhanced transparency and trust in food supply chains (Kouhizadeh & Sarkis, 2018; Pournader et al., 2020). These technologies influence the purchasing decisions of digital natives by providing detailed product information on sourcing methods, nutritional value, and environmental impact. Incorporating data-driven strategies into the Nutri-cereal supply chain can improve efficiency, reduce waste, and ensure better access to high-quality products. For instance, AI-driven logistics and precision agriculture optimize resource utilization and enhance consumer access to Nutri-cereals (Liu et al., 2023; Zhang et al., 2017). When combined with targeted marketing strategies on social media platforms, this approach effectively engages digital natives by aligning with their environmental values and digital lifestyles. By reimagining the values of the Nutri-cereal supply chain to match the preferences of digital natives, stakeholders can promote healthier eating habits, support environmental sustainability, and create economic opportunities for smallholder farmers. In a rapidly digitizing world, this alignment lays the foundation for achieving nutritional and health sustainability.

1.1 Overview of Nutri-Cereals and Health Benefits

1.1.1 Nutri-Cereals

Millets are otherwise termed as a Nutri- Cereals a subhead consists of Sorghum (jowar), Pearl millet (bajra), Finger Millet (ragi), Banyard Millet, Proso Millet, Kodo Millet, Buckwheat, Amaranthus and Foxtail Millet. For the millions of Indians, it is a great source of vital nutrientsthey are also called as 'nutritious cereals. The Indian Millets are nutritionally superior to wheat and rice as they are rich in protein, vitamins and minerals. They are also gluten-free and have a low glycemic index, making them ideal for people with celiac disease or diabetes. India is the world's largest producer of Millets with the share of 38.40% of worlds production (FAO, 2021). A significant amount of the human diet is made up of cereals, which are also a good source of starch and other dietary carbohydrates (dietary fibre), which have a significant impact on a person's nutritional intake and energy needs. The millets have a higher fibre content, and their mineral makeup and protein quality greatly enhance nutritional security of a substantial portion of the populace living in millet-growing regions, who are thought to be the most marginalized groups (Yadav et al., 2021).

Figure 1. Millets Map

Source: APEDA

1.1.2 Health Benefits of Nutri-Cereals

Millets are coarse grains that resemble later crops found in the Indian subcontinent, such as rice and wheat. Millets provide a variety of key nutrients that are critical for human health, making them nutritional powerhouses. Their high dietary fiber content facilitates digestion, increases feelings of fullness, and aids in maintaining a healthy weight. Additionally, millets are a great source of protein, minerals including iron, calcium, magnesium, and zinc, and important vitamins, especially the B complex vitamins. These nutrients are essential for a number of body processes, including immune system and energy metabolism. By adding millets to diets, one can enhance overall nutritional status and fill in nutrient gaps. The grain is also abundant in phytochemicals, such as phytate, which millets contain, and phytic corrosive, which is thought to lower cholesterol (Coulibaly et al., 2011).

Figure 2. Health benefits

1.2 Sustainable Sourcing and Production

Making sure that sourcing and production methods are sustainable is one of the most crucial aspects of reworking the Nutri-cereal supply chain. Transparency in sourcing and the effects of the products they use on the environment are important to digital natives.

1.2.1 Sustainable Farming Practices

Purchasing raw ingredients from farms that use regenerative farming methods is the first stage in producing a sustainable Nutri-cereal product. By concentrating on biodiversity, soil health, and lowering carbon emissions, these methods go beyond organic farming. A more sustainable product can be produced, for example, by collaborating with farmers who practice crop.

Regenerative farming is crucial for combating climate change, according to studies conducted by the Food and Agriculture Organization (FAO) in 2021. In addition to lessening their environmental effect, nutri-cereal companies that source their ingredients from regenerative farms also appeal to consumers who prioritize ethical consumption.

1.2.2 Ethical Sourcing of Ingredients

Brands that show a dedication to ethical sourcing are especially appealing to digital natives,Consumer trust can be further increased by certifications like Fair Trade and Rainforest Alliance, which guarantee that producers use ethical and sustainable practices. Customers can feel more secure knowing that their purchases are promoting fair salaries and working conditions for farmers in addition to environmental sustainability thanks to these certifications.

1.2.3 Waste Reduction and Resource Efficiency

Digital natives are becoming more and more concerned about reducing waste, whether that means using less packaging or disposing of waste properly. Brands of nutri-cereals can spend money on closed-loop methods that reduce or reuse production waste.

Reducing food waste during manufacturing can result in more effective resource usage, which directly speaks to digital natives' sustainability principles, according to the Ellen MacArthur Foundation (2022).

1.3 Digital Transformation of Supply Chain Operations

With the development of technology, nutri-cereal companies have a rare chance to improve customer satisfaction and optimize their business processes. By guaranteeing transparency and maximizing efficiency, digital solutions like blockchain, artificial intelligence (AI), and the Internet of Things (IoT) have the potential to completely transform the supply chain (Rejeb et al., 2021; Liu et al., 2023).

1.3.1 Blockchain Technology for Openness

By providing a means of tracking the movement of raw materials, blockchain technology guarantees transparency throughout the whole production process. Nutri-cereal companies may give customers certified information about the origins of their components, from the farm to the factory, by putting blockchain technology into practice. For digital natives, who expect brands they support to be accountable, this transparency is a major selling feature. 73% of Gen Z and millennial consumers are willing to spend more for products that are transparently manufactured and sourced sustainably, according to a 2023 IBM survey. The infrastructure required to verify these claims is provided by blockchain, enabling nutri-cereal enterprises to gain the trust of their customers.

1.3.2 Artificial Intelligence and Data Analytics

Supply chain management is changing as a result of AI and data analytics. Businesses may eliminate waste, cut down on surplus inventory, and more precisely forecast demand by using predictive analytics. By making sure that manufacturing meets demand without going overboard, this not only streamlines the supply chain but also supports environmental objectives.

AI can also aid in production process optimization, which lowers carbon emissions and energy use. AI can be used by nutri-cereal companies to track energy consumption in real time and spot inefficiencies that can be fixed to lessen their environmental impact.

1.3.3 Internet of Things (IoT) for Real-Time Monitoring

Manufacturing facilities can use IoT devices to track everything from equipment maintenance to energy usage. Real-time data transmission from these devices enables operators to make resource and energy-saving modifications. Food waste can be decreased and supply chain forecasting accuracy increased by using IoT to track agricultural conditions in real-time.

1.4 Personalized Nutrition and Digital Engagement

Attracting digital natives requires integrating digital tools that support tailored nutrition. This generation looks for products that support their personal health objectives, whether those objectives be general well-being, muscle growth, or weight loss.

1.4.1 Personalized Nutrition

Digital natives can be successfully attracted by using technology to provide customized cereal selections depending on their dietary requirements and interests. For instance, nutri-cereal companies can develop platforms or apps that let users enter their dietary needs and health objectives.

According to a Nielsen analysis from 2021, customers are looking for more individualized experiences, which may lead to an increase in personalized health and wellness goods. Brands of nutri-cereals that provide this level of personalization can build closer relationships with their customers.

1.4.2 Gamification and Interactive Content

Digital natives are used to interacting with brands via gamified and interactive material. Brands of nutri-cereals can design virtual communities, fitness tracking integrations, or online challenges that let consumers monitor their health objectives while advertising the product. A company might, for example, design a monthly "health challenge" in which participants record how much cereal they eat and how much exercise they do each day, then post their results on social media. This encourages healthy living and builds a sense of community in addition to promoting the product.

1.4.3 Influencer Partnerships and Social Media Marketing

Digital natives' purchase decisions are greatly influenced by influencers. Reach and credibility can be raised by collaborating with wellness and health influencers who share the brand's beliefs. Influencers are more trusted by digital natives than traditional ads, and their recommendations. Since digital natives spend the majority of their time on platforms like YouTube, Instagram, and TikTok, brands should concentrate on producing shareable, bite-sized content for these platforms. The brand's dedication to sustainability might be reinforced by this content, which could include short recipe videos or behind-the-scenes recordings of the cereal's production process.

2. REVIEW OF LITERATURE AND FRAMEWORK

2.1 Sustainable Supply Chain

Seuring and Müller (2008) define sustainable supply chain management as the process of managing material, information, and capital flows, along with fostering cooperation among companies within the supply chain. This management approach considers the goals of all three dimensions of sustainable developmenteconomic, environmental, and social. These goals are guided by the requirements of customers and stakeholders. The authors emphasize that supply chain members must meet environmental and social criteria to remain part of the chain. At the same time, competitiveness is sustained by fulfilling customer needs and adhering to related economic criteria. Supply chains play a crucial role in advancing the broader adoption and development of sustainability. Supply chains encompass the entire lifecycle of products, from raw material sourcing to final delivery to the end customer. The trade of ethical products initially emerged as an alternative to the traditional market system (Waldman & Kerr, 2014). However, it has recently been adopted by major networks as a strategy for differentiation and corporate social responsibility. In theory, this shift involves transforming relationships throughout the value chain, emphasizing trust and ethical practices with both suppliers and customers. By creating value through relationships, sustainability influences how buyers and suppliers interact and adapt to customer demands. Consequently, sustainable practices reshape the nature of buyer-supplier relationships, aligning them with principles of trust, responsibility, and responsiveness.

2.2 Nutritional and Health Benefits

Millets, often referred to as Nutri-cereals, are gaining recognition for their exceptional nutritional and health benefits, with an increasing number of studies emphasizing their potential to combat lifestyle diseases and enhance dietary health. Porwal et al. (2023) and Saleh et al. (2013) provide a detailed analysis of millets' rich protein, dietary fiber, and micronutrient content, which make them effective in managing malnutrition and reducing the risks of chronic diseases such as diabetes and obesity. Bellad and Belavadi (2023) further highlight the anti-inflammatory and antioxidant properties of millets, underlining their role in disease prevention and overall health improvement. The adaptability of underutilized millet varieties to diverse agro-climatic conditions, as discussed by Kumar et al. (2021), contributes significantly to dietary diversity and food security.

The global focus on promoting millet consumption is exemplified by initiatives like the International Year of Millets 2023, explored by Achinna and Rao (2023), which emphasize their contribution to sustainable food systems and malnutrition reduction. In their analysis of millet production growth trends, Pillai et al. (2023) demonstrate how these crops can support national nutrition and food security policies. To improve the nutritional content of dairy products and increase fiber and micro-nutrient intake, Prasad (2023) investigates novel strategies, such as incorporating millets into these products.Innovations in technology are essential for improving the supply chain and promoting millet. Research by Jagtap et al. (2022) and Kamilaris et al. (2019) highlights the value of IoT, blockchain, and digitization in enhancing the traceability and transparency of millet supply chains. Chen et al. (2018) explore the role of mobile health applications in encouraging tech-savvy individuals to consume millet, demonstrating a shift towards digital-native consumer engagement. Aung and Chang (2021) further emphasize the importance of traceability systems in ensuring the quality and safety of millet products. Policy actions are equally crucial for promoting millet. In their discussion of the shortcomings of certification programs in commodity crop production, Waldman and Kerr (2014) advocate for improved safeguards to enhance environmental sustainability and protect human health. According to Bossert et al. (1998), institutional changes can transform millet supply chains, making them more consumer-focused and efficient. Taken together, these studies highlight the diverse ways in which millets can promote sustainability, nutrition, and health while emphasizing the need for further research and technical advancements to fully realize their potential.

Rajasekharan et al. (2023) note that Nutri-cereals, also known as little millets, are considered smart foods predicted to revolutionize the food industry and diets to provide nutritional security. Nutri-cereals are both nourishing and climate-adaptable. This review highlights the importance of little millets, their cultural heritage values, and their future potential. It also examines the nutritional and medicinal qualities of little millets to support the creation of sustainable diets in the near future. Bellad et al. (2023) suggest that millets are an excellent food for diabetics due to their low glycemic index. Additionally, they are more environmentally friendly, requiring less water than crops like wheat and rice, making them ideal for areas with water scarcity. Pillai et al. (2023) also emphasize these benefits.

2.3 Challenges in Current Nutri-Cereal Supply Chains

Porwal et al. (2023) identify the lack of modern technologies and insufficient government support as significant barriers to growth in the Nutri-cereal supply chain. Similarly, Prasad (2023) emphasizes the untapped potential for value addition through creative processing and product integration. Aung and Chang (2021) highlight how fragmented systems compromise the safety and quality of Nutri-cereal products, while Jagtap et al. (2022) advocate for digitization to improve supply chain efficiency and traceability. Kamilaris et al. (2019) argue that blockchain technology has the potential to revolutionize the Nutri-cereal supply chain by addressing inefficiencies and boosting stakeholder confidence.

Additionally, L. et al. (2023) suggest that advancements in genomics and genetics can significantly enhance production quality and reduce post-harvest losses, thereby overcoming critical bottlenecks. Both Waldman and Kerr (2014) and Porwal et al. (2023) point out flaws in existing certifications and standards, calling for more robust mechanisms to ensure sustainability and efficiency. Collectively, these studies provide a comprehensive understanding of the challenges facing the Nutri-cereal supply chain, emphasizing the need for innovative technologies, supportive legislation, and collaborative international efforts to address these barriers.Historical data indicates that during the past three decades, the green revolution has led to a decline in both acreage and productivity of millet farming. However, over the last two decades, there has been a noticeable increase in output, driven by the introduction of high-yielding cultivars resistant to pests and diseases.

This study aims to analyse the growth trends in millet production over time and provide recommendations for strategies to increase the area, production, and productivity of millet farming in India.Waldman and associates (2014) highlight that the nature of corn and soybean production, distribution, and consumptioncharacterized by numerous sales outlets and the widespread use of these crops in processed foodsmakes the implementation of supply chain standards extremely challenging.

They further conclude that certification schemes aimed at reducing agricultural pollution may be impractical under current conditions. There is also a lack of effective digital integration, which hinders efficient distribution and complicates the management of supply chains for nutri-cereal products (Rejeb et al., 2021).

Smallholder farmers, who are crucial to the production of nutri-cereals, often face challenges accessing reliable markets and obtaining fair trade opportunities (Patel et al., 2022). The competition with more widely known grains like rice and wheat, along with logistical issues in reaching urban centers, further limits the growth potential of nutri-cereals (Chaudhary et al., 2023).

Additionally, the lack of government support and policies to incentivize the cultivation and promotion of these products limits their potential for large-scale adoption (Kumar et al., 2020). The inconsistent supply and seasonal availability of nutri-cereals also pose challenges in ensuring year-round access, which impacts their market appeal (Krishnan et al., 2022). Finally, without proper digital traceability systems, there is an inherent risk of concerns over product authenticity and quality, which affects consumer trust and adoption (Bosona & Gebresenbet, 2013).

2.4 Digitalization in Food Supply Chain

Digital technology has revolutionized food supply chains by enhancing operational efficiency, traceability, and transparency. Kamilaris et al. (2019) claim that blockchain technology has the potential to completely transform the agriculture sector by promoting trust and ensuring supply chain traceability. Similarly, X et al. (2021) highlight the importance of digital traceability systems in ensuring food safety and quality, reducing fraud, and boosting consumer confidence. Liu et al. (2023) expand this perspective by exploring AI applications that improve supply chain efficiency through better demand forecasting, quality assurance, and predictive analytics.Tsolakis et al. (2014) and Zhang et al. (2019) emphasize the integration of Internet of Things (IoT) technology, noting its ability to enhance traceability, reduce logistical inefficiencies, and collect real-time data, particularly for perishable goods.

Hobbs (2020) provides valuable insights into resilient future food systems by highlighting how digital platforms can mitigate supply chain disruptions during crises like the COVID-19 pandemic.Kouhizadeh and Sarkis (2018) analyse blockchain's benefits for sustainability, showing how the technology can enhance data exchange and traceability in agri-food supply chains. Bosona and Gebresenbet (2013) also emphasize the critical role of traceability in ensuring food quality and safety. Bumblauskas et al. (2020) investigate the integration of RFID and IoT technologies, demonstrating their potential to improve supply chain traceability and performance. Carvalho et al. (2018) examine advanced technologies like digital twins, highlighting their importance in predictive maintenance and process optimization.

Espiñeira and Santaclara (2016) discuss advancements in digital food authentication systems that enhance traceability. Pournader et al. (2021) further emphasize the benefits of digitalization, illustrating how the strategic integration of blockchain and artificial intelligence (AI) fosters efficient and sustainable food systems while improving risk management and resilience in food supply chain. This study explores how digital disruption highlights Generation Z's uniqueness as digital natives and impacts their attitudes toward rarely seen products. It finds that while Gen Z relies more on digital media than previous generations, social networks have a greater influence across all generations. Generational differences from digital disruption can be mitigated through practice, as factors like work requirements shape behaviors.

The findings provide insights into digital innovation's effects and offer a foundation for future research and practical applications (Chang & Chang, 2023). The rapid digital transformation of the agri-food industry is enhancing supply chain transparency and efficiency. Blockchain technology plays a crucial role by ensuring product traceability, providing consumers with verified information about product origins, and strengthening supply chain trust (Pournader et al., 2020; Kouhizadeh & Sarkis, 2018). Additionally, IoT devices are increasingly being used to monitor crop conditions in real time, helping to optimize harvesting times and improve the overall quality and efficiency of agricultural supply chains (Rejeb et al., 2021).

Artificial intelligence (AI) further enhances agri-food systems by predicting demand and assisting businesses in allocating resources more effectively, leading to improved planning and reduced waste (Gereffi et al., 2022). Digital platforms facilitate real-time data exchange between farmers, wholesalers, and retailers, minimizing waste and delays while ensuring timely product delivery. Moreover, e-commerce platforms are transforming how consumers access niche food products, such as Nutri-cereals, by removing traditional distribution barriers and enabling direct interactions between producers and health-conscious buyers (Kapoor & Dwivedi, 2022). Mobile applications are also reshaping the meal delivery industry by promoting healthier food choices and helping consumers make more informed purchasing decisions (Kapoor & Dwivedi, 2022). By providing transparency regarding product sourcing and sustainability, blockchain technology not only reinforces consumer trust but also encourages ethical purchasing. Digital platforms play a key role in educating consumers and raising awareness about food products by fostering direct communication between farmers and consumers (Patel et al., 2022).

Furthermore, AI and machine learning help predict consumer preferences, improving customer engagement with healthier food options and offering personalized meal recommendations (Liu et al., 2023). IoT and AI-powered smart logistics solutions streamline transportation, ensuring that perishable goods like nutri-cereals maintain their quality and freshness during transit (Gereffi et al., 2022).

Additionally, digital finance solutions such as smart contracts and mobile payment systems empower farmers by enabling faster payments, ensuring fair trade opportunities, and improving smallholder farmers' access to markets (Patel et al., 2022). Cloud-based systems also facilitate collaboration among agri-food supply chain stakeholders, increasing efficiency and reducing costs (Rejeb et al., 2021).

By accurately forecasting demand and ensuring that products are supplied in the right quantities, real-time data exchange helps minimize food waste. Digital supply chain solutions further enhance the sustainability of agri-food systems by reducing waste and improving energy efficiency through AI-driven demand forecasting and resource management.

2.5 Consumer Preferences and Digital Natives

Millennials and Gen Z, as digital natives, are reshaping consumer habits by prioritizing environmentally friendly and ethically sourced products. When making purchasing decisions, they increasingly rely on social media, digital platforms, and online reviews (Kapoor & Dwivedi, 2022). Social media significantly influences food choices, with influencers playing a key role in promoting sustainable and health-conscious options (Kapoor & Dwivedi, 2022).

Furthermore, these consumers value supply chain transparency, seeking detailed information about sourcing, production methods, and sustainability credentials (Hansen et al., 2018). As sustainability and health become central to their purchasing decisions, digital natives are looking for personalized food experiences through technology-driven platforms that offer tailored dietary advice (Kapoor & Dwivedi, 2022).

Research has shown that integrating gamification and interactive content into digital platforms effectively engages consumers and encourages healthier eating habits (Kapoor & Dwivedi, 2022). Additionally, meal-tracking mobile applications are growing in popularity, allowing users to monitor their nutritional intake and receive recommendations for improving their diets (Chopra et al., 2022). Direct-to-consumer sales and subscription-based models are gaining traction, providing easier access to nutritious food products such as Nutri-cereals (Kapoor & Dwivedi, 2022). Personalized recommendations based on past purchases, along with mobile-based health and wellness platforms, cater to the demand for convenient and specialized food options (Liu et al., 2023). Moreover, an increasing number of apps and digital tools track the sustainability and health impact of food choices, empowering consumers to make informed decisions and adopt healthier diets (Chopra et al., 2022).

Integrating digital technology across the supply chain is essential for increasing the adoption of Nutri-cereals. One such innovation is smart packaging, which utilizes blockchain technology and QR codes to enhance product authenticity and traceability, thereby strengthening consumer trust (Aung & Chang, 2021). Additionally, direct-to-consumer business models, such as subscription services and online marketplaces, improve consumer access to nutri-cereal products, enhancing convenience (Kapoor & Dwivedi, 2022).

AI-powered personalized nutrition platforms offer individualized dietary recommendations based on users' unique health profiles, further boosting engagement and consumption (Liu et al., 2023). Digital marketing, particularly through influencers and social media, has been instrumental in promoting the benefits of Nutri-cereals and raising awareness about their nutritional and sustainability advantages (Kapoor & Dwivedi, 2022). Digital agro-advisory services also play a crucial role in strengthening the supply side by providing farmers with access to market insights, best practices, and demand forecasts, enabling them to meet consumer needs effectively (Patel et al., 2022).

Additionally, mobile applications that track food intake and suggest healthier alternatives can encourage consumers to incorporate more nutri-cereals into their diets (Chopra et al., 2022). Blockchain technology can further enhance transparency in the food supply chain by ensuring the traceability, sustainability, and ethical sourcing of nutri-cereals (Bosona & Gebresenbet, 2013; Pournader et al., 2020).

Furthermore, digital financial solutions, such as smart contracts and mobile payment platforms, can support smallholder farmers by improving market access, ensuring fair pricing, and reducing risks associated with market volatility (Patel et al., 2022). By implementing these strategies, the nutri-cereal industry can better serve digital-native consumers while strengthening the supply chain for sustainable growth.

2.6 Conceptual Framework

Figure 3.

Figure 3.

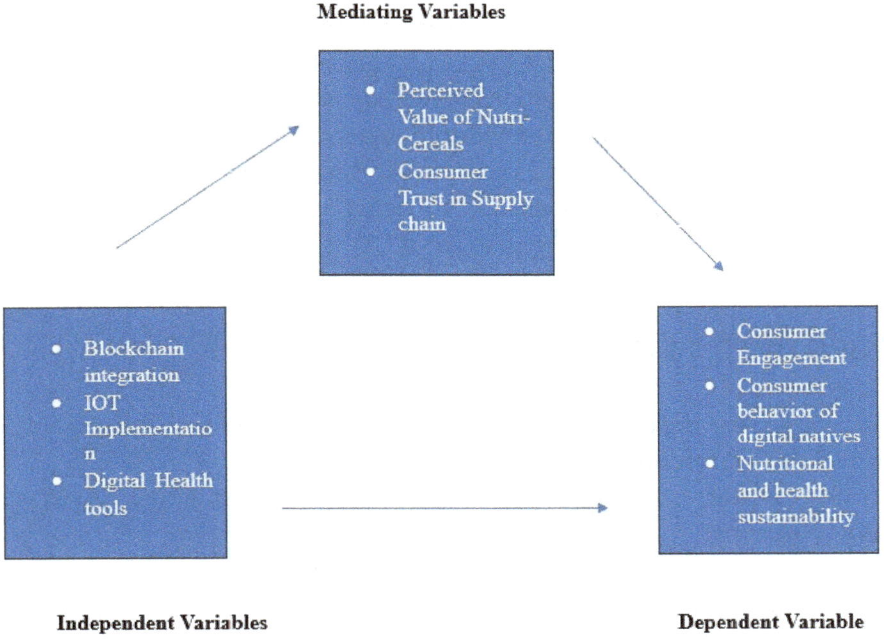

3. RESEARCH GAP

The integration of digital technologies such as blockchain, IoT, and AI into the Nutri-cereal supply chain offers a transformative pathway to enhance transparency, sustainability, and consumer engagement. This approach is particularly appealing to tech-savvy and health-conscious digital natives. Blockchain technology has shown immense potential in ensuring traceability, building consumer trust, and promoting sustainable practices in agricultural supply chains (Pournader et al., 2020; Kouhizadeh & Sarkis, 2018). Similarly, IoT has demonstrated its ability to improve operational efficiency and real-time visibility, which is critical for preserving the quality and freshness of perishable goods like Nutri-cereals (Rejeb et al., 2021; Zhang et al., 2017). AI also plays a pivotal role in optimizing food supply chains through predictive analytics, accurate demand forecasting, and robust quality control systems, thereby contributing to greater efficiency and transparency (Liu et al., 2023). Additionally, digital health tools are influencing consumer preferences by providing personalized, data-driven dietary recommendations, which encourage healthier eating habits (Chen et al., 2018). By incorporating these advanced technologies, the Nutri-cereal supply chain can meet modern consumer demands for traceable, sustainable, and convenient food options. This alignment is increasingly critical as consumers prioritize ethical production and transparency in their food choices (Aung & Chang, 2021). Leveraging such tools not only enhances consumer trust but also improves health outcomes and supports environmental sustainability. To bridge the existing research gap, further exploration is needed to understand how these technologies can be effectively implemented to modernize the Nutri-cereal supply chain. Such advancements could significantly encourage digital natives to adopt healthier and more sustainable dietary habits (Rejeb et al., 2021).

4. OBJECTIVES OF THE STUDY

To analyse the impact of supply chain strategies on consumer engagement with Nutri-cereals among digital natives.

To evaluate the relationship between nutritional awareness and perceived value of Nutri-cereals.

To assess the role of digital technologies in enhancing efficiency in the Nutri-cereal supply chain.

5. RESEARCH METHODOLOGY

5.1 Instrument Development

This study differs from related research as it evaluates the key factors influencing the implementation of supply chain practices alongside digital technologies in the Nutri-cereal industry. A structured questionnaire was designed, utilizing a five-point Likert scale to assess the perceptions of respondents.Secondary data was sourced from journals, government websites and newspaper etc., to gain in-depth insights into the Nutri-cereal supply chain. The questionnaire incorporated sections addressing general company information and specific factors related to the adoption of digital technologies, health nutritional and sustainability and consumer engagement and behaviour in Nutri-cereal processing and distribution.

5.2 Reliability of Analysis

Cronbach's alpha was used to assess the reliability of the constructs, with values greater than 0.70 indicating strong reliability. According tc the results, the results suggest that all constructs are highly reliable, as their Cronbach's alpha values exceed 0.70.

Table 1. Mean Ranking Analysis- Blockchain Integration

Factors	Number of Items	Cronbach's alpha
Blockchain Integration	5	.812
IoT Implementation	5	.783
Digital Health Tools	5	.863
Consumer Engagement and Behaviour	6	.814

Source: Primary Data

5.3 Sampling

The study conducted in Tamil Nadu assessed the adoption of digital technologies in the Nutri-cereals supply chain, covering production, processing, and distribution. Major Nutri-cereal-producing regions, including Madurai, Chennai, Coimbatore, and Trichy, were selected for their significant contributions to cereal cultivation, processing, and value addition.To ensure robust findings, a total of 370 samples were collected using a proportionate stratified random sampling method. The respondents included producers, distributors, and consumers, with equitable representation from each category based on their role in the Nutri-cereal ecosystem.Data collection involved surveys and semi-structured interviews, conducted both in-person and online, depending on the respondents' accessibility and digital literacy levels.

6. ANALYSIS AND INTERPRETATION

Table 2.

Descriptive Statistics	Mean	Std. Deviation	Rank
I value knowing the origin of Nutri-cereals I purchase.	3.10	1.243	**2**
Blockchain technology improves my trust in the traceability of Nutri-cereal products.	3.41	1.223	**1**
I am more likely to trust a brand that uses blockchain for transparency.	2.83	1.261	**3**
Transparent supply chain data increases my confidence in product quality.	2.79	1.232	**5**
Blockchain promotes environmentally sustainable practices in the Nutri-cereal supply chain.	2.81	1.260	**4**

Interpretation

The descriptive statistics highlight consumer perceptions of blockchain technology in the Nutri-cereal supply chain. The statement "Blockchain technology improves my trust in the traceability of Nutri-cereal products" ranks highest (mean = 3.41, SD = 1.223), indicating strong agreement and moderate variability, suggesting that blockchain significantly enhances trust in traceability. Conversely, "Transparent supply chain data increases my confidence in product quality" ranks lowest (mean = 2.79, SD = 1.232), reflecting relatively lower agreement and indicating that supply chain transparency is less strongly linked to perceived product quality. Consumers moderately value knowing the origin of Nutri-cereals (mean = 3.10, rank 2), while blockchain's role in promoting environmentally sustainable practices (mean = 2.81, rank 4) and building brand trust through transparency (mean = 2.83, rank 3) shows potential but less pronounced importance. Overall, the findings emphasize blockchain's critical role in trust and traceability, with opportunities to strengthen its perceived impact on sustainability and product quality.

Table 3. IOT Implementation

Descriptive Statistics	Mean	Std. Deviation	Rank
IoT technology improves the efficiency of Nutri-cereal production and delivery.	3.10	1.243	**1**
IoT ensures better management of resources in the supply chain.	2.99	1.395	**3**
I find real-time tracking of Nutri-cereal products valuable.	3.03	1.349	**2**

continued on following page

Table 3. Continued

Descriptive Statistics	Mean	Std Deviation	Rank
IoT-enabled visibility reassures me about product freshness.	2.90	1.405	4
IoT technology helps maintain the quality of Nutri-cereals during transportation.	2.90	1.350	4

Source: Primary Data

Interpretation

The table reveal that consumer perceptions of IoT technology in the Nutri-cereal supply chain, with "IoT technology improves the efficiency of Nutri-cereal production and delivery" ranking highest (mean = 3.10, SD = 1.243), indicating a strong recognition of its role in enhancing efficiency. The value of real-time tracking is also acknowledged, ranking second (mean = 3.03, SD = 1.349), suggesting that consumers appreciate the ability to monitor products in transit. However, statements about IoT ensuring better resource management (mean = 2.99, SD = 1.395) and reassuring product freshness or maintaining quality during transportation (mean = 2.90, SD = 1.405 and SD = 1.350, respectively) rank lower, reflecting comparatively less enthusiasm about these aspects. Overall, the findings underscore the perceived value of IoT in improving efficiency and enabling real-time tracking, while indicating potential to better communicate its benefits in resource management and quality assurance.

Table 4. Digital Health tools

Descriptive Statistics	Mean	Std. Deviation	Rank
Digital tools enhance my interaction with Nutri-cereal brands.	3.10	1.243	2
I engage more with brands that provide data-driven health insights.	3.41	1.223	1
Digital health tools encourage me to adopt a healthier diet.	2.83	1.261	3
Nutri-cereals promoted through health tools influence my purchasing decisions.	2.79	1.232	5
I would trust a Nutri-cereal brand that provides personalized health advice.	2.81	1.260	4

Source: Primary Data

Interpretation

The table shows that consumer perceptions of digital tools in their interaction with Nutri-cereal brands. The statement "I engage more with brands that provide data-driven health insights" ranks highest (mean = 3.41, SD = 1.223), indicating strong consumer interest in health insights as a key engagement driver. Similarly, "Digital tools enhance my interaction with Nutri-cereal brands" ranks second (mean = 3.10, SD = 1.243), reflecting the importance of digital interaction. However, statements about digital health tools encouraging healthier diets (mean = 2.83, rank 3), influencing purchasing decisions (mean = 2.79, rank 5), and fostering trust through personalized health advice (mean = 2.81, rank 4) received lower rankings, suggesting room to enhance the perceived value of these features. Overall, the findings emphasize the significant role of data-driven insights in consumer engagement while indicating opportunities to strengthen the influence of digital health tools on trust, dietary behaviour, and purchasing decisions.

Table 5. Chi- Square test on Location and Consumer Engagement and Behaviour

Chi-Square Tests			
Pearson Chi-Square	**Value**	**df**	**Asymptotic Significance (2-sided)**
	2.738	8	.950

Source: Primary Data

Interpretation

The Chi-Square test result shows a Pearson Chi-Square value of 2.738 with 8 degrees of freedom and an asymptotic significance (p-value) of 0.950. Since the p-value is much greater than the standard significance threshold (e.g., 0.05), we fail to reject the null hypothesis. This indicates that there is no statistically significant association between the location and consumer engagement are being analysed.

Table 6. Chi- Square test on Age and Digital health tools

Chi-Square Tests			
Pearson Chi-Square	**Value**	**df**	**Asymptotic Significance (2-sided)**
	45.417	12	.000

Source: Primary Data

Interpretation

The Chi-Square test result shows a Pearson Chi-Square value of 45.417 with 12 degrees of freedom and an asymptotic significance (p-value) of 0.000. Since the p-value is less than the standard significance threshold (e.g., 0.05), we reject the null hypothesis. This indicates a statistically significant association between the age and digital health tools are being analysed.

DTNCB - Digital tools enhance my interaction with Nutri-cereal brands.

IBDHI- I engage more with brands that provide data-driven health insights.

DHAHD -Digital health tools encourage me to adopt a healthier diet.

NPHPD - Nutri-cereals promoted through health tools influence my purchasing decisions.

INCPHD-I would trust a Nutri-cereal brand that provides personalized health advice.

Table 7. Correlation analyses between variables of Digital Health Tools

		AGE	DTNCB	IBDHI	DHAHD	NPHPD	INCPHD
AGE	PC	1					
	Sig.						
	N	370					
DTNCB	PC	.030	1				
	Sig.	.511					
	N	370	370				
IBDHI	PC	.003	.048	1			
	Sig.	.950	.290				
	N	370	370	370			
DHAHD	PC	.019	.028	.114*	1		
	Sig.	.683	.543	.013			
	N	370	370	370	370		
NPHPD	PC	.002	-.009	.013	-.108*	1	
	Sig.	.961	.849	.783	.018		
	N	370	370	370	370	370	
INCPHD	PC	-.001	.000	.011	.003	.193**	1
	Sig.	.988	.995	.804	.948	**.000**	
	N	370	370	370	370	370	370

*. Correlation is significant at the 0.05 level (2-tailed).

**. Correlation is significant at the 0.01 level (2-tailed).

Source: Primary Data

Interpretation

The table shows that Most correlations are weak and non-significant, indicating limited linear relationships between the variables. Notably, Digital health tools encourage me to adopt a healthier diet. shows a weak but statistically significant positive correlation with I engage more with brands that provide data-driven health insights. (r = .114, p = .013), suggesting a slight association between these variables. Additionally, I would trust a Nutri-cereal brand that provides personalized health advice exhibits a weak but significant positive correlation with Nutri-cereals promoted through health tools influence my purchasing decisions. (r = .193, p <.001), implying a modest relationship between these two variables. The other correlations are either negligible or non-significant, as evidenced by their p-values exceeding the 0.05 threshold.

IRCNHB -I regularly consume Nutri-cereals for health benefits.

DEENP - Digital engagement encourages me to try Nutri-cereal products

TPEPV -Traceable products enhance my perception of value.

IPNTSS - I prefer Nutri-cereals that are traceable and sustainably sourced.

SIDPNC - Sustainability influences my decision to purchase Nutri-cereals

Table 8.Correlation analyses between variables of Consumer Engagement and Behaviour

Correlations							
		INCOME	IRCNHB	DEENP	TPEPV	IPNTSS	SIDPNC
INCOME	PC	1					
	Sig.						
	N	370					
IRCNHB	PC	.030	1				
	Sig.	.511					
	N	370	370				
DEENP	PC	.003	.048	1			
	Sig.	.950	.290				
	N	370	370	370			
TPEPV	PC	.019	.028	.114*	1		
	Sig.	.683	.543	.013			
	N	370	370	370	370		
IPNTSS	PC	.002	-.009	.013	-.108*	1	
	Sig.	.961	.849	.783	.018		
	N	370	370	370	370	370	
SIDPNC	PC	-.001	.000	.011	.003	.193**	1

Source: Primary Data

Interpretation

The table reveals that the relationships among six variables. Notable findings include a weak positive correlation between Traceable products enhance my perception of value and Digital engagement encourages me to try Nutri-cereal products (PC = .114, Sig. = .013) and a weak negative correlation between Traceable products enhance my perception of value and I prefer Nutri-cereals that are traceable and sustainably sourced. (PC = -.108, Sig. = .018), both statistically significant at the 0.05 level. Additionally, Sustainability influences my decision to purchase Nutri-cereals shows a moderate positive correlation with itself (PC = .193, Sig. = .003), likely a methodological control.

H_0- There is no significant relationship between age and digital health tools

Table 9.ANOVA – Test for Age and Digital health tools

ANOVA						
		Sum of Squares	df	Mean Square	F	Sig.
Digital tools enhance my interaction with Nutri-cereal brands.	Between Groups	2.422	2	1.211	.782	.458
	Within Groups	568.075	367	1.548		
	Total	570.497	369			
I engage more with brands that provide data-driven health insights.	Between Groups	.038	2	.019	.013	.987
	Within Groups	551.519	367	1.503		
	Total	551.557	369			
Digital health tools encourage me to adopt a healthier diet.	Between Groups	.160	2	.080	.050	.951
	Within Groups	586.770	367	1.599		
	Total	586.930	369			
Nutri-cereals promoted through health tools influence my purchasing decisions.	Between Groups	10.904	2	5.452	3.642	.027
	Within Groups	549.485	367	1.497		
	Total	560.389	369			
I would trust a Nutri-cereal brand that provides personalized health advice.	Between Groups	1.652	2	.826	.519	.596
	Within Groups	584.480	367	1.593		
	Total	586.132	369			

Source: Primary Data

Interpretation

The ANOVA table evaluates the differences between groups for five statements related to digital tools and Nutri-cereal brands. Most variables show no significant differences between groups, as indicated by high significance values (Sig. > .05).

For instance, the statements on digital tools enhancing interaction (Sig. = .458), engaging with brands offering data-driven health insights (Sig. = .987), encouraging healthier diets (Sig. = .951), and trusting personalized Nutri-cereal brands (Sig. = .596) reveal no significant variance. However, the statement "Nutri-cereals promoted through health tools influence my purchasing decisions" shows a statistically significant difference between groups (F = 3.642, Sig. = .027), suggesting that group differences exist for this particular perception.

H_0- There is no significant relationship between location and IOT implementation

Table 10.ANOVA – Test forlocation and IOT implementation

ANOVA						
		Sum of Squares	**df**	**Mean Square**	**F**	**Sig.**
IoT technology improves the efficiency of Nutri-cereal production and delivery.	Between Groups	.657	2	.329	.212	.809
	Within Groups	569.840	367	1.553		
	Total	570.497	369			
IoT ensures better management of resources in the supply chain.	Between Groups	.643	2	1.323	.679	.508
	Within Groups	715.311	367	1.949		
	Total	715.954	369			
I find real-time tracking of Nutri-cereal products valuable.	Between Groups	.942	2	.471	.258	.773
	Within Groups	670.787	367	1.828		
	Total	671.730	369			
IoT-enabled visibility reassures me about product freshness.	Between Groups	.687	2	.006	.007	.993
	Within Groups	417.236	367	.875		
	Total	417.248	369			
IoT technology helps maintain the quality of Nutri-cereals during transportation.	Between Groups	.148	2	.074	.060	.942
	Within Groups	589.644	367	1.236		
	Total	589.792	369			

Source: Primary data

Interpretation

The ANOVA results indicate no significant differences between groups across all five statements related to the impact of IoT technology on Nutri-cereal production, delivery, and quality assurance. This is evident from the high significance values (Sig. > .05) for each statement: improving efficiency in production and delivery (Sig. = .809), better supply chain resource management (Sig. = .508), the value of real-time tracking (Sig. = .773), reassurance about product freshness (Sig. = .993), and maintaining quality during transportation (Sig. = .942). These findings suggest that perceptions regarding the role of IoT in these aspects are consistent across the groups analysed.

H_0- There is no significant relationship between location and Consumer Engagement and Behaviour

Table 11.ANOVA – Test forlocation and Consumer Engagement and Behaviour

ANOVA						
		Sum of Squares	df	Mean Square	F	Sig.
I regularly consume Nutri-cereals for health benefits.	Between Groups	.224	2	.112	.072	.930
	Within Groups	570.273	367	1.554		
	Total	570.497	369			
Digitalengagement encourages me to try Nutri-cereal products.	Between Groups	22.973	2	11.486	6.066	.003
	Within Groups	694.984	367	1.894		
	Total	717.957	369			
I am willing to pay more for Nutri-cereals with transparent sourcing.	Between Groups	.224	2	.112	.072	.930
	Within Groups	570.273	367	1.554		
	Total	570.497	369			
Traceable products enhance my perception of value.	Between Groups	6.911	2	3.456	2.328	.099
	Within Groups	544.646	367	1.484		
	Total	551.557	369			
I prefer Nutri-cereals that are traceable and sustainably sourced.	Between Groups	.173	2	.087	.054	.947
	Within Groups	586.756	367	1.599		
	Total	586.930	369			
Sustainability influences my decision to purchase Nutri-cereals.	Between Groups	12.901	2	6.451	4.324	.014
	Within Groups	547.488	367	1.492		
	Total	560.389	369			

Source: Primary data

Interpretation

The ANOVA results show significant group differences for two statements. Digital engagement encouraging consumers to try Nutri-cereal products has a significant effect (F = 6.066, Sig. = .003), and sustainability influencing purchasing decisions is also significant (F = 4.324, Sig. = .014), indicating these perceptions vary across groups. However, no significant differences are observed for regularly consuming Nutri-cereals for health benefits (Sig. = .930), willingness to pay more for transparent sourcing (Sig. = .930), preference for traceable and sustainably sourced Nutri-cereals (Sig. = .947), and traceable products enhancing value perception (Sig. = .099). These results suggest that while sustainability and digital engagement significantly influence certain consumer behaviours, other factors are perceived similarly across groups.

7. MAJOR FINDING AND SUGGESTIONS

7.1 Impact of Blockchain Technology

Blockchain technology enhances supply chain transparency, increasing consumer trust in the legitimacy of Nutri-cereal products. While it fosters confidence, consumers do not strongly associate blockchain with improvements in sustainability and product quality, as its perceived impact in these areas remains moderate.

7.2 Role of IoT in the Supply Chain

The adoption of IoT improves supply chain visibility and efficiency by enhancing logistics and real-time monitoring. However, its lesser-known role in optimizing resource management and ensuring product quality highlights the need for better communication to stakeholders about its benefits in these areas.

7.3 Influence of Digital Tools on Consumer Engagement

Digital tools effectively engage consumers by providing valuable insights into nutrition and health, increasing their awareness of the benefits of Nutri-cereals. However, personalized health recommendations have a limited impact on trust-building and purchasing decisions, indicating that while consumers appreciate the information.

7.4 Statistical Analysis of Consumer Perceptions

Statistical analyses reveal those linear relationships between digital adoption and consumer perceptions, indicating the significant correlations. However, Chi-Square and ANOVA results show that consumer perceptions are generally consistent across demographic groups, with notable exceptions for digital engagement and sustainability, which have a significant impact on purchasing behaviour.

To strengthen blockchain's impact, businesses should enhance transparency initiatives by demonstrating tangible benefits in sustainability and product quality assurance. IoT adoption should be accompanied by effective communication strategies to highlight its role in improving resource management and ensuring product freshness. Digital engagement strategies should emphasize the practical benefits of health tools in influencing dietary behaviour and purchasing decisions. Given the varying perceptions of sustainability and digital engagement, targeted marketing strategies can address specific consumer concerns. Finally, rural consumers' higher preference for product origin transparency suggests the need for region-specific messaging that aligns with their trust and purchasing priorities.

8. MANAGERIAL IMPLICATIONS

Enhancing consumer trust- Integrate blockchain for verified sourcing information to build consumer trust and reinforce ethical practices and use blockchain to provide clear insights into sourcing, production processes, and transportation, building credibility.

Implementation of Digital Technologies - Implement IoT devices for real-time monitoring and predictive analytics for better demand forecasting and reduced waste and use AI to analyse data for quality control, ensuring food safety and freshness during storage and transport and also offer tailored nutrition advice through digital platforms to cater to individual health needs.

Regenerative agriculture partnership-Use gamification and interactive content to engage consumers and enhance brand connection.Partner with influencers to increase product visibility and trust, promoting brand credibility and also focus on regenerative agriculture partnerships and ethical sourcing for product development.

Marketing campaigns - Drive marketing campaigns that emphasize transparency, sustainability, and the health benefits of Nutri-cereals. Use digital platforms to enhance product visibility and educate consumers on the nutritional advantages, to adopt circular economy practices like closed-loop production systems to minimize waste and maximize resource efficiency.

Market Integration - Ensure packaging is eco-friendly, reducing environmental impact and aligning with consumer values and to provide smallholder farmers with access to digital platforms for better market integration and visibility.

Promote Policies- Actively promote policies that support the sustainable development of smallholder farmers in the Nutri-cereal supply chain to focus on educating consumers about the health benefits of Nutri-cereals, especially through digital and social media channels.

Training and Resources -Provide training and resources to farmers on sustainable practices, helping to build a resilient supply chain to implement subscription services offering personalized meal plans to cater to modern health-conscious consumers also include health tracking features to enhance consumer experience and foster long-term brand loyalty.
Digital Innovation-Align digital innovations with sustainable, ethical sourcing and consumer engagement strategies to ensure long-term business success.Drive both sustainability and economic growth within the Nutri-cereal industry by adopting these strategies.

9. CONCLUSION

The digital transformation of the Nutri-cereal supply chain presents a rare opportunity to align sustainable farming methods with the demands of digital-native consumers. Blockchain, IoT, and AI technologies enhance efficiency, traceability, and transparency, boosting consumer confidence in ethically sourced products. Digital engagement strategies and personalized nutrition tools further encourage customer acceptance, while sustainability certifications and targeted marketing help brands stand out in an increasingly competitive market. However, for widespread adoption, challenges such as limited market access for smallholder farmers, inadequate regulatory support, and a lack of technical integration must be addressed. According to the study's findings, a consumer-centric, digitally enhanced approach is essential to advancing nutritional sustainability, improving health outcomes, and promoting economic growth in the Nutri-cereal sector.

REFERENCES

Achinna, P., & Rao, P. P. (2023). The International Year of Millets-2023, Millets as Nutri-cereals of 21st Centenary for Health and Wellness. *AATCC Review*.

Aung, M. M., & Chang, Y. S. (2021). Traceability in a food supply chain: Safety and quality perspectives. *Food Control*, *123*, 107730.

Bellad, A., & Belavadi, S. (2023). *Nutritional and Health Benefits of Millets*. AYUSHDHARA., DOI: 10.47070/ayushdhara.v10i5.1317

Bosona, T., & Gebresenbet, G. (2013). Food traceability as an integral part of logistics management in food and agricultural supply chain. *Food Control*, *33*(1), 32–48. DOI: 10.1016/j.foodcont.2013.02.004

Bossert, T., Hsiao, W., Barrera, M., Alarcon, L., Leo, M., & Casares, C. (1998). Transformation of ministries of health in the era of health reform: The case of Colombia. *Health Policy and Planning*, *13*(1), 59–77. https://www.jstor.org/stable/45089471. DOI: 10.1093/heapol/13.1.59 PMID: 10178186

Bumblauskas, D., Mann, A., Dugan, B., & Rittmer, J. (2020). A blockchain use case in food distribution: Do you know where your food has been. *International Journal of Information Management*, *52*, 102008. DOI: 10.1016/j.ijinfomgt.2019.09.004

Carvalho, N., Chaim, O., Cazarini, E., & Gerolamo, M. (2018). Manufacturing in the fourth industrial revolution: A positive prospect in sustainable manufacturing. *Procedia Manufacturing*, *21*, 671–678. DOI: 10.1016/j.promfg.2018.02.170

Chang, C. W., & Chang, S. H. (2023). The Impact of Digital Disruption: Influences of Digital Media and Social Networks on Forming Digital Natives' Attitude. *SAGE Open*, *13*(3), 21582440231191741. DOI: 10.1177/21582440231191741

Chaudhary, J., Shelar, R., Thakur, K., & Singh, R. (2023). Millets in India: Production, Consumption and Impact on Food Security. Asian Journal of Agricultural Extension. *Economia e Sociologia*, *41*(8), 151–162.

Chen, J., Guo, F., & Wang, W. (2018). Mobile health applications and their influence on healthy eating behaviour: A systematic review. *JMIR Health and Health*, *6*(10), e12379.

Chopra, S., Gupta, R., & Mehra, R. (2022). Role of personalized nutrition apps in promoting healthier food choices among digital natives. *Health Informatics Journal*, *28*(3), 1–14.

Coulibaly, A., Kouakou, B., & Chen Jie, C. J. (2011). Phytic acid in cereal grains: structure, healthy or harmful ways to reduce phytic acid in cereal grains and their effects on nutritional quality.

Espiñeira, M., & Santaclara, F. J. (Eds.). (2016). *Advances in food traceability techniques and technologies: improving quality throughout the food chain*. Woodhead Publishing.

FAO. (2021). *Regenerative Agriculture for Climate Resilience*. Food and Agriculture Organization.

Gereffi, G., Humphrey, J., & Sturgeon, T. (2022). The digital transformation of global value chains: Implications for food security and sustainability. *World Development*, *154*, 105896.

Hansen, T., Sørensen, M. I., & Eriksen, M. L. R. (2018). Understanding consumer values and behavior towards organic food through social media analytics. *Journal of Retailing and Consumer Services*, *42*, 110–120.

Hobbs, J. E. (2020). Food supply chains during the COVID-19 pandemic. *Canadian Journal of Agricultural Economics/Revue canadienne d'agroeconomie, 68*(2), 171-176.

Kapoor, K. K., & Dwivedi, Y. K. (2022). Consumer engagement in digital food marketing: A review and research agenda. *Journal of Business Research*, *146*, 187–202.

Kouhizadeh, M., & Sarkis, J. (2018). Blockchain practices, potentials, and perspectives in greening supply chains. *Sustainability (Basel)*, *10*(10), 3652. DOI: 10.3390/su10103652

Krishnan, R., Arshinder, K., & Agarwal, R. (2022). Robust optimization of sustainable food supply chain network considering food waste valorization and supply uncertainty. *Computers & Industrial Engineering*, *171*, 108499. DOI: 10.1016/j.cie.2022.108499

Kumar, A., Singh, R. K., & Shankar, R. (2020). Value chain strategies for the sustainability of millets: A systematic review. *Agricultural Systems*, *178*, 102740.

Liu, Z., Wang, S., Zhang, Y., Feng, Y., Liu, J., & Zhu, H. (2023). Artificial intelligence in food safety: A decade review and bibliometric analysis. *Foods*, *12*(6), 1242. DOI: 10.3390/foods12061242 PMID: 36981168

Patel, S., Kumar, N., & Sharma, P. (2022). Digital advisory services for smallholder farmers: Opportunities and challenges. *Agricultural Systems*, *198*, 103376.

Porwal, A., Bhagwat, G., Sawarkar, J., & Kamble, P. (2023). An overview of millets-the nutri-cereals: Its nutritional profile, potential health benefits, and sustainable cultivation approach. *International Journal of Science and Research Archive*, *10*(1), 841–859. DOI: 10.30574/ijsra.2023.10.1.0828

Pournader, M., Shi, Y., Seuring, S., & Koh, S. L. (2020). Blockchain applications in supply chains, transport and logistics: A systematic review of the literature. *International Journal of Production Research*, *58*(7), 2063–2081. DOI: 10.1080/00207543.2019.1650976

Rejeb, A., Rejeb, K., Abdollahi, A., Zailani, S., Iranmanesh, M., & Ghobakhloo, M. (2021). Digitalization in food supply chains: A bibliometric review and key-route main path analysis. *Sustainability (Basel)*, *14*(1), 83. DOI: 10.3390/su14010083

Rothgerber, H. (2020). A plant-based diet and health sustainability: The role of consumer attitudes. *Appetite*, *148*, 104617.

Tsolakis, N. K., Keramydas, C. A., Toka, A. K., Aidonis, D. A., & Iakovou, E. T. (2014). Agrifood supply chain management: A comprehensive hierarchical decision-making framework and a critical taxonomy. *Biosystems Engineering*, *120*, 47–64. DOI: 10.1016/j.biosystemseng.2013.10.014

Waldman, K. B., & Kerr, J. M. (2014). Limitations of Certification and Supply Chain Standards for Environmental Protection in Commodity Crop Production. *Annual Review of Resource Economics*, *6*(1), 429–449. DOI: 10.1146/annurev-resource-100913-012432

Yadav, S., Singh, H. C., & Singh, D. R. (2021). Nutritional quality of millets and their value-added products with the potential health benefits: A review. *International Journal of Current Microbiology and Applied Sciences*, *10*(10), 163–175. DOI: 10.20546/ijcmas.2021.1010.019

Zhang, Y., Ren, S., Liu, Y., & Si, S. (2017). A big data analytics architecture for cleaner manufacturing and maintenance processes of complex products. *Journal of Cleaner Production*, *142*, 626–641. DOI: 10.1016/j.jclepro.2016.07.123

Chapter 8

The Essential Role of Logistics in Driving Customer Satisfaction in E-Commerce

Aarthi Dakshana J. D.
Dhanalakshmi Srinivasan University, India

ArunKumar Asaithambi
http://orcid.org/0000-0002-7393-2007
International Institute of Business Studies, India

C. Kruthika Devi
http://orcid.org/0009-0008-7042-2870
Maruthu Pandiyar College, India

S. Balaji Naik
International Institute of Business Studies, India

ABSTRACT

It can be argued that the development in logistics services has developed into one of the most vital determinants of customer satisfaction while purchasing from online stores: it relates mainly to the development of e-commerce and changing trends of shopping. The present study intends to assess the attributes of importance affecting the satisfaction of online young e-commerce users while shopping online. Timely update of delivery information, delivery options, and the return policy made a significant contribution to building satisfaction among users, based on the analysis

DOI: 10.4018/979-8-2600-1855-2.ch008

of the data. A correlational analysis showed that the ease of delivery was related positively and significantly to satisfaction, thus indicating that e-commerce platforms need to improve their logistics.

1. INTRODUCTION

E-commerce is a dynamic and vital sector driving economic growth and competitiveness, fueled by expanding internet access, mobility, and the rise of portable devices (Wakil et al., 2020). E-commerce is another key engine for economic growth powered by expanding internet access, increasing mobility, and widespread use of portable devices (Liu et al., 2008; Singh and Srivastava, 2019). E-commerce saves customers money as it connects them directly to manufacturers without involving wholesalers and distributors as intermediaries. E-commerce creates value through competitive prices, shop accessibility 24/7, and various payment options; that is really the catch (Chen and Zhang, 2015). In recent years, e-commerce has experienced dynamic growth, propelled by advancements in technology, expanded accessibility to the internet, and the advent of mobile devices. Formerly, online shopping took up a very small market share because of the distrust and limited knowledge of virtual transactions. Recognizing the outsize potential of the internet as a tool for reaching consumers has since brought about drastic changes to the landscape (Gajewska, 2009). E-commerce expands markets globally and enhances efficiency by replacing traditional paper-based processes with digital ones, thereby boosting industry competitiveness. It also opens the door to more trips in cargo carriers but with smaller sizes, which might increase rates charged. Alongside these, e-commerce tends to lower the demand and cost of storage, allowing for better pricing (Tseng et al., 2005). The rapid development of e-commerce and its bright prospects have attracted the interested attention of logistics operators, especially in the CEP sector. Logistics has always been a key competitive factor for the e-commerce sector (Ambroziak and Tkaczyk, 2015). Logistics are an intrinsic part of e-commerce, and a delay, damage or poor delivery of service may dissuade customers from making repeat purchases(Vakulenko et al.,2019). Managers understand the importance of logistics customer service and give it more thought in their priorities than ever before. In order to make their services more efficient, they usually outsource the process of delivery into the hands of specialized companies. This would help them achieve a delivery that is reliable and satisfying (Delfmann et al., 2002; Moagar-Poladian et al., 2017). With an increasing emphasis on shipment tracking in real-time, returns made friendly, and delivery options at the discretion of the customer, the nature of the industry of engagement plays a huge role in how logistics are actually expected to function. The above-mentioned factors build various service levels that, in the long-run, have a great impact on customer satisfaction. Still, scant attention had been paid to a study of e-commerce logistics in different industries. The different industry-related specifics of e-commerce adoption and efficiency should have their own grounds of variations (Saridakis et al., 2018). E-commerce customers often face logistics issues, as sellers fail to meet delivery expectations, leading to negative feedback and lower store ratings. These challenges impact customer satisfaction, prompting buyers to switch between multiple stores in search of reliable sellers with better logistics services. Analyzing these logistics problems is crucial to improving customer experience and retention(Kim et al., 2013). In this regard, the this research investigates the role of logistics which is perhaps one of the most important aspects since it governs the satisfaction levels of customers. The logistics challenges being experienced by online shoppers will be analyzed in order to identify the most important drivers of consumer behavior. Grasping these topical issues might deliver higher efficiency to logistics while developing the e-commerce landscape.

2. REVIEW OF LITERATURE

Properties such as time and process efficiency are said to encompass the LSQ reference model that affects customer satisfaction through emotion across different market segments, according to Mentzer et al. (1997) Bian et al. (2011). To retain customers in the B2C market, good LSQ components such as the return procedure, timely delivery, tracking system, and packaging should always be improved (Hua & Jing, 2015). According to what Draycott & Kline (1994) have mentioned, it is one of the central elements of building customer satisfaction. Mentzer et al. (2001) later elaborated on the conceptual model of LSQ to include definitions of delivery reliability, shipping cost, return policy, and e-customer satisfaction. The link between LSQ constructs and customer satisfaction manifests a theoretical framework through the identification of very significant dimensions (Jarvenpaa & Todd, 1996). The top factors are privacy, merchandising, convenience, trust, delivery, usability, and product quality, while security is considered a basic attribute (Belanche et al.,2021).

2.1 Convenient Place of Delivery

Convenient e-commerce logistics truly give customers an enjoyable shopping experience, uninterrupted by physical movement in any place or at any time, from any device (Yazdanparast et al., 2010). It completely involves flexible delivery and return options and real-time tracking to enable better communication. Time and flexibility also play a key role in improving delivery experience overall (Kaswengi and Lambey-Checchin, 2020). By choosing the location where he or she wants his or her order to be delivered, the consumer takes the whole operation between the exit point and the entry point into account in his or her value chain. Orders are accepted in several different varieties, like a direct delivery by a professional to the address (Zhang, 2020). With the added option of the out-of-home, where customers can pick up the consignment from desired locations, the delivery is really flexible. All these convenient delivery options increase customer satisfactions and the likelihood of repeat purchases (Kawa, 2020). Thus, the researcher hypothesize that:

H1: convenient place of delivery has a positive impact on customer satisfaction.

2.2 Time and Flexibility of Delivery

Timely delivery is one of the advantages of online shopping-when it comes to getting goods, of course (Vakulenko et al., 2019). When there is guarantee of safe transport and accurate delivery time frames, a deal will be sounded almost trustworthy. If the clients are well updated about the status of their shipment, assumptions won't come into play, and understanding will be established. Any delay or mishandling is a great negative that from then on will affect buying decisions. There will not be direct contact between buyers and sellers; so, time really is an important part of value (Faugere and Montreuil, 2016). Restive searching of products, obtaining information, replying to simple questions, and meeting the requirements of orders will pay special attention to rapid delivery, of utmost importance for customer satisfaction (Joong-Kun Cho et al., 2008). Thus, effective management by the seller of order processing, including timing for prep and delivery, is essential. Offering flexibility in delivery choices to customers can impact overall processing time (Koufteros et al., 2014). Hence, the researcher posits that:

H2: time and flexibility of delivery has a positive impact on customer satisfaction.

2.3 Delivery Monitoring

With advancing technologies, buyers are able to place orders from online portals and receive their chosen item at specified destinations, given the right details, such as those of "landmarks" near the destination and some contact information, to allow seamless delivery. Setting customer addresses also eases the way to make future choices of orders amongst many with fewer repetitions of questions (Westland, 2010). Sellers ought to send order fulfillment updates and delivery information through various channels including emails, SMS, Websites, or Mobile Apps. Customers are given the capability to track their orders live, with logistics providers, payment services, and marketplaces being part of the status update (Zhang et al., 2020). Timely relevant information given, select the right moments, and match rate expectations to make the buyer feel secure, therefore enhancing trust in the seller should equally increase the probability of new purchases (Janjevic and Winkenbach, 2020). Therefore, the researcher propounds that:

H3: delivery monitoring has a positive impact on customer satisfaction.

2.4 Convenience of Return

Online shopping carries the risk of dissatisfaction, incorrect fit, or a change of mind, often leading to product returns, sometimes mandated by regulations. However, the return process is generally inconvenient (XiaoYan et al., 2012). Convenient returns help build young buyers' trust in e-tailers due to the lack of face-to-face dealings with which building trust becomes harder (Dutta et al., 2019). No-hassle-return policies supplement time saving and enhance repurchase intentions; therefore, convenience becomes the determining factor in online shopping. For managers, fostering trust is essential to driving repeat purchases (Kumar, 2019; Zhao et al., 2018). Customers usually return products due to mismatches, not seller issues, but a complicated process can add frustration. A smooth return experience enhances satisfaction, encouraging repeat purchases from the same retailer (Vakulenko et al., 2019). Trust is crucial for e-commerce growth, and seamless service recovery enhances buyer satisfaction, fostering trust. Buyers feel more confident when e-tailers address their concerns and resolve issues effectively, strengthening long-term relationships (Amoako et al., 2023; Javed and Wu, 2020). Therefore, researcher proposed the following hypothesis:

H4: Convenience of return, has a positive impact on customer satisfaction.

3. METHODOLOGY

3.1 Method and Measurement

The research employs a quantitative research approach in analyzing the determining factors of purchase intentions among youth consumers. A structured research framework has been developed in order to identify crucial determinants of LSQ affecting customer satisfaction among e commerce users. In catering to the objective of the study, handling both primary and secondary data sources are very essential in gaining a full insight of the research problems. The primary data for the study were collected through self-administered questionnaires distributed through e-mail surveys and interaction on social media with respondents in Bangalore. The respondents included in the study were those who have prior experience using E-commerce. In addition to this, secondary data was gathered from various journal articles, newspapers, websites, and industry reports of repute that provided insights on logistic value in e commerce. Youngsters were contacted for questionnaire filling using purposive sampling for this non-probability sampling technique, making sure respondents had relevant purchases made from e-commerce sites. The respondent sample size is 117. This structured questionnaire was developed from a thorough review of the secondary literature. The questionnaire was composed of 20 clear items, divided into Delivery Monitoring, Convenient Place of Delivery, Convenience of Return, Time and Flexibility of Delivery, and Customer Satisfaction (Kawa and Światowiec-Szczepańska, 2021). Using five-point Likert scale questions, which ranged from 1 for "strongly disagree" to 5 for "strongly agree", all these dimensions were measured.

Figure 1.

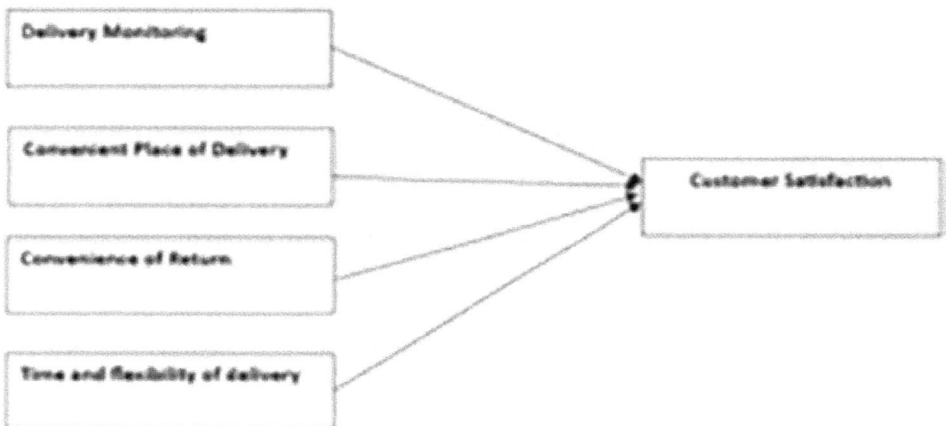

Research Model Adapted from Kawa and Świątowiec-Szczepańska (2021)

4. ANALYSIS AND INTERPRETATION

4.1 Reliability Analysis of the Variables Used in the Study

Table 1.

Reliability Statistics			
S.No	**Variables**	**Cronbach's Alpha**	**N of Items**
1	Delivery Monitoring	.607	4
2	Convenient place of delivery	.629	4
3	Convenience of return	.637	4
4	Time and flexibility of delivery	.693	4
5	Customer Satisfaction	.721	4

The reliability analysis assesses the internal consistency of the variables using Cronbach's Alpha, which indicates how well the items within each construct measure the same concept. Generally, a Cronbach's Alpha value above 0.7 is considered acceptable, while values between 0.6 and 0.7 suggest moderate reliability. In this study, the independent variables—Delivery Monitoring, Convenient Place of Delivery, Convenience of Return, and Time and Flexibility of Delivery—have reliability values ranging from 0.607 to 0.693, indicating moderate internal consistency. The dependent variable, Customer Satisfaction, has the highest Cronbach's Alpha value of 0.721, signifying strong internal consistency among its items.

Among the independent variables, Time and Flexibility of Delivery shows the highest reliability score of 0.693, indicating that the items within this category are relatively consistent. Convenience of Return (0.637) and Convenient Place of Delivery (0.629) demonstrate moderate reliability, suggesting that while they measure their respective constructs adequately, there may be some variation in responses. Delivery Monitoring has the lowest reliability score of 0.607, which suggests that the items in this category may need improvement. This could involve refining the wording of the items, increasing the number of items, or ensuring better alignment with the overall construct to improve reliability.

The dependent variable, Customer Satisfaction, has the highest Cronbach's Alpha value of 0.721, indicating good internal consistency among its items. This suggests that the questions used to measure customer satisfaction are well-structured and provide reliable data. Although the independent variables exhibit moderate reliability, Delivery Monitoring shows the greatest need for refinement. To enhance the measurement accuracy of these constructs, future studies may consider revising or expanding the items used in the questionnaire. By improving the reliability of the independent variables, the overall consistency of the study can be strengthened, leading to more precise and dependable results.

4.2 Descriptive Statistics Analysis

Table 2.

Descriptive Statistics						
S.No	**Items**	**N**	**Minimum**	**Maximum**	**Mean**	**Std. Deviation**
1	Customers prefer online sellers that provide shipment tracking .	117	1	5	3.08	1.043
2	Customers choose online sellers who keep them informed about their order status .	117	1	5	3.15	1.069
3	Customers buy from online sellers who collaborate with couriers to provide delivery time updates .	117	1	5	3.07	1.065
4	Customers prefer online retailers that work with couriers to ensure timely deliveries .	117	1	5	3.15	1.124
5	Customers opt for online sellers that offer deliveries to PUDO (Pick-Up Drop-Off) points, such as traffic kiosks or gas stations .	117	1	5	3.24	1.096
6	Customers prefer online sellers that deliver to self-service terminals, like parcel lockers	117	1	5	3.27	1.103
7	Customers buy from online sellers that allow order pickup at their branches	117	1	5	3.34	0.911
8	Customers choose online sellers that provide postal delivery service	117	1	5	3.59	1.035
9	Customers favor online sellers that offer free product returns	117	1	5	3.28	0.99
10	Customers prefer online sellers with a hassle-free return process	117	1	5	2.91	0.928
11	Customers opt for online sellers that allow product returns beyond 14 days	117	1	5	2.91	0.982
12	Customers choose online sellers that accept returns of used products	117	1	5	3.15	1.069
13	Customers prefer online sellers that provide delivery within two hours	117	1	5	3.02	1.017
14	Customers buy from online retailers that ensure same-day delivery	117	1	5	2.88	1.052
15	Customers appreciate online retailers that allow them to choose their preferred delivery time	117	1	5	3.08	1.084
16	Customers opt for online retailers that offer delivery options on non-working days	117	1	5	3.13	1.087

The analysis of descriptive statistics offers crucial insights into the role of logistics in enhancing customer satisfaction within e-commerce. With data collected from 117 respondents, it is evident that transparency in delivery services significantly influences consumer preferences. Customers appreciate sellers who provide shipment tracking (Mean = 3.08) and keep them updated about order status (Mean = 3.15), indicating that clear communication throughout the delivery process is highly valued. Additionally, collaboration with couriers to ensure accurate delivery time updates (Mean = 3.07) and timely deliveries (Mean = 3.15) further emphasize the importance of efficiency and reliability in e-commerce logistics.

Convenience in delivery also plays a vital role in shaping customer choices. The preference for sellers offering deliveries to Pick-Up Drop-Off (PUDO) points (Mean = 3.24) and self-service terminals (Mean = 3.27) suggests that customers seek flexible and accessible delivery options. The relatively higher mean score of 3.34 for order pickup at seller branches highlights that consumers appreciate having multiple options for receiving their orders. Interestingly, the highest mean value (3.59) corresponds to postal delivery services, reinforcing the continued preference for reliable and well-established shipping methods.

Return policies also influence customer satisfaction. Sellers offering free product returns (Mean = 3.28) and hassle-free return processes (Mean = 2.91) attract more buyers, as flexible return policies reduce purchase risk. The option to return products beyond 14 days received the same mean score of 2.91, indicating that while extended return periods are valued, they may not be a top priority for all consumers. Meanwhile, accepting returns of used products (Mean = 3.15) suggests that customers appreciate leniency in return conditions.

Delivery speed is another factor that impacts purchasing decisions. The preference for two-hour deliveries (Mean = 3.02) and same-day shipping (Mean = 2.88) shows that while fast shipping is desirable, other logistical factors, such as reliability and return flexibility, might hold greater importance. Allowing customers to choose their preferred delivery time (Mean = 3.08) and offering delivery services on non-working days (Mean = 3.13) reinforce the demand for convenience in modern e-commerce logistics.

In conclusion, the findings highlight that a well-structured logistics strategy is essential for enhancing customer satisfaction. E-commerce businesses can gain a competitive advantage by implementing efficient tracking systems, ensuring timely deliveries, offering flexible pickup and return options, and providing reliable shipping services. By aligning logistics operations with customer expectations, online retailers can improve service quality and foster long-term customer loyalty.

4.3 Correlation Analysis of the Independent Variables With Customer Satisfaction

Table 3.

		Customer Satisfaction
Customer Satisfaction	Pearson Correlation	1
	Sig. (2-tailed)	
	N	117
Customers prefer online sellers that provide shipment tracking .	Pearson Correlation	-.010
	Sig. (2-tailed)	.917
	N	117
Customers choose online sellers who keep them informed about their order status .	Pearson Correlation	.633**
	Sig. (2-tailed)	.000
	N	117
Customers buy from online sellers who collaborate with couriers to provide delivery time updates .	Pearson Correlation	.743**
	Sig. (2-tailed)	.000
	N	117
Customers prefer online retailers that work with couriers to ensure timely deliveries .	Pearson Correlation	.628**
	Sig. (2-tailed)	.000
	N	117
Customers opt for online sellers that offer deliveries to PUDO (Pick-Up Drop-Off) points, such as traffic kiosks or gas stations .	Pearson Correlation	.702**
	Sig. (2-tailed)	.000
	N	117
Customers prefer online sellers that deliver to self-service terminals, like parcel lockers	Pearson Correlation	.732**
	Sig. (2-tailed)	.000
	N	117
Customers buy from online sellers that allow order pickup at their branches	Pearson Correlation	.441**
	Sig. (2-tailed)	.000
	N	117
Customers choose online sellers that provide postal delivery service	Pearson Correlation	.213*
	Sig. (2-tailed)	.021
	N	117
Customers favor online sellers that offer free product returns	Pearson Correlation	.556**
	Sig. (2-tailed)	.000
	N	117

continued on following page

Table 3. Continued

		Customer Satisfaction
Customers prefer online sellers with a hassle-free return process	Pearson Correlation	.212*
	Sig. (2-tailed)	.022
	N	117
Customers opt for online sellers that allow product returns beyond 14 days	Pearson Correlation	.219*
	Sig. (2-tailed)	.018
	N	117
Customers choose online sellers that accept returns of used products	Pearson Correlation	.633**
	Sig. (2-tailed)	.000
	N	117
Customers prefer online sellers that provide delivery within two hours	Pearson Correlation	.455**
	Sig. (2-tailed)	.000
	N	117
Customers buy from online retailers that ensure same-day delivery	Pearson Correlation	.300**
	Sig. (2-tailed)	.001
	N	117
Customers appreciate online retailers that allow them to choose their preferred delivery time	Pearson Correlation	.317**
	Sig. (2-tailed)	.000
	N	117
Customers opt for online retailers that offer delivery options on non-working days	Pearson Correlation	.636**
	Sig. (2-tailed)	.000
	N	117

The correlation analysis table provides insights into the relationship between various factors related to online shopping and delivery services with customer satisfaction. The Pearson correlation coefficient measures the strength and direction of these relationships, with values ranging from -1 to 1. A positive value indicates that as one factor increases, customer satisfaction also tends to increase, while a negative value suggests an inverse relationship. The significance level, represented by p-values, determines whether these relationships are statistically meaningful. A p-value below 0.05 indicates statistical significance, while a value below 0.01 indicates a highly significant correlation.

One of the most notable findings is the correlation between order status updates and customer satisfaction, which shows a strong positive relationship with a correlation coefficient of 0.633 and a p-value of 0.000. This suggests that customers who receive frequent updates about their order status tend to have higher levels of satisfaction. Similarly, collaboration with couriers for delivery time updates exhibits a very strong positive correlation of 0.743 with a p-value of 0.000. This highlights the importance of sellers working closely with courier services to keep customers informed about expected delivery times, as it greatly influences their overall satisfaction. Another crucial factor is the effort made by sellers to ensure timely deliveries, which also has a strong positive correlation of 0.628, reinforcing the idea that prompt and on-time delivery plays a vital role in enhancing customer satisfaction.

Another significant factor that contributes positively to customer satisfaction is the availability of pick-up drop-off (PUDO) points, which shows a correlation of 0.702. This means that customers appreciate the option of picking up their orders from designated locations such as kiosks or gas stations, as it provides them with greater convenience. Similarly, the provision of self-service terminals, such as parcel lockers, demonstrates an even stronger positive correlation of 0.732, indicating that customers highly prefer flexible delivery options that allow them to collect their packages at their convenience. In contrast, the option of order pickup at branches has a moderate correlation of 0.441, which suggests that while some customers find it beneficial, it is not as strong a determinant of satisfaction as other flexible delivery methods.

The study also highlights the role of return policies in shaping customer satisfaction. Free product returns show a moderate positive correlation of 0.556, meaning that customers are more satisfied when they do not have to bear additional costs for returning products. Similarly, the hassle-free return process, though having a weaker correlation of 0.212, still shows a statistically significant positive impact. This suggests that while customers do prefer a smooth return process, it is not as influential as other factors. Another noteworthy finding is the extended return policy, which has a weak positive correlation of 0.219, indicating that while customers appreciate having more time to return products, it does not significantly impact their overall satisfaction. However, the acceptance of used product returns has a strong positive correlation of 0.633, demonstrating that customers place high value on sellers who allow them to return used items, likely because it provides them with a sense of security when making purchases.

Delivery speed is another crucial factor that influences customer satisfaction. The ability to receive a delivery within two hours exhibits a moderate positive correlation of 0.455, indicating that customers are significantly more satisfied when they receive their orders quickly. Similarly, same-day delivery shows a weaker correlation of 0.300, suggesting that while it does improve satisfaction, it is not as impactful as ultra-fast delivery options. Additionally, allowing customers to select their preferred delivery time has a moderate positive correlation of 0.317, which implies that flexibility in choosing delivery schedules enhances their experience to a certain extent.

One surprising finding in the analysis is the correlation between shipment tracking and customer satisfaction, which is almost negligible at -0.010 with a p-value of 0.917. This indicates that providing shipment tracking does not significantly affect customer satisfaction, suggesting that customers may prioritize other factors, such as delivery speed and status updates, over tracking features. Similarly, postal delivery service shows a weak but statistically significant correlation of 0.213, meaning that while some customers value postal delivery, it does not have a major influence on overall satisfaction.

In conclusion, the correlation analysis suggests that factors such as frequent order updates, collaboration with couriers, timely deliveries, and flexible delivery options have the strongest positive impact on customer satisfaction. Additionally, return policies, especially free returns and acceptance of used product returns, also play a vital role in enhancing the shopping experience. While ultra-fast delivery options such as two-hour delivery improve satisfaction significantly, same-day delivery has a relatively weaker impact. Surprisingly, shipment tracking does not appear to be a major determinant of satisfaction, indicating that customers may prioritize real-time updates and flexibility over simple tracking information. These findings provide valuable insights for e-commerce businesses aiming to improve customer satisfaction by focusing on the most impactful factors.

4.4 Multiple Regression Analysis of the Independent Variables With Customer Satisfaction

4.4.1 Model Summary Analysis of the regression

Table 4.

Model Summary				
Model	**R**	**R Square**	**Adjusted R Square**	**Std. Error of the Estimate**
1	.967[a]	.935	.925	.220

The Model Summary provides crucial insights into the strength and effectiveness of the regression model. The R-value of 0.967 indicates a very high correlation between the independent variables and customer satisfaction, suggesting a strong linear relationship. The R-squared value of 0.935 reveals that 93.5% of the variation in customer satisfaction can be explained by the independent variables included in the model, demonstrating that the model is highly effective in predicting customer satisfaction. The adjusted R-squared value of 0.925, slightly lower than R-squared, accounts for the number of predictors and confirms that the model remains robust and reliable even after adjusting for the number of variables. Additionally, the standard error of the estimate is 0.220, which suggests that the predicted values of customer satisfaction are closely aligned with the actual values, indicating that the model's predictions are precise with minimal deviations.

4.4.2 Anova Analysis of the regression

Table 5.

ANOVA						
Model		Sum of Squares	df	Mean Square	F	Sig.
1	Regression	69.983	15	4.666	96.566	.000[b]
	Residual	4.880	101	.048		
	Total	74.863	116			

The ANOVA (Analysis of Variance) results further validate the reliability and significance of the regression model. The total sum of squares is 74.863, which represents the total variation in customer satisfaction. Out of this, 69.983 is explained by the regression model, while the residual sum of squares, which represents the unexplained variation, is only 4.880. This indicates that the model accounts for a substantial portion of the variation in customer satisfaction, with very little left unexplained. The F-statistic value of 96.566 is extremely high, which suggests that the overall model is statistically significant and not due to random chance. The significance value (p-value) of 0.000 confirms that at least one of the independent variables significantly impacts customer satisfaction. Since this p-value is well below the conventional threshold of 0.05, it strongly supports the conclusion that the regression model is highly effective in explaining variations in customer satisfaction.

4.4.3 Coefficient Analysis of the regression

Table 6.

Coefficients

Model		Unstandardized Coefficients		Standardized Coefficients		
		B	Std. Error	Beta	t	Sig.
1	(Constant)	.062	.127		.487	.627
	Customers prefer online sellers that provide shipment tracking .	-.024	.022	-.032	-1.116	.267
	Customers buy from online sellers who collaborate with couriers to provide delivery time updates .	.219	.029	.290	7.659	.000
	Customers prefer online retailers that work with couriers to ensure timely deliveries .	.225	.021	.314	10.619	.000
	Customers opt for online sellers that offer deliveries to PUDO (Pick-Up Drop-Off) points, such as traffic kiosks or gas stations .	.192	.025	.261	7.703	.000
	Customers prefer online sellers that deliver to self-service terminals, like parcel lockers	.217	.026	.297	8.243	.000
	Customers buy from online sellers that allow order pickup at their branches	-.049	.034	-.055	-1.450	.150
	Customers choose online sellers that provide postal delivery service	.035	.023	.045	1.506	.135
	Customers favor online sellers that offer free product returns	.057	.031	.070	1.852	.067
	Customers prefer online sellers with a hassle-free return process	.035	.030	.041	1.161	.249
	Customers opt for online sellers that allow product returns beyond 14 days	-.017	.028	-.020	-.599	.550
	Customers choose online sellers that accept returns of used products	-.753	.121	-1.002	-6.237	.000
	Customers prefer online sellers that provide delivery within two hours	.052	.034	.066	1.559	.122
	Customers buy from online retailers that ensure same-day delivery	-.010	.032	-.014	-.325	.746
	Customers appreciate online retailers that allow them to choose their preferred delivery time	-.010	.028	-.013	-.349	.728
	Customers opt for online retailers that offer delivery options on non-working days	.818	.114	1.107	7.194	.000

a. Dependent Variable: Customer Satisfaction

The Coefficients table provides detailed insights into the individual impact of each predictor on customer satisfaction. Positive coefficients indicate that an increase in the predictor variable leads to an increase in customer satisfaction, while negative coefficients suggest a decrease. Key significant positive predictors include delivery on non-working days (B = 0.818, p = 0.000), ensuring timely deliveries (B = 0.225, p = 0.000), collaboration with couriers for delivery updates (B = 0.219, p = 0.000), and deliveries to self-service terminals (B = 0.217, p = 0.000). These findings suggest that customers highly value flexible and efficient delivery options. Conversely, a significant negative predictor is the acceptance of used product returns (B = -0.753, p = 0.000), which negatively impacts satisfaction, possibly due to concerns about product quality. Other variables, such as shipment tracking (B = -0.024, p = 0.267), same-day delivery (B = -0.010, p = 0.746), and the ability to choose a preferred delivery time (B = -0.010, p = 0.728), are statistically insignificant, indicating that while they may be valued by customers, they do not have a substantial impact on overall satisfaction. These results highlight that online retailers should prioritize flexible delivery options, timely deliveries, and efficient courier collaborations while reconsidering return policies to enhance customer satisfaction effectively.

4. CONCLUSION

The study examined the relationship between various delivery-related factors and customer satisfaction in the e-commerce sector. The reliability analysis indicated moderate consistency among the independent variables, with Time and Flexibility of Delivery demonstrating the highest reliability. The dependent variable, Customer Satisfaction, exhibited strong internal consistency, reinforcing the reliability of the measurement scale. While most independent variables showed acceptable reliability levels, Delivery Monitoring had the lowest score, suggesting potential improvements in item refinement for future research.

The descriptive analysis revealed that customers highly value shipment tracking, timely delivery updates, and multiple delivery options such as PUDO points and postal services. Additionally, a seamless return policy, including free returns and extended return periods, emerged as a key factor in influencing purchase decisions. Although fast delivery options like same-day shipping were appreciated, their impact on customer satisfaction appeared to be less significant compared to factors like reliability, flexibility, and communication.

The correlation analysis demonstrated a strong positive relationship between customer satisfaction and key delivery factors, particularly delivery updates, flexible pickup options, and return policies. Among these, collaboration with couriers for timely updates and providing self-service delivery terminals showed the highest correlation. These findings emphasize that efficient logistics strategies—focused on communication, flexibility, and convenience—play a crucial role in enhancing customer satisfaction and loyalty.

To remain competitive, e-commerce businesses should invest in real-time tracking systems, reliable courier partnerships, and hassle-free return policies. Future research could explore additional variables, such as customer trust and technological advancements in logistics, to gain deeper insights into evolving consumer preferences. By continuously optimizing their delivery frameworks, online retailers can strengthen customer relationships and drive long-term business growth.

REFERENCES

Ambroziak, T., & Tkaczyk, S. (2015). The selection of transportation means for technological processes. *Archives of transport, 36*(4), 7-20.

Amoako, G. K., Caesar, L. D., Dzogbenuku, R. K., & Bonsu, G. A. (2023). Service recovery performance and repurchase intentions: The mediation effect of service quality at KFC. *Journal of Hospitality and Tourism Insights*, *6*(1), 110–130. DOI: 10.1108/JHTI-06-2021-0141

Belanche, D., Casaló, L. V., Flavián, C., & Pérez-Rueda, A. (2021). The role of customers in the gig economy: How perceptions of working conditions and service quality influence the use and recommendation of food delivery services. *Service Business*, *15*(1), 45–75. DOI: 10.1007/s11628-020-00432-7

Bian, W. L., Ju, S. D., Xu, J., & Ding, J. Z. (2011). An empirical research on online B2C customer perceptions of logistics services and related factors. *Guanli Gongcheng Xuebao*, *25*(2), 14–20.

Chen, Q., & Zhang, N. (2015). Does e-commerce provide a sustained competitive advantage? An investigation of survival and sustainability in growth-oriented enterprises. *Sustainability (Basel)*, *7*(2), 1411–1428. DOI: 10.3390/su7021411

Delfmann, W., Albers, S., & Gehring, M. (2002). The impact of electronic commerce on logistics service providers. *International Journal of Physical Distribution & Logistics Management*, *32*(3), 203–222. DOI: 10.1108/09600030210426539

Draycott, S. G., & Kline, P. (1994). Further investigation into the nature of the BIP: A factor analysis of the BIP with primary abilities. *Personality and Individual Differences*, *17*(2), 201–209. DOI: 10.1016/0191-8869(94)90026-4

Dutta, P., Suryawanshi, P., Gujarathi, P., & Dutta, A. (2019). Managing risk for e-commerce supply chains: An empirical study. *IFAC-PapersOnLine*, *52*(13), 349–354. DOI: 10.1016/j.ifacol.2019.11.143

Faugere, L., & Montreuil, B. (2016, June). Hyperconnected city logistics: smart lockers terminals & last mile delivery networks. In *Proceedings of the 3rd International Physical Internet Conference,* Atlanta, GA, USA (Vol. 29, p. 5).

Hua, W., & Jing, Z. (2015). An empirical study on e-commerce logistic service quality and customer satisfaction. *WHICEB Proceedings*, 269–275.

Janjevic, M., & Winkenbach, M. (2020). Characterizing urban last-mile distribution strategies in mature and emerging e-commerce markets. *Transportation Research Part A, Policy and Practice*, *133*, 164–196. DOI: 10.1016/j.tra.2020.01.003

Jarvenpaa, S. L., & Todd, P. A. (1996). Consumer reactions to electronic shopping on the World Wide Web. *International Journal of Electronic Commerce*, *1*(2), 59–88. DOI: 10.1080/10864415.1996.11518283

Javed, M. K., & Wu, M. (2020). Effects of online retailer after delivery services on repurchase intention: An empirical analysis of customers' past experience and future confidence with the retailer. *Journal of Retailing and Consumer Services*, *54*, 101942. DOI: 10.1016/j.jretconser.2019.101942

Joong-Kun Cho, J., Ozment, J., & Sink, H. (2008). Logistics capability, logistics outsourcing and firm performance in an e-commerce market. *International Journal of Physical Distribution & Logistics Management*, *38*(5), 336–359. DOI: 10.1108/09600030810882825

Kaswengi, J., & Lambey-Checchin, C. (2020). How logistics service quality and product quality matter in the retailer–customer relationship of food drive-throughs: The role of perceived convenience. *International Journal of Physical Distribution & Logistics Management*, *50*(5), 535–555. DOI: 10.1108/IJPDLM-01-2019-0036

Kawa, A. (2020). Out-of-Home Delivery as a Solution of the Last Mile Problem in E-commerce. *Smart and Sustainable Supply Chain and Logistics–Trends, Challenges. Methods and Best Practices*, *1*, 25–40.

Kawa, A., & Światowiec-Szczepańska, J. (2021). Logistics as a value in e-commerce and its influence on satisfaction in industries: A multilevel analysis. *Journal of Business and Industrial Marketing*, *36*(13), 220–235. DOI: 10.1108/JBIM-09-2020-0429

Kim, D., Cavusgil, S. T., & Cavusgil, E. (2013). Does IT alignment between supply chain partners enhance customer value creation? An empirical investigation. *Industrial Marketing Management*, *42*(6), 880–889. DOI: 10.1016/j.indmarman.2013.05.021

Koufteros, X., Droge, C., Heim, G., Massad, N., & Vickery, S. K. (2014). Encounter satisfaction in e-tailing: Are the relationships of order fulfillment service quality with its antecedents and consequences moderated by historical satisfaction? *Decision Sciences*, *45*(1), 5–48. DOI: 10.1111/deci.12056

Kumar, A. (2019). Exploring young adults' e-waste recycling behaviour using an extended theory of planned behaviour model: A cross-cultural study. *Resources, Conservation and Recycling*, *141*, 378–389. DOI: 10.1016/j.resconrec.2018.10.013

Liu, X., He, M., Gao, F., & Xie, P. (2008). An empirical study of online shopping customer satisfaction in China: A holistic perspective. *International Journal of Retail & Distribution Management, 36*(11), 919–940. DOI: 10.1108/09590550810911683

Mentzer, J. T., Flint, D. J., & Hult, G. T. M. (2001). Logistics service quality as a segment-customized process. *Journal of Marketing, 65*(4), 82–104. DOI: 10.1509/jmkg.65.4.82.18390

Mentzer, J. T., Rutner, S. M., & Matsuno, K. (1997). Application of the means-end value hierarchy model to understanding logistics service value. *International Journal of Physical Distribution & Logistics Management, 27*(9/10), 630–643. DOI: 10.1108/09600039710188693

Moagar-Poladian, S., Dumitrescu, G. C., & Tanase, I. A. (2017). Retail e-Commerce (E-tail)-evolution, characteristics and perspectives in China, the USA and Europe. *Global Economic Observer, 5*(1), 167.

Saridakis, G., Lai, Y., Mohammed, A. M., & Hansen, J. M. (2018). Industry characteristics, stages of E-commerce communications, and entrepreneurs and SMEs revenue growth. *Technological Forecasting and Social Change, 128*, 56–66. DOI: 10.1016/j.techfore.2017.10.017

Singh, S., & Srivastava, S. (2019). Engaging consumers in multichannel online retail environment: A moderation study of platform type on interaction of e-commerce and m-commerce. *Journal of Modelling in Management, 14*(1), 49–76. DOI: 10.1108/JM2-09-2017-0098

Tseng, Y. Y., Yue, W. L., & Taylor, M. A. (2005, January). The role of transportation in logistics chain. Eastern Asia Society for Transportation Studies.

Vakulenko, Y., Shams, P., Hellström, D., & Hjort, K. (2019). Service innovation in e-commerce last mile delivery: Mapping the e-customer journey. *Journal of Business Research, 101*, 461–468. DOI: 10.1016/j.jbusres.2019.01.016

Vakulenko, Y., Shams, P., Hellström, D., & Hjort, K. (2019). Service innovation in e-commerce last mile delivery: Mapping the e-customer journey. *Journal of Business Research, 101*, 461–468. DOI: 10.1016/j.jbusres.2019.01.016

Wakil, K., Alyari, F., Ghasvari, M., Lesani, Z., & Rajabion, L. (2020). A new model for assessing the role of customer behavior history, product classification, and prices on the success of the recommender systems in e-commerce. *Kybernetes, 49*(5), 1325–1346. DOI: 10.1108/K-03-2019-0199

Westland, J. C. (2010). Lower bounds on sample size in structural equation modeling. *Electronic Commerce Research and Applications*, *9*(6), 476–487. DOI: 10.1016/j.elerap.2010.07.003

XiaoYan, Q., Yong, H., Qinli, D., & Stokes, P.XiaoYan. (2012). Reverse logistics network design model based on e-commerce. *The International Journal of Organizational Analysis*, *20*(2), 251–261. DOI: 10.1108/19348831211227864

Yazdanparast, A., Manuj, I., & Swartz, S. M. (2010). Co-creating logistics value: A service-dominant logic perspective. *International Journal of Logistics Management*, *21*(3), 375–403. DOI: 10.1108/09574091011089808

Zhang, X., Zhou, G., Cao, J., & Wu, A. (2020). Evolving strategies of e-commerce and express delivery enterprises with public supervision. *Research in Transportation Economics*, *80*, 100810. DOI: 10.1016/j.retrec.2019.100810

Zhao, S., Wu, F., Jia, T., & Shu, L. (2018). The impact of product returns on price and delivery time competition in online retailing. *Computers & Industrial Engineering*, *125*, 658–667. DOI: 10.1016/j.cie.2018.01.007

Chapter 9

Mapping the Convergence: A Bibliometric and Trend Analysis of Artificial Intelligence and Supply Chain Optimization in Microinsurance

S. Poorani Mithila
http://orcid.org/0000-0001-6695-9175
Alagappa University, India

Gurupandi M.
Alagappa University, India

ABSTRACT

The study explores the potential of artificial intelligence and supply chain integration in optimizing aspects of Microinsurance, such as transparency, operational efficiency, and inclusivity. It uses Knowledge spill over theory, Network theory, and Resilience theory to address the impact of AI and supply chain integration in the sector. The research is based on 1240 research papers from 2014 to 2024, focusing on authorship networks, citation dynamics, keyword co-occurrences, and theme grouping. The study predicts an increase in interest in this area in the past decade, focusing on predictive analytics of AI and addressing practical issues like data privacy and regulatory implications. The study aims to address research gaps in practical applications and long-term socioeconomic effects of insurance, providing actionable recommendations for academics, policymakers, and industry leaders to advance innovation and inclusivity.

DOI: 10.4018/979-8-2600-1855-2.ch009

1. INTRODUCTION

1.1 Overview of Microinsurance and Its Importance for Financial Inclusion

Microinsurance is a subset of insurance that aims to provide low-cost risk protection to low-income individuals, particularly in emerging countries. It is a crucial instrument for financial inclusion, allowing vulnerable individuals to withstand financial shocks caused by illness, natural catastrophes, crop loss, or unemployment. In contrast to traditional insurance, which often involves complex underwriting procedures and high premiums, microinsurance aims to provide simple, low-cost products to persons with little disposable money (Churchill, 2006). Despite its potential benefits, microinsurance remains unaffordable due to various structural challenges, including high operating costs, inadequate financial literacy, poor risk assessment models, and delays in claims processing. According to Lloyd's (2018), most microinsurance plans have substantial administrative costs per policy, making them unsustainable in the long run. Trust concerns arise as a result of claim settlement delays and a lack of openness in policy terms, which deters potential policyholders (Tadesse & Brans, 2012). A number of studies highlight the role of technology in increasing microinsurance acceptance and efficiency. For example, Feyen et al. (2021) argue that digitalisation, especially through Artificial Intelligence (AI) and Supply Chain Optimisation (SCO), can eliminate inefficiencies in microinsurance operations. Insurers may use data-driven automation to improve risk assessment, automate policy distribution, avoid fraud, and provide a better client experience.

1.2 The Effects of AI and Supply Chain Optimisation on Microinsurance

1.2.1 Artificial Intelligence (AI) in Microinsurance

Artificial intelligence (AI) has proven to be a game changer in the insurance industry, enabling better data analysis, fraud detection, automated claim settlement, and customisable premium charges. AI applications in microinsurance cover various key areas. For example, in risk pricing and assessment, predictive analytics algorithms use artificial intelligence to appropriately price insurance based on the policyholder's risk profile (Deloitte, 2020). Detection of Fraud: AI can detect telltale signals of fraudulent claims, significantly reducing insurance losses. Genuine policyholders can get timely reimbursements, enhancing the credibility of microinsurance programs (Accenture, 2021). Automated Claims Processing: Machine learning algorithms and AI-powered chatbots automate claim verification and settlement, reducing processing time from weeks to hours (Brynjolfsson and McAfee, 2017). Mills (2022) found that AI-based chatbots in African microinsurance marketplaces improved policyholder contact and claim settlement efficacy, particularly in low-literacy areas.

1.2.2 Supply Chain Optimisation (SCO) in Microinsurance

Supply chain optimisation (SCO) is critical for successful insurance distribution, premium collection, and claim management. Traditional insurance supply chains are hampered by sluggish claim settlement, extensive documentation, and a lack of real-time monitoring (Christopher 2016). Combining AI-powered SCO techniques improves operational efficiency by automated policy distribution: AI-powered digital systems provide simple policy enrolment over mobile networks, reducing dependency on human agents. Blockchain for Claims Management, as demonstrated by Donthu et al. (2021), blockchain-enabled smart contracts automate claim settlement, making it faster and more secure. Optimised Logistics for Disaster Relief Claims: AI- and IoT-based supply chains provide real-time monitoring of covered assets (for example, crop health using satellite data), allowing farmers affected by disasters to receive rapid claims payment (Feyen et al., 2021). AI-SCO integration, as reported by Accenture (2021), can reduce claims processing expenses by up to 40% while increasing customer satisfaction. All of these factors strengthen the viability and attraction of microinsurance to marginalised groups.

1.3 Objectives

The purpose of this book chapter is to investigate the intersection of AI and supply chain optimisation in microinsurance, covering the most significant technology advancements, research initiatives, and commercial applications. The goals are:

To examine how AI improves microinsurance efficiency through automation, predictive analytics, and fraud detection.
To examine the impact of supply chain optimisation on insurance distribution and claims management improvement.
To conduct a bibliometric study of scholarly contributions in AI-powered microinsurance supply networks.
To investigate emerging trends such as blockchain, IoT, and big data for microinsurance models.
To emphasise problems and ethical concerns such as data privacy, AI bias, and legislative constraints.
To provide strategic guidance to insurers, legislators, and technology providers on AI-SCO integration.

This study is critical in light of the growing demand for digital innovation in microinsurance. With the evolution of the insurance sector, it is critical to investigate technology solutions that improve accessibility, reduce operating costs, and encourage equitable and timely claim settlements.

1.4 Methodology

A Bibliographic and Trend Analysis Approach. This study employs a bibliometric analysis methodology, which is a standard way for examining trends in scientific publications, the effect of research, and knowledge gaps within a certain subject. Bibliometric analysis enables quantitative and qualitative examination of research papers by examining: Citation networks identify renowned authors, institutions, and research collaborations. Keyword co-occurrence mapping helps identify important topics, trends, and technical breakthroughs. Publication trends across time: Mapping the evolution of AI and supply chain utilisation in microinsurance.

This study uses Scopus, Web of Science, IEEE Xplore, and industry publications to gather data on AI, supply chain optimisation, and microinsurance. Network mapping and trend graphing are performed using bibliometric tools such as VOSviewer and Biblioshiny. Furthermore, the trend analysis technique is utilised to investigate the actual application of AI-enabled supply chains within microinsurance. This includes examining case studies of AI use in microinsurance markets.

Examining policy papers from international financial organisations (e.g., World Bank, IFC, and OECD) on digital insurance adoption. Identifying industry breakthroughs such as blockchain-based smart contracts and IoT-based risk assessment algorithms. This two-pronged approach provides a thorough examination of both academic research trends and real-world commercial advancements in AI-powered microinsurance.

1.5 Chapter Structure

To provide a systematic examination of AI and supply chain optimisation for microinsurance, the chapter has the following structure:

Section 2- discusses the fundamentals of microinsurance and supply chain optimisation, as well as the present problems and industry trends.

Section 3- examines the application of AI in microinsurance, focusing on risk assessment, fraud detection, and claims automation.

Section 4- provides a bibliometric analysis, highlighting notable research tendencies, gaps, and noteworthy contributions.

Section 5-investigates future developments, including blockchain, IoT, and AI-based policy distribution.

Section 6-investigates difficulties and ethical considerations, including data privacy, algorithmic prejudice, and legislative impediments. Section 7 provides policy suggestions and future directions, outlining strategic approaches for implementing AI-based microinsurance.

2. UNDERSTANDING MICROINSURANCE AND SUPPLY CHAIN OPTIMIZATION

2.1 Definition and Features of Microinsurance

Microinsurance is a specialised financial product that offers affordable risk protection to low-income individuals excluded from traditional insurance markets, safeguarding them against various financial risks (Churchill, 2006). It plays a crucial role in financial inclusion by providing security against health crises, natural disasters, and livelihood disruptions. According to the Microinsurance Network (2020), microinsurance plans typically have the following features:

Affordability: Low premiums are maintained, making them accessible to those with little discretionary cash.

Simplified Policy Structures: Terms in policies that are easy to understand for people with low financial literacy.

Rapid Claims Processing: Claims in microinsurance are efficiently processed through streamlined procedures, occasionally utilising computerised verification methods for swift resolution.

Policies are often delivered through microfinance institutions (MFIs), cooperatives, non-governmental organisations (NGOs), or mobile networks. Unlike traditional insurance that relies on extensive underwriting, microinsurance products predominantly utilise parametric models for payout calculation, linking indemnity to external events like weather patterns or satellite data (Skees & Barnett, 2006).

Review of Microinsurance as a Financial Inclusion Tool

Some research suggests that microinsurance has the ability to decrease poverty and improve economic resilience. According to Morduch (1999), uninsured risks exacerbate poverty traps by forcing poor households without financial buffers to sell assets or borrow at excessive interest rates during crises. Roth et al. (2007) argue that microinsurance can prevent income shocks by providing timely financial help, allowing low-income households to recover rapidly from unforeseen events. However, according to Lloyd's (2018) research, despite the enormous potential of microinsurance, low adoption rates are due to mistrust, a lack of understanding, and complex claims. This necessitates new distribution strategies and technological solutions to increase accessibility and efficiency.

2.2 Key Stakeholders in Microinsurance Supply Chain

2.2.1 Insurers and Reinsurers

The term insurance refers to a contract between two parties, the insurer and the insured, in which the insurer agrees to cover certain losses experienced by the insured in return for an acceptable value, i.e. a premium. The insured is the person seeking insurance coverage, whereas the insurer is the party responsible for mitigating the other's risk. Einsurance is a reinsurance contract between a ceding insurance company and a reinsurer, where the ceding company transfers a portion of its risk to the reinsurer in exchange for compensation as outlined in the agreement. The ceding company is the first insurance company that agreed to indemnify the risk and then 'cede' or transfer the risk/liability to another insurance company. The reinsurer, in this context, is the insurance company that assumes a portion of the risk from the ceding company through the Einsurance agreement. An insurance policy is a legal document that specifies the coverage, limitations, and conditions of the insurance agreement between the insurer and the insured. It describes the sorts of losses covered by the insurance and the maximum amount payable in the event of death or loss.

2.2.2 Distribution Channels

Due to limited rural penetration by typical insurance brokers, microinsurance must employ different distribution channels, such as: Microfinance institutions (MFIs): Combining microinsurance and microloans has a wide reach (Churchill & Matul, 2012). Mobile Network Operators (MNOs) offer pay-as-you-go insurance via mobile money platforms such as Kenya's M-Pesa (GSMA, 2020). Agricultural cooperatives and non-governmental organisations (NGOs) enable farmers and low-income persons to get insurance in bulk at a lower rate.

2.2.3 Policyholders (End Users)

The target audience consists of low-income earners, small-scale farmers, informal sector workers, and marginalised groups. They tend to have poor financial knowledge; thus, simplicity of use and trust must be prioritised for widespread adoption.

Review: Mobile Technologies' Role in Expanding Microinsurance

According to the GSMA (2021), mobile insurance has emerged as a very successful avenue for distributing microinsurance products. According to research, mobile-based microinsurance schemes such as BIMA (Ghana) and Telenor (Pakistan) have helped millions of previously uninsured people gain coverage. According to Matul et al. (2013), using mobile networks reduces administrative costs while also allowing for automated insurance enrolment and electronic claims administration.

2.3 Challenges of Microinsurance Distribution and Claims Management

Although promising, microinsurance has several operational obstacles that make it difficult to maintain and develop.

2.3.1 Distribution Costs are High

Conventional insurance employs physical salesmen, which is costly in rural microinsurance markets. Other channels, such as mobile phone-based insurance and web platforms, show potential but need significant initial technological expenditures.

2.3.2 There is Limited Awareness and Trust

Most low-income people are unaware of insurance products or believe they are untrustworthy due to previous experiences with late or rejected claims. Matul et al. (2013) argue that improving financial literacy through education initiatives and public outreach is critical for increasing adoption rates.

2.3.3 Fraud and Adverse Selection Risks

Microinsurance is also very susceptible to fraud since manual claims procedures are easily misused through fake reporting and exaggerated claims (Dercon & Kirchberger, 2008). AI-powered fraud detection systems, such as machine learning-based anomaly detection, can help to avoid such fraud.

Review: Blockchain's Role in Reducing Microinsurance Fraud

According to recent literature, blockchain technology has the potential to improve transparency and security in microinsurance. Donthu et al. (2021) discovered that smart contracts on the blockchain significantly reduced claim processing time and eliminated fraudulent claims by making records tamper-proof. Companies like

Acre Africa have successfully deployed blockchain-based agriculture insurance for smallholder farmers.

2.4 Supply Chain Optimisation: Principles and Applications in Microinsurance

2.4.1 Principles of Supply Chain Optimisation (SCO)

In microinsurance, Supply Chain Optimisation (SCO) comprises improving the efficiency of policy distribution, premium collection, and claims settlement. The main principles are:

Process Automation: Using AI-powered automation to reduce paperwork and expedite claim validation.

Real-Time Data Sharing: Providing stakeholders (insurers, MFIs, claim valuers) with instant access to policyholder information to allow for faster decision-making.

Lean Operations: By streamlining operations, we may eliminate administrative redundancy and improve the policyholder experience.

2.4.2 Uses of SCO in Microinsurance

i) Risk Assessment Models Powered by AI

AI-based predictive analytics algorithms use past claims data and external variables to estimate risk (for example, weather forecasts and satellite photos for crop insurance). This leads to more precise pricing and lower losses for the insurer.

ii) AI-guided Automated Claims Processing

Lemonade and AXA's Fizzy use AI-led claims adjudication to pay out policyholders in minutes rather than weeks (Brynjolfsson & McAfee, 2017).

iii) Blockchain for Full Supply Chain Visibility

Blockchain eliminates paperwork, creates tamper-proof transaction records, and increases trust in the claims process. InsurTech companies such as Etherisc have tried blockchain-based weather insurance for farmers.

According to research, integrating AI-SCO can increase operational efficiency by 30-40%, while also lowering administrative costs and increasing policyholder satisfaction (Accenture, 2021). Mills (2022) demonstrated that artificial intelligence-enabled supply chains significantly improve microinsurance uptake by eliminating inefficiencies in policy enrolment and claims processing.

3. THE ROLE OF ARTIFICIAL INTELLIGENCE IN MICROINSURANCE

3.1 Introduction

Low-income persons confront several barriers to receiving financial goods. To address these barriers, various microinsurance-related innovations have been developed. Furthermore, there is an increasing number of reference publications that emphasise the changing intersections between the actuarial profession and technology innovation. This literature analysis offers insights into technologies that intersect with the actuarial profession in microinsurance. The aim is to establish a framework that actuaries can utilize in their professional endeavors. Its objective is to captivate readers and ignite a vision of how microinsurance and related technologies could influence the future of the actuarial profession. By comprehending the potential impact of these technologies, actuaries can proactively anticipate industry trends and sustain competitiveness in the changing landscape. In the face of ongoing technological advancements in the actuarial profession, maintaining awareness and a proactive approach will be essential for achieving success. Actuaries need to proactively embrace new tools and methodologies to adeptly navigate the evolving microinsurance landscape. Through maintaining awareness and a proactive stance, actuaries can establish themselves as leaders in incorporating technology into their profession.

3.2 AI Applications for Microinsurance

3.2.1 AI for Underwriting and Risk Assessment

Underwriting is the foundation of all insurance models. Previously, underwriting was based on historical data and actuarial risk models, which are typically constrained in microinsurance markets. AI enhances underwriting by scanning massive data sets with machine learning algorithms to identify risk patterns not detected by standard actuarial techniques. Alternative Data Sources: AI uses non-traditional data sources such as mobile phone behaviour, geographical analysis, and social trends to assess risk among the uninsured. Automated Decision-Making: AI enables real-time underwriting by cross-checking data in real-time, reducing manual involvement and processing times. Review: According to Kumar et al. (2020), AI-powered risk estimate models increased underwriting precision by 40% compared to traditional underwriting, especially in health and agriculture microinsurance. Further research undertaken by the GSMA (2021) discovered that AI-enabled mobile underwriting provided insurance coverage to over 50 million individuals in Sub-Saharan Africa and Southeast Asia.

3.2.2 AI Fraud Detection

Fraudulent claims are a major concern in microinsurance, causing higher expenses and financial losses. AI enhances fraud detection through pattern recognition: AI systems identify irregularities in claim patterns, which may indicate fraud. NLP in Document Verification: AI-powered NLP systems check text-based claims for anomalies in policyholder statements. Computer Vision: AI checks and scans identity papers, medical records, and claim-related photos to detect forgery or manipulation. According to a McKinsey (2022) research, AI-based fraud detection reduced erroneous claims by 50%, hence increasing insurers' financial soundness. Acko Insurance (India) effectively adopted AI-based fraud detection, reducing manual verification time significantly.

3.2.3 AI for Claims Processing

Claims processing is sluggish and inefficient, particularly in microinsurance, where human documentation and verification delay reimbursements. AI speeds claim handling through: Automated Claim Verification: AI models use policyholder data, incident reports, and submitted papers to automatically accept or deny claims. Chatbots for Claims Assistance: AI-powered chatbots help clients fill out claim forms, increasing efficiency and user experience. Smart Contracts for Claims Settlement: AI paired with blockchain-based smart contracts allows for rapid payouts depending on predefined parameters. Acko, an India-based digital-first insurance company, used AI to automate 95% of its claim process, reducing payment time from weeks to minutes. This has been especially beneficial in health and vehicle microinsurance plans, resulting in increased client satisfaction and decreased operating costs.

3.3 AI-Driven Supply Chain Optimisation for Microinsurance

Supply chain optimisation (SCO) in microinsurance ensures that insurance products are supplied efficiently and claims are resolved quickly. AI improves supply chain efficiency in microinsurance by using predictive analytics to forecast demand for policies and optimise resource allocation. AI chatbots engage customers by informing them, assisting with onboarding, and facilitating premium payments via mobile channels. Blockchain and AI Integration: Combining AI and blockchain technology allows for tamper-proof and transparent policy management and claims processing. Donthu et al. (2021) found that AI-based supply chain models in microinsurance reduced distribution costs by 35% while increasing claim efficiency by 50%. AI-based mobile models adopted by BIMA (Ghana) and MicroEnsure (Kenya) have improved the availability of microinsurance products in rural regions.

3.4 Machine Learning Models and Predictive Analytics for Microinsurance

Machine learning (ML) and predictive analytics are revolutionising the microinsurance industry by enhancing risk estimation, fraud detection, pricing strategies, and client retention rates. With microinsurance complexity (policyholders without traditional financial records), artificial intelligence (AI)-based models provide insurers with another method of risk assessment, pricing, and detecting fraudulent claims. Machine learning algorithms empower insurers to make informed, data-driven decisions, enhancing operational efficiency, cutting losses, and promoting financial inclusion for underserved populations through in-depth analysis of vast datasets, historical claims, and consumer behaviour. Neural networks play a crucial role in fraud detection within microinsurance, effectively identifying fraudulent activities such as fabricated claims and suspicious patterns. Utilising Predictive Pricing Models to Optimise Premiums These models are crucial for enhancing the efficiency and cost-effectiveness of microinsurance operations.

3.4.1 Risk Assessment using Decision Trees and Random Forests

Risk assessment forms the bedrock of insurance models. While traditional microinsurance underwriting relies on imprecise and inconsistent actuarial tables and manual data, machine learning tools like decision trees and random forests offer a flexible, data-driven method for categorising risks. How Do Decision Trees and Random Forests Work in Microinsurance? Decision trees categorise clients into risk categories based on a variety of factors such as income level, health history, employment, geography, and prior insurance claims. The tree splits the data at each level, resulting in an easy-to-understand framework for identifying high-risk vs. low-risk policyholders. Random forests, as an ensemble technique, amalgamate multiple decision trees to enhance accuracy and mitigate overfitting, crucial in microinsurance scenarios characterised by fragmented or inadequate data. Real-World Application of Microinsurance Bharadwaj et al. (2022) found that using random forest models in agricultural microinsurance increased claim prediction accuracy by 35%, allowing insurers to price policies more effectively. Similarly, BIMA (Ghana) used decision trees to classify clients based on mobile usage data, allowing for more accurate premium pricing and policy customisation.

Key Benefits:

Improve risk segmentation.
Faster underwriting and policy issuance.
Improved fraud detection using anomaly detection.

3.4.2 Neural Networks for Fraud Detection

The use of Graph Neural Networks (GNNs) into financial fraud detection systems has considerable practical benefits for financial organisations, notably in terms of improving fraud detection accuracy, lowering false positives, and guaranteeing regulatory compliance. Unlike traditional fraud detection models, which rely on rule-based heuristics and transaction-level characteristics, GNN-based models leverage relational connections within financial transaction networks, offering a comprehensive and adaptable approach to fraud detection.

Maintaining a high recall in fraud detection is challenging as it aims to identify as many fraudulent operations as possible while minimizing false positives. False positives can lead to genuine transactions being wrongly denied. False positives pose a significant operational risk as they not only result in customer dissatisfaction and reputational damage but also lead to financial losses due to unnecessary transaction holds. Many existing fraud detection frameworks rely on static rule-based thresholds, which are unable to react to the dynamic nature of financial crime.

Key Advantages:

Scalable automatic fraud detection.
Streamlined genuine claims processing.
Improved financial stability for microinsurance enterprises.

3.4.3 Predictive Pricing Models

Predictive pricing is a data-driven pricing method in which businesses set prices based on acquired and analysed data such as customer purchasing history and market trends. Predictive analytics, the backbone of predictive pricing, employs contemporary technology to collect and analyze data, generate insights on customer behavior, and provide forecasts that assist company executives in setting prices at an ideal level for profitability, revenue optimization, and current market trends. Although some organizations use forecasts to determine fixed rates, predictive pricing, unlike traditional forecasting, primarily focuses on dynamic pricing and automation. Because it involves the use of AI and machine learning algorithms to analyze customer behavior patterns and market trends, the full process of predictive pricing is sometimes executed without direct human intervention. Predictive pricing is at the crossroads of business strategy and data science; by integrating historical sales data with predictive analytics models, organizations can accurately estimate future demand and set optimal prices for their products. Most modern businesses leverage predictive analytics in at least some of their pricing strategies to enhance decision-making, improve pricing accuracy, and adapt to changing market conditions. Given the continual enhancement and widespread availability of artificial intelligence and machine learning models, they have quickly become one of the most effective methods for businesses to stay agile and boost revenues, such as by optimizing pricing strategies based on real-time market data.

Key Benefits:

Reduced microinsurance premiums.
Increased policy adoption in underserved markets.
Real-time premium modification based on cu.

Future of AI in Microinsurance The application of machine learning models and predictive analytics is altering microinsurance by improving: Use decision trees and random forests for accurate risk assessment, Effectiveness of fraud detection with CNNs and RNNs, Improved affordability and accessibility via predictive pricing approaches. Despite these advances, difficulties persist, such as data privacy issues, legal barriers, and the digital gap in underdeveloped countries. To realise AI's full potential, insurers must invest in AI literacy programs, enhance data protection measures, and work with regulators to adopt AI-friendly policies.

3.5 Case Studies for AI Adoption in Microinsurance

3.5.1 BIMA (Ghana)

Mobile AI-Powered Microinsurance AI utilises mobile activity for underwriting and fraud prevention at BIMA (Ghana). Chatbots respond to client enquiries and claims over mobile networks. Effect: Over 35 million low-income clients are insured, with a 70% decrease in claims processing time.

3.5.2 MicroEnsure (Kenya)

AI-powered Weather-Based Crop Insurance Artificial intelligence uses satellite photos and climatic data to identify crop loss automatically. Effect: Over 300,000 smallholder farmers are insured, with faster reimbursements thanks to blockchain connectivity.

3.5.3 AXA Fizzy

AI and Blockchain-Based Parametric Insurance AI monitors real-time flight delays and initiates automatic adjustment. Impact: Removed manual claim handling and reduced Artificial intelligence is transforming microinsurance by enhancing underwriting precision, fraud detection, claim processing, and supply chain optimisation. Artificial intelligence models such as machine learning, natural language processing, and blockchain-enabled smart contracts have demonstrated real-world advances in insurance affordability and accessibility. Despite its promise, AI applications in microinsurance face challenges such as data privacy, legislation, and the digital divide. To ensure long-term growth, microinsurance businesses must prioritise: Establishing governance systems for AI to ensure that consumer data is used responsibly. Increasing AI literacy among insurance professionals and policyholders. Increased investment in AI-enabled microinsurance settings. As AI advances, its use in microinsurance models will be critical to improving financial inclusion, risk resilience, and social protection for low-income people worldwide.

4. BIBLIOMETRIC ANALYSIS OF AI AND SCO IN MICROINSURANCE

Figure 1. Co-Authorship Analysis of Authors (average norm citation)

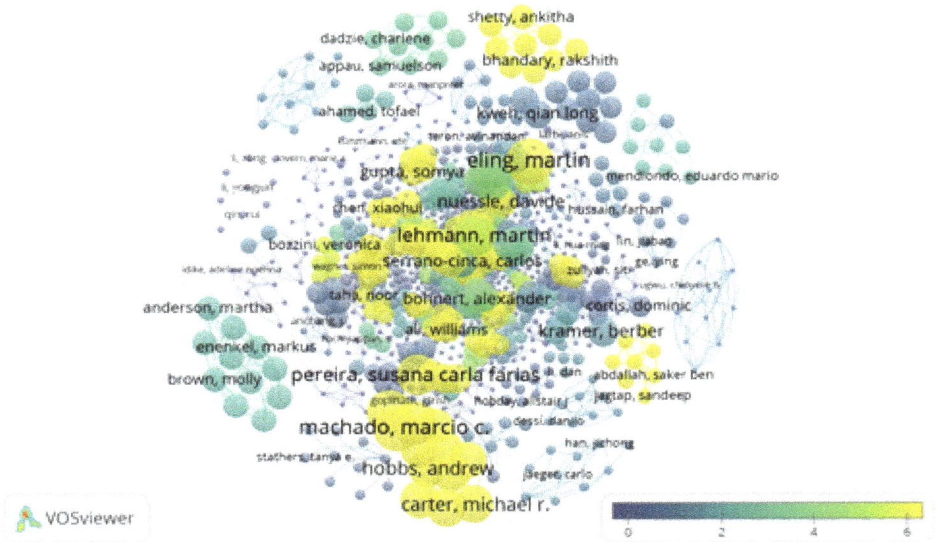

Figure 1 Illustrates the VOS viewer visualisation of a bibliometric network map that depicts co-authorship or citation relationships among researchers using Dimensions, with findings applicable to Scopus and Web of Science (WoS). Researchers are represented by nodes in the visualisation, while the lines linking them signify collaboration or citation ties. The colour-coded clusters depict distinct research networks: blue nodes represent researchers with fewer connections or citations, green nodes indicate those with medium impact, and yellow nodes indicate very influential authors with many citations and dense collaboration networks. Leading authors such as Lehmann, Martin, Eiling, and Machado, Marcio show significant figures in the discipline with a high level of connectedness. Densely packed clusters reflect established research groups, whereas outlying nodes may represent creative researchers or expert contributions by individuals. Dimensions data focuses on contemporary and multidisciplinary trend research, Scopus chooses experienced experts with extensive publication records, and WoS emphasises influential scholars. This visual provides valuable insight into dominant authors, prolific research teams, and future directions in the literature, making it an ideal resource for updating literature reviews, identifying collaboration opportunities, and directing research

agendas towards high-impact studies, enhancing research efficiency and fostering interdisciplinary collaborations.

Figure 2. Citation Analysis of Documents

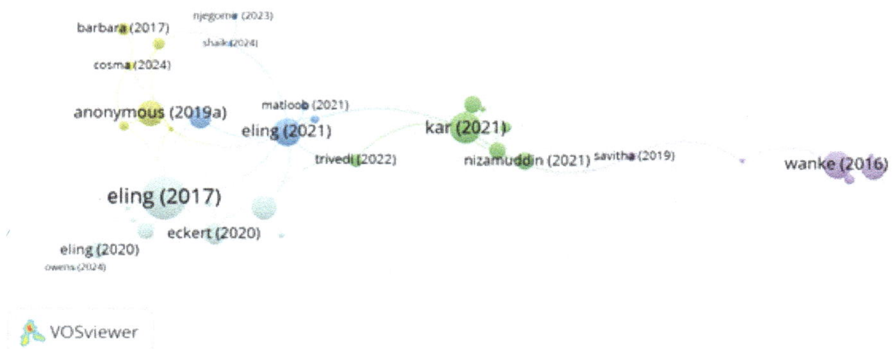

As in Figure 2 The VOS viewer visualisation illustrates a bibliometric network map of citation and co-authorship links between researchers using Dimensions, with Scopus and Web of Science (WoS) insights being relevant. Individual writers are shown as nodes, with lines connecting them indicating cooperation or citation links. The colour-coded clusters distinguish research networks: green nodes indicate moderately related authors, blue nodes identify established academics with high citation rates, while purple nodes reflect isolated or specialised study groups. Eling (2017), Kar (2021), and Wanke (2016) are important contributors who represent well-known research or huge collaborative networks. The existence of interconnected nodes like Anonymous (2019) and Barbara (2017) indicates crucial reference points in the research network. While Dimensions emphasises developing topics and cross-disciplinary collaboration, Scopus prefers established scientists with a good citation history, and WoS frequently emphasises key publications published in well-regarded journals. The cluster from Wanke (2016) to Kar (2021) indicates a research trajectory that may reflect evolving themes or methodological breakthroughs. This visualisation is useful for recognising important scholars, following academic trends, and matching research efforts to relevant publications in various databases.

Figure 3. Citation Analysis of Authors

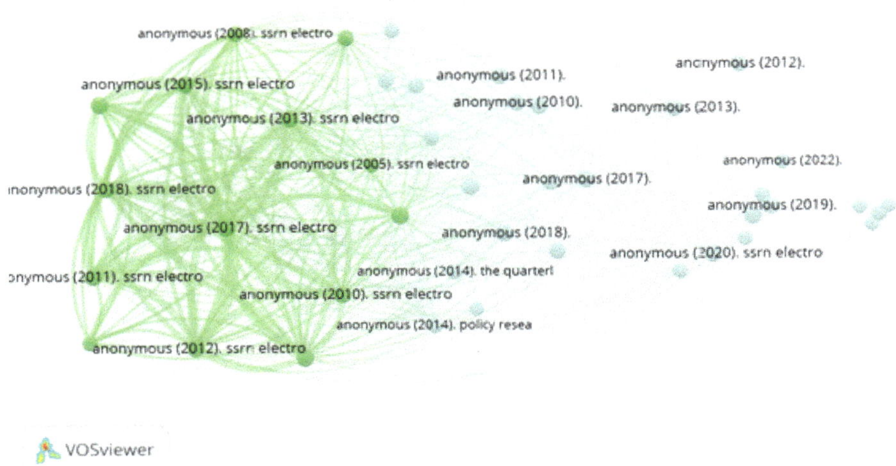

Figure 3 is a VOS viewer visualization that presents a citation network analysis of authors, highlighting its relevance to Dimensions, Scopus, and Web of Science. Nodes represent individual writers, and the connecting lines show citation links, illustrating the flow of knowledge and influence. The dense cluster on the left, featuring repeated occurrences of 'anonymous (2012)' and 'SSRN electro,' suggests a closely interconnected research group with frequent cross-referencing, probably centered around a specific theme or topic. The presence of multiple 'anonymous' citations could indicate collaborative efforts, institutional publications, or references to highly cited grey literature. Green nodes with thicker links indicate authors with greater citation influence or foundational research in the network, while lighter nodes represent newer or less-cited work. The scattered pattern on the right side indicates either newly emerging research or work that has not developed significant citation networks yet. In terms of database differences, Dimensions emphasises current research patterns and interdisciplinary citations, making it excellent for identifying upcoming academic trends. Scopus offers a larger citation monitoring horizon, focused on notable authors who make long-term contributions. In contrast, WoS prefers high-impact publications and well-established research subjects. This network visualisation is incredibly useful for identifying major contributors, following noteworthy research, and looking into potential gaps or developing patterns in the literature. For strategic research planning, researching the highly linked writers may provide insights into core notions, while analysing the disconnected nodes may provide suggestions about under-researched or speciality topics.

Figure 4. Bibliographic Coupling of Documents

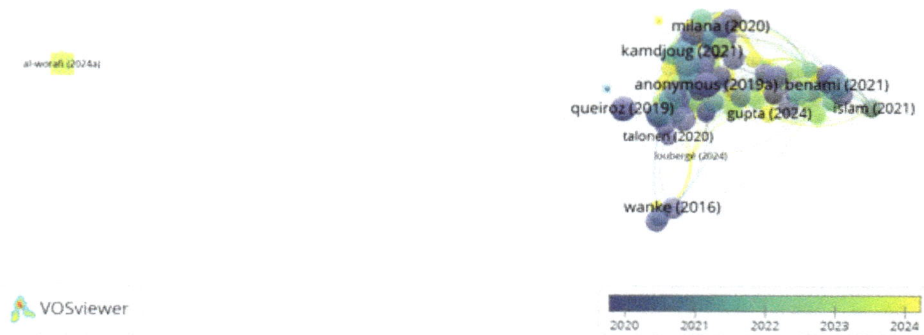

Figure 4 depicts that the nodes are individual writers, and the lines that connect them reflect citation or co-authorship ties. The gradient colour distinguishes publishing history, with blue nodes indicating older publications (e.g., Wanke (2016)) and yellow nodes representing recent contributions (e.g., Al-Worafi (2024)). The dense cluster on the right portrays a closely linked group of researchers, including Milana (2020), Benammi (2021), and Gupta (2024), indicating dense collaboration patterns or shared study problems. This type of rich structure is common in well-established fields like economics and sociology, which involve continuous cross-referencing. *Al-Worafi (2024a), on the other hand, stands alone, possibly due to pioneering research or innovative contributions that are still in the early stages of collaboration.* Dimensions focuses on emerging trends and cross-disciplinary contributions, Scopus on mature research outputs with a lengthy citation history, and Web of Science on key research papers published in respected journals. Al-Worafi's (2024a) distinct but more recent contribution might indicate novel information or early-stage research with future potential. In contrast, the dense cluster centred on Wanke (2016) indicates an established field of study with foundational research projects. This visualisation can help academics discover important writers, assess changing research paths, and explore cooperation opportunities across various scholarly resources.

Figure 5. Co-Authorship Network Visualisation

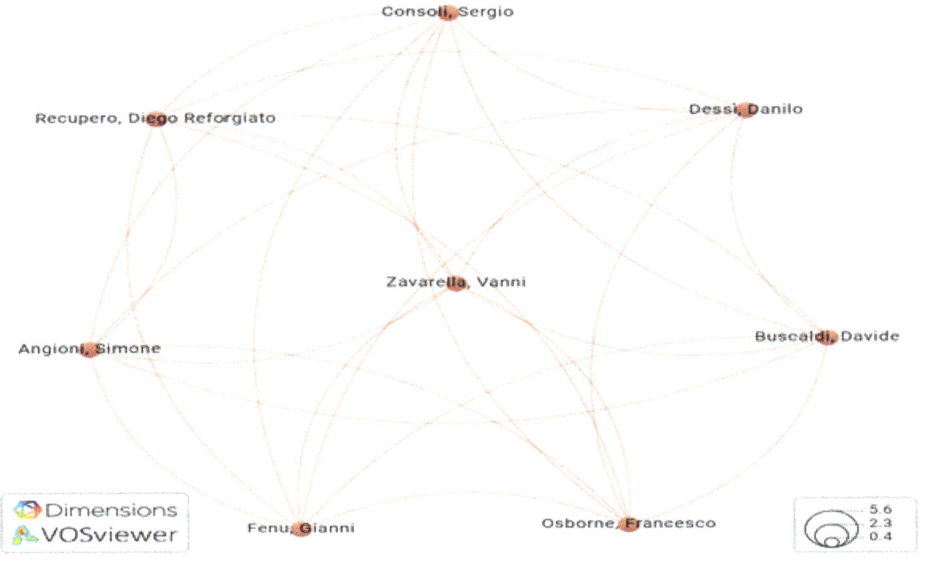

Figure 5 illustrates a Dimensions-created co-authorship network analysis, and the conclusions are congruent with data from Scopus and the Web of Science. Each node represents an author, and the lines linking them indicate significant collaborative relationships established through co-authored publications. Larger nodes, such as Consoli, Sergio, Dessi, Danilo, and Osborne, Francesco, represent notable scholars who have made major contributions in the field, evidenced by their significant citation influence. The dense network of superimposed linkages demonstrates a tightly knit research group and frequent active cooperation, indicating a particular research emphasis or topic specialisation. The diameters of the various nodes in the legend, ranging from 0.4 to 5.6, correspond to different levels of impact citations or publication numbers. In contrast to Scopus, which detects broad citation patterns, and WoS, which focuses on top journal citations, Dimensions accurately captures emerging linkages and transdisciplinary changes, such as the evolution of interdisciplinary research themes. This network is an invaluable tool for identifying notable writers, such as emerging scholars or prolific researchers, tracking collaborative ties, and facilitating new partnerships in specific scholarly areas.

Figure 6. Publications in Research Categories

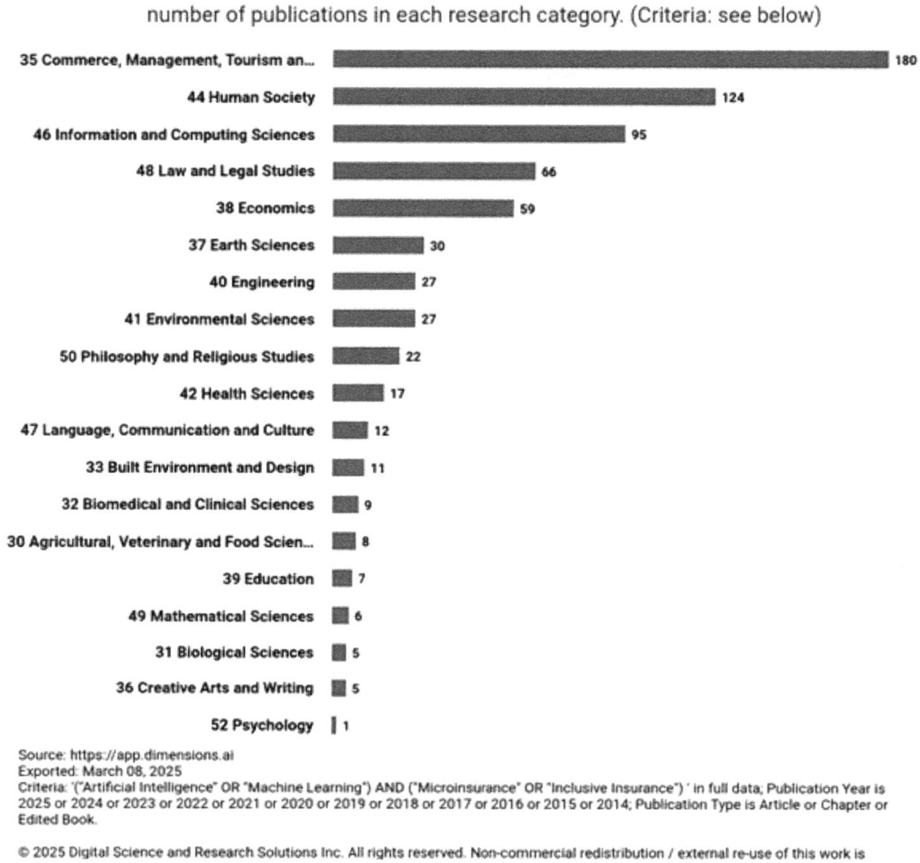

Figure 6 demonstrates the data comprising research outputs on Artificial Intelligence (AI), Machine Learning (ML), Microinsurance, and Inclusive Insurance published between 2014 and 2025. Commerce, Management, Tourism, and Services has the most concentrated output (180 papers), indicating extensive study on AI applications in financial services, insurance markets, and business innovation. Human Society (124) and Information and Computing Sciences (95) underscore the integration of social sciences, AI-driven decision-making, and computational science in the context of AI and microinsurance research. Disciplines like Law and Legal Studies (66) and Economics (59) have also witnessed an increase in discussion on regulatory settings, policy considerations, and economic implications of microinsurance AI implementation. In instances, issue areas such as environmental sciences, health sciences, and engineering contribute little to the discourse, despite the increasing presence of AI in those fields. The low number of publications in categories such as Psychology (1), Creative Arts (5), and Mathematical Sciences (6) indicates a dearth of research on AI and microinsurance concepts within these fields. While Dimensions emphasises emerging interdisciplinary research, Scopus prioritises recent academic publications with robust citation indices, and WoS concentrates on high-impact research featured in top-tier journals. This emphasises the growing importance of artificial intelligence and microinsurance in business, computing, and social sciences, while also highlighting untapped opportunities in fields such as psychology and the creative arts, influencing research pathways and avenues for exploration. This information is crucial for academics looking to discover influential subjects for future research or expand into other research areas.

Table 1. Publications published in each year

	2016	2017	2018	2019	2020	2021	2022	2023	2024	2025
Publications (total)	17	12	21	35	322	226	214	96	148	26

The visualization shows the number of publications published in each year

The table 1 depicts the annual number of publications from 2016 to 2025, exhibiting a clear trend in research effort over time. The data show a large increase in publications on Artificial Intelligence (AI), Machine Learning (ML), Microinsurance, and Inclusive Insurance, with notable oscillations. From 2016 to 2018, publication rates were relatively low, ranging from 17 to 21 per year, suggesting a period with limited research interest or significant advancements. However, there was a substantial surge in 2019 with 35 articles, signifying a notable rise in academic interest. The most significant surge is observed in 2020, where publications skyrocketed to 322, primarily due to the swift growth of AI and digital solutions amid the COVID-19 pandemic, driving innovation in financial services, insurance technology, and risk management. After this peak, publications fell steadily in 2021 (226) and 2022 (214), but they remained much higher than before 2020, showing that AI and microinsurance research was continuing strong long after the first rush had subsided. The decline in 2023 (96 publications) could suggest a transition towards consolidating or improving existing research findings. The data for 2024 (148 publications) indicates a growth in interest or the emergence of new trends, potentially associated with progress in AI-based insurance models or regulatory advancements. The lower figure in 2025 (26 publications, as of early data export) shows either incomplete data collection for the year or articles that are currently pending evaluation. This tendency is corroborated by Scopus and Web of Science (WoS) data, which show that fast expansion is frequently accompanied by revolutionary developments, followed by stabilisation and tuning. According to the numbers, 2020 is a significant year for AI and microinsurance research, with renewed expansion in 2024 indicating new trends or technical developments to investigate.

5. TREND ANALYSIS AND FUTURE DIRECTIONS

5.1 Emerging Trends in AI-Driven Microinsurance Supply Chains

AI-based microinsurance value chains are experiencing significant shifts in operations as machine learning, predictive analytics, and automation advance rapidly. AI-based underwriting systems are replacing traditional risk assessment methods by leveraging vast datasets to analyse risk profiles with greater precision. The increased utilisation of AI-powered chatbots and virtual assistants has enhanced client engagement through rapid assistance in policy issuance, claims settlement, and enquiries. AI is facilitating the creation of personalised and on-demand microinsurance solutions that address individual consumer requirements by leveraging behavioural and transactional data. Moreover, AI-powered fraud detection tools are revolutionising fraud prevention by analysing historical claim patterns, identifying anomalies, and consequently reducing the number of false claims while enhancing insurer trust. AI integration in microinsurance promotes financial inclusion through the creation of affordable microinsurance products customised for low-income groups, reducing administrative expenses, and simplifying policy management.

The incorporation of artificial intelligence (AI) into microinsurance supply chains is revolutionising the industry by increasing efficiency, accuracy, and convenience. Several new developments are transforming the AI-powered microinsurance supply chain environment.

Automated Underwriting and Risk Assessment - Predictive analytics and machine learning systems based on artificial intelligence improve risk assessment accuracy. These algorithms evaluate massive databases to assess policyholder risks, allowing insurers to customise policies to specific needs while lowering underwriting costs and increasing policy affordability.

AI-powered claims processing and fraud detection - Intelligent automation, which employs natural language processing (NLP) and image recognition, accelerates claim processing. AI models can also detect false claims through behavioural and historical data analysis, boosting confidence and lowering microinsurance losses.

Individualised and Inclusive Insurance Products - Insurance companies can use AI to develop dynamic and adaptable policies based on demographics, economic conditions, and client behaviour. Microinsurance companies use artificial intelligence to tailor plans to low-income customers, increasing their financial inclusion.

AI Chat Bots and Virtual Assistants for Customer Engagement - AI-powered virtual assistants and chatbots enhance customer service by providing real-time policy information, claims assistance, and premium payment reminders. These apps reduce human intervention while providing microinsurance services to underserved communities.

AI-powered, parametric insurance models - AI enables the development of parametric insurance by analysing climate, health, and finance data to automatically initiate payouts based on specified factors, such as weather or agricultural yields, to assist vulnerable populations in developing countries.

5.2 Role of Blockchain, IoT, and Big Data in Microinsurance and SCO

The integration of blockchain, the Internet of Things (IoT), and big data with microinsurance and supply chain optimisation (SCO) improves transparency, efficiency, and security.

Blockchain technology facilitates secure and transparent transactions - Blockchain technology boosts microinsurance reliability and confidence by employing decentralised, tamper-proof smart contracts. Smart contracts streamline claim settlement processes, reducing delays and friction between insurers and policyholders.

Examples: IoT devices like wearable health monitors and smart sensors use real-time data to develop personalised microinsurance policies. For agricultural microinsurance, IoT-enabled weather sensors monitor weather conditions and trigger insurance payouts upon identifying adverse weather.

Big data analysis - plays a crucial role in developing accurate risk pricing models and assessment strategies. Big data analytics enables insurers to examine massive volumes of data, such as satellite images, financial transactions, and behavioural patterns. This enables dynamic risk pricing models, which offer more precise premium structures to individual policyholders.

Supply Chain Visibility and Anti-Fraud Blockchain and AI - improves supply chain visibility while lowering operational inefficiencies and fraud. Blockchain is utilised by microinsurance companies to authenticate transactions on supply chain networks, ensuring that only eligible customers receive insurance.

Smart Contracts for Claims Settlement - Automated smart contracts based on blockchain settle insurance claims, lowering administrative costs and boosting transparency. These contracts enhance efficiency and eliminate payment delays, particularly in remote and disadvantaged regions.

5.3 Policy and Regulatory Considerations for AI Adoption

As AI deployment in microinsurance grows, regulatory settings must keep up with resolving ethical, legal, and operational concerns. Policy and regulatory priorities include the following:

Data Privacy and Security Regulations - Regulatory settings must assure compliance with data protection regulations, such as the General Data Protection Regulation (GDPR). To safeguard consumer information, AI-based microinsurance models must employ robust encryption methods like AES-256 and anonymisation techniques such as differential privacy.

AI Ethics and Bias Prevention - AI models used in microinsurance must be created to prevent algorithmic bias. Regulatory bodies must set criteria for fairness, openness, and accountability in AI-driven decision-making to avoid discrimination in policy approval and pricing.

Legalisation of Smart Contracts - Governments must establish legal frameworks to ensure the enforcement of blockchain-based smart contracts. This will expedite claims settlement and make digital insurance contracts legally binding.

Consumer Protection and Transparency in AI - Policymakers should require transparency in AI algorithms to help policyholders comprehend the factors influencing their premiums and claims decisions. Transparency in AI-driven procedures can foster confidence and promote microinsurance acceptance.

Cross-Border Regulation of AI-Powered Insurance - Because AI and blockchain are worldwide, authorities must establish cross-border agreements to assure consistent AI-powered microinsurance policies.

6. FUTURE RESEARCH DOMAINS AND EMERGING TECHNOLOGY DISRUPTIONS

The future of technology-driven microinsurance and supply chain optimisation will be affected by new research fields and technical breakthroughs. Some of the most significant domains for future research include:

Explainable Artificial Intelligence (XAI) for Insurance Decision-Making Future research should focus on developing explainable AI models to enhance transparency and intelligibility in underwriting and claims administration, thereby boosting confidence and regulatory compliance in technology-based microinsurance. This will boost confidence and regulatory compliance in technology-based microinsurance.

DeFi can enable blockchain-based insurance frameworks, allowing policyholders to pool funds and share risk through decentralised, community-based insurance models.

Quantum Computing can revolutionize risk modeling by processing complex insurance data sets at extraordinary rates, enabling real-time risk evaluation and policy modifications. Quantum computing has the potential to revolutionise risk modelling by effectively processing complex insurance data sets at extraordinary rates, allowing for real-time risk evaluation and policy modifications.

Integrating AI with Climate Risk Insurance can improve microinsurance products by anticipating and mitigating the financial risks associated with extreme weather occurrences. With climate change affecting impoverished communities, AI-based climate risk models might improve microinsurance products by anticipating and mitigating the financial risks associated with extreme weather occurrences.

AI-Powered Behavioural Insurance Models, which combine AI with behavioral economics, offer the potential to create responsive insurance models that monitor policyholder behavior in real time, incentivizing healthier and risk-averse behaviors. Combining AI with behavioural economics offers the potential to create responsive insurance models that monitor policyholder behaviour in real time, incentivising healthier and risk-averse behaviours.

Blockchain-powered Peer-to-peer Microinsurance can lead to significant and cost-effective insurance solutions by reducing reliance on traditional insurers and promoting community-based insurance models. Studies of decentralised blockchain-based peer-to-peer microinsurance models can lead to significant and cost-effective insurance solutions that reduce reliance on traditional insurers.

Future studies should look into how AI and IoT might affect usage-based microinsurance plans, in which premiums are dependent on real-time behavioural data from IoT devices.

Research should aim to develop ethical AI governance frameworks that adhere to international norms, promoting justice, accountability, and transparency in AI-based insurance models.

Research should seek to develop ethical AI governance frameworks that adhere to international norms and promote justice, accountability, and transparency in AI-based insurance models.

7. CHALLENGES AND ETHICAL CONSIDERATIONS

7.1 Data Security and Privacy Issues

Data privacy and security are crucial aspects of AI-based microinsurance supply chains. As more AI and blockchain are adopted, enormous amounts of customer data, such as personal, financial, and behavioural data, are gathered and processed. Securing this data against breaches and cyberattacks is imperative to ensure trust and regulatory compliance.

Data Breaches and Cybersecurity Risks

Microinsurance companies keep confidential information that is usually the target of cybercrime. Data breaches can lead to identity theft, financial losses, and damage to reputation. Implementing strong encryption, multi-factor authentication, and blockchain-based security measures can avert these issues.

Regulatory Compliance

Adherence to international and local data protection legislation, including GDPR, HIPAA, and India's Personal Data Protection Bill, is necessary. Failure to comply may lead to legal sanctions and consumer distrust. AI models should be developed to conform to data minimisation practices, where only relevant information is gathered and processed.

Data Ownership and Consent

Ensuring that policyholders have control over their data is fundamental. AI-driven microinsurance platforms should implement transparent consent mechanisms, allowing users to understand how their data is being used and enabling them to opt out if desired.

7.2. Algorithmic Bias and Fairness in AI-Driven Microinsurance

AI algorithms used in microinsurance underwriting, fraud detection, and risk assessment may inadvertently introduce biases, leading to unfair treatment of certain demographic groups.

Sources of Algorithmic Bias

Bias in AI systems can arise from: Historical Data- Past data, if they mirror systemic biases, can be reproduced by AI models. Feature Selection- Some demographic characteristics can have a disproportionate effect on risk computations. Model Training- Inappropriate training methods can result in biased outcomes favouring one group at the expense of another.

Fairness and Transparency

Fairness in AI-based microinsurance is ensured by Bias Auditing- Periodic checks on AI models to identify and rectify biases. Explain ability - Offering transparent AI decision-making mechanisms so users know why specific decisions were taken. Regulatory Oversight- Establishing governance structures to promote fairness in AI-based decision-making.

Inclusive Insurance Access

Bias in AI-based underwriting can lock out marginalized groups. Ensuring diverse training data and incorporating human oversight can guarantee equitable outcomes in AI-based microinsurance.

7.3. Ethical Considerations in AI-Based Decision-Making

AI-based microinsurance systems need to comply with ethical principles, making decisions fair, transparent, and accountable.

The Role of Human Oversight

Even though AI can perform many tasks for microinsurance automatically, human oversight is required to: Avoid Unfair Denials- AI-based claim denials need to be audited by human experts. Offer Appeals Procedures- Policyholders must have mechanisms to appeal against AI-based decisions. Assure Accountability- The insurance provider needs to be held responsible for AI-based decisions.

Ethical AI Design Principles

To keep ethical AI-based microinsurance, the below principles must be applied: Transparency- AI decision-making should be explainable. Non-Discrimination- AI models should not disproportionately disadvantage any group. Beneficence- AI should improve customer experiences and issue fair risk assessments.

Overcoming Moral Hazards

AI-based automation could lead to ethical risks, such as policyholders engaging in fraudulent activities or insurers prioritizing profit over customer well-being. Ethical mitigants, such as ethical AI deployment and stakeholder involvement, can reduce such risks.

Overcoming Challenges in AI Adoption for Microinsurance Supply Chains

AI implementation in microinsurance supply chains faces challenges such as technological limitations, operational constraints, and cultural resistance.

7.4 Data Quality and Availability

Quality data is necessary for training precise AI models. Issues are: Inaccurate or Incomplete Data- Inadequate data quality can undermine AI reliability. Data Fragmentation- Isolated data among several insurers can restrict AI effectiveness. Limited Historical Data- New markets might not have adequate historical data for AI training.

Technological Infrastructure

Limited Internet Access, AI implementation depends on cloud computing and digital platforms. High Implementation Expenses- Creating and sustaining AI systems is capital-intensive. Legacy System Integration- Insurers have largely retained old IT systems that do not necessarily have the capacity for AI integration.

Resistance to Change

Organizational and cultural resistance can be an obstacle to AI adoption. To overcome this, one needs: Training and Capacity Building- Employee and stakeholder education on AI advantages. Change Management Strategies- Adoption of formalized strategies to AI adoption. Regulatory Support- Governments and regulatory agencies need to set forth clear guidelines for AI integration into their systems.

Ethical Use of AI in Supply Chains

Ensuring the ethical use of AI in microinsurance supply chains involves, Stakeholder Engagement- Holding talks with consumers, regulators, and insurers about the deployment of AI. Sustainable AI Practices- Reducing AI's environmental effect, such as excessive energy use during model training. Continuous Monitoring and Adaptation- AI models are regularly updated to account for changes in market conditions and moral standards.

While AI-powered microinsurance can improve efficiency and accessibility, it also introduces significant hurdles and ethical considerations. Overcoming data privacy concerns, making AI decision-making fair, preserving ethical AI practices, and overcoming technological and cultural barriers are all critical for successful AI adoption. AI-based microinsurance can help to create a more equitable and resilient insurance environment by implementing robust governance frameworks, engaging stakeholders, and being transparent.

8. CONCLUSIONS AND POLICY RECOMMENDATIONS

The combination of artificial intelligence (AI) and supply chain optimisation offers the potential to improve the microinsurance industry by enhancing efficiency, transparency, and accessibility. Key breakthroughs and future research directions were identified through bibliometric and trend analysis, emphasizing the transformative effects of AI-powered automation and blockchain-based smart contracts on enhancing supply chain resilience.

Summary of Key Findings:

Improved Risk Analysis and Pricing: AI-powered models, particularly machine learning algorithms, have considerably increased the precision of risk assessment, allowing insurers to provide personalised and equitable pricing schemes.

Automated claims verification through AI and blockchain smart contracts accelerates processing, prevents fraud, and enhances customer satisfaction.

Supply Chain Resilience: The integration of AI and supply chain optimisation enables effective resource allocation, real-time tracking, and predictive analytics, reducing operational inefficiencies in microinsurance.

Financial Inclusion: AI solutions increase accessibility by allowing low-income people to acquire microinsurance products via digital channels, removing entrance obstacles.

legal and Ethical Challenges: While AI and blockchain provide several advantages, data privacy, legal, and algorithmic bias problems remain essential and require smart government intervention.

8.1 Policy Proposals to Regulators and Industry Stakeholders

AI-Driven Insurance Regulatory Framework: Governments and regulators must establish clear criteria for employing AI in microinsurance that are consistent with ethical AI principles, data protection laws, and consumer rights.

Blockchain Interoperability Standardisation: It is crucial for industry stakeholders to collaborate in creating interoperable blockchain standards that facilitate seamless integration across various insurance and banking systems.

Public-Private Partnerships: Governments should encourage insurers, technology companies, and research institutions to work together to promote innovation, support pilot projects, and extend AI-powered microinsurance solutions.

Fraud Prevention tools: Regulators must require the use of AI-powered fraud detection tools while maintaining transparency and accountability in claims management.

Financial Literacy and Digital Inclusion: Initiatives should prioritize educating low-income communities about the advantages of AI-based microinsurance and the utilization of digital insurance platforms.

Sustainability and ESG Compliance: Policymakers must encourage the use of AI-based insurance solutions that meet environmental, social, and governance (ESG) criteria, ensuring that microinsurance aligns with sustainable development objectives.

CONCLUSION

The combination of AI and supply chain optimisation marks a paradigm shift in the microinsurance industry. As technology progresses, the usage of AI-driven solutions will be critical for improving risk prediction, simplifying procedures, and expanding insurance coverage to underserved populations. However, achieving these benefits requires a complete approach that addresses legislative, ethical, and infrastructural concerns. Future study should concentrate on refining AI models, enhancing data governance, and investigating DeFi application cases in microinsurance. The industry can fully exploit the potential of AI and supply chain convergence by creating and executing well-thought-out regulatory measures that will create a more robust, inclusive, and transparent microinsurance environment.

ACKNOWLEDGMENT

The author gratefully acknowledges the support provided by the ICSSR through the Post- Doctoral Fellowship, which has significantly contributed to the successful completion of this research.

REFERENCES

Accenture. (2021). AI in Insurance: Driving Efficiency and Customer Engagement. Accenture Strategy Report.

Brynjolfsson, E., & McAfee, A. (2017). The Business of Artificial Intelligence. *Harvard Business Review.*

Christopher, M. (2016). Logistics & Supply Chain Management. Pearson Education.

Churchill, C. (2006). *Protecting the Poor: A Microinsurance Compendium.* International Labour Organization.

Cosma, S., & Rimo, G. (2024). Redefining insurance through technology: Achievements and perspectives in Insurtech. *Research in International Business and Finance, 70*, 102301. DOI: 10.1016/j.ribaf.2024.102301

De Leeuw, J., Vrieling, A., Shee, A., Atzberger, C., Hadgu, K. M., Biradar, C. M., Keah, H., & Turvey, C. (2014). The potential and uptake of remote sensing in insurance: A review. *Remote Sensing (Basel), 6*(11), 10888–10912. DOI: 10.3390/rs61110888

Deloitte. (2020). *The Future of AI in Insurance: Transforming Underwriting and Claims Processing*. Deloitte Insights.

Donthu, N., Kumar, S., Pattnaik, D., & Lim, W. M. (2021). AI in Insurance: Reducing Fraud and Optimizing Supply Chains. *Journal of Financial Services Marketing, 26*(3), 345–362.

Donthu, N., Kumar, S., Pattnaik, D., & Lim, W. M. (2021). A Bibliometric Review of Research on Artificial Intelligence Applications in Business. *Journal of Business Research, 123*, 389–404.

Eshun, B. T. B., Chan, A. P., & Osei-Kyei, R. (2021). Conceptualizing a win–win scenario in public–private partnerships: Evidence from a systematic literature review. *Engineering, Construction, and Architectural Management, 28*(9), 2712–2735. DOI: 10.1108/ECAM-07-2020-0533

Feyen, E., Lester, R., & Rocha, R. (2021). *The Digital Transformation of Microinsurance*. World Bank Publications.

Ganeshkumar, C., Jena, S. K., Sivakumar, A., & Nambirajan, T. (2023). Artificial intelligence in agricultural value chain: Review and future directions. *Journal of Agribusiness in Developing and Emerging Economies*, *13*(3), 379–398. DOI: 10.1108/JADEE-07-2020-0140

Gebauer, H., & Reynoso, J. (2013). An agenda for service research at the base of the pyramid. *Journal of Service Management*, *24*(5), 482–502. DOI: 10.1108/JOSM-04-2013-0090

Gebrekidan, B. H., Agaba, M., & Dhehibi, B. Adoption of Climate-Smart Agricultural Technologies and Practices in Fragile and Conflict-Affected Settings: A Review and Meta-Analysis.

GSMA. (2021). *AI and Mobile-Based Insurance in Emerging Markets*. GSMA Research.

Joshi, S., & Sharma, M. (2023). Assessment of implementation barriers of blockchain technology in public healthcare: Evidences from developing countries. *Health Systems (Basingstoke, England)*, *12*(2), 223–242. DOI: 10.1080/20476965.2023.2206446 PMID: 37234469

Kalfin, S., Sukono, , Supian, S., & Mamat, M. (2022). Insurance as an alternative for sustainable economic recovery after natural disasters: A systematic literature review. *Sustainability (Basel)*, *14*(7), 4349. DOI: 10.3390/su14074349

Kar, A. K., & Navin, L. (2021). Diffusion of blockchain in insurance industry: An analysis through the review of academic and trade literature. *Telematics and Informatics*, *58*, 101532. DOI: 10.1016/j.tele.2020.101532

Lloyd's. (2018). Insuring the Frontier: The Role of Insurance in Emerging Markets. Lloyd's of London.

McKinsey. (2022). *The Role of AI in Fraud Detection and Claims Processing*. McKinsey Insights.

Mills, C. (2022). The Role of AI in Optimizing Insurance Supply Chains. *Insurance & Technology Journal*, *18*(2), 45–62.

Tadesse, M., & Brans, J. P. (2012). Risk and Insurance in Developing Countries: A Study on Microinsurance. *The Journal of Risk and Insurance*, *79*(3), 811–835.

Compilation of References

Abhulimen, A., & Ejike, O. (2024). Solving supply chain management issues with AI and Big Data analytics for future operational efficiency. Computer Science & IT Research Journal. https://doi.org/.DOI: 10.51594/csitrj.v5i8.1396

Accenture. (2021). AI in Insurance: Driving Efficiency and Customer Engagement. Accenture Strategy Report.

Achinna, P., & Rao, P. P. (2023). The International Year of Millets-2023, Millets as Nutri-cereals of 21st Centenary for Health and Wellness. *AATCC Review*.

Addo-Tenkorang, R., & Helo, P. (2016). Big data applications in operations/supply-chain management: A literature review. *Computers & Industrial Engineering*, *101*, 528–543. DOI: 10.1016/j.cie.2016.09.023

Adewusi, A. O., Komolafe, A. M., Ejairu, E., Aderotoye, I. A., Abiona, O. O., & Oyeniran, O. C. (2024). The role of predictive analytics in optimizing supply chain resilience: A review of techniques and case studies. *International Journal of Management & Entrepreneurship Research*, *6*(3), 815–837. DOI: 10.51594/ijmer.v6i3.938

Agyabeng-Mensah, Y., Afum, E., Acquah, I. S. K., & Baah, C. (2023). How does supply chain knowledge enhance green innovation? The mediation mechanisms of corporate reputation and non-supply chain learning. *Journal of Business and Industrial Marketing*, *38*(4), 852–868. DOI: 10.1108/JBIM-04-2021-0192

Ahmed, H. N., Ahmed, S., Khan, M. A., & Ali, S. M. (2024). Sustainable supply chain in emerging economies during and post COVID-19 pandemic: A systematic literature review and future research directions. *International Journal of Emerging Markets*, *19*(9), 2472–2498. DOI: 10.1108/IJOEM-01-2022-0092

Aladaileh, M. J., Lahuerta-Otero, E., & Aladayleh, K. J. (2024). Mapping sustainable supply chain innovation: A comprehensive bibliometric analysis. *Heliyon*, *10*(7), e29157. DOI: 10.1016/j.heliyon.2024.e29157 PMID: 38623205

Al-Faouri, E. H., Huson, Y. A., Alkrarha, A. S., Aljawarneh, N. M., & Alqmoo, T. J. (2025). Mapping the landscape: A bibliometric analysis of digital leadership, service quality, and supply chain management. *Uncertain Supply Chain Management, 13*(3), 543–556. DOI: 10.5267/j.uscm.2024.8.013

Alonge, E. O., Eyo-Udo, N. L., Ubanadu, B. C., Daraojimba, A. I., Balogun, E. D., & Ogunsola, K. O. (2023). Real-time data analytics for enhancing supply chain efficiency. *Journal of Supply Chain Management and Analytics*, *10*(1), 49–60.

Al-Samad, K., Sufian, M. A., Haque, S., Faruq, O., Hossain, M. A., Talukder, T., & Shayed, A. U. (2024). Leveraging IoT for Enhanced Supply Chain Management in Manufacturing. AIJMR-Advanced International Journal of Multidisciplinary Research, 2(5).

Alzate, I. C., Manotas, E. C., Manotas, E. M., & Boada, A. (2022). Impact of supply chain dynamic capabilities (SCDC) and horizontal collaboration over supply chain resilience for SME's sustainability in emerging economies. *Polish Journal of Management Studies, 25.*

Ambroziak, T., & Tkaczyk, S. (2015). The selection of transportation means for technological processes. *Archives of transport, 36*(4), 7-20.

Ameh, B. (2024). Technology-integrated sustainable supply chains: Balancing domestic policy goals, global stability, and economic growth. *International Journal of Science and Research Archive*, *13*(2), 1811–1828. DOI: 10.30574/ijsra.2024.13.2.2369

Amoako, G. K., Caesar, L. D., Dzogbenuku, R. K., & Bonsu, G. A. (2023). Service recovery performance and repurchase intentions: The mediation effect of service quality at KFC. *Journal of Hospitality and Tourism Insights*, *6*(1), 110–130. DOI: 10.1108/JHTI-06-2021-0141

Amoozad Mahdiraji, H., Yaftiyan, F., Garza-Reyes, J. A., Razavi Hajiagha, S. H., & Kazancoglu, Y. (2024). Decarbonised closed-loop supply chains resilience: Examining the impact of COVID-19 toward risk mitigation by a fuzzy multi-layer decision-making framework. *Annals of Operations Research.* Advance online publication. DOI: 10.1007/s10479-024-06093-3

Anagnostakos, P. (2024). *Balancing resilience and sustainability: Tensions, trade-offs, and strategies for multinational enterprises in a complex global landscape.* https://doi.org/DOI: 10.2139/ssrn.5074123

Apeji, U. D., & Sunmola, F. T. (2023). Sustainable supply chain visibility assessment and proposals for improvements using fuzzy logic. *Journal of Modelling in Management*, *18*(3), 701–726. DOI: 10.1108/JM2-08-2021-0181

Aslam, F., & Calghan, J. (2023). Using NLP to enhance supply chain management systems. *Journal of Engineering Research and Reports, 25*(9), 211–219. DOI: 10.9734/jerr/2023/v25i9994

Aung, M. M., & Chang, Y. S. (2021). Traceability in a food supply chain: Safety and quality perspectives. *Food Control, 123*, 107730.

Awasthi, S. (2024). Artificial Intelligence in Supply Chain Management. Journal of Student Research. https://doi.org/.DOI: 10.47611/jsrhs.v13i1.5996

Azzi, R., Kilany, R., & Sokhn, M. (2019). The power of a blockchain-based supply chain. *Computers & Industrial Engineering, 135*, 582–592. DOI: 10.1016/j.cie.2019.06.042

Babashahi, L., Barbosa, C. E., Lima, Y., Lyra, A., Salazar, H., Argôlo, M., Almeida, M. A., & Souza, J. M. D. (2024). AI in the workplace: A systematic review of skill transformation in the industry. *Administrative Sciences, 14*(6), 127. DOI: 10.3390/admsci14060127

Bamia, A., & Bamia, F. (2025). SCRGD: Supply chain resilience in the face of global disruptions. *International Business Research, 18*(2), 80. DOI: 10.5539/ibr.v18n2p80

Banaee, H., Ahmed, M. U., & Loutfi, A. (2013). Data mining for wearable sensors in health monitoring systems: A review of recent trends and challenges. *Sensors (Basel), 13*(12), 17472–17500. DOI: 10.3390/s131217472 PMID: 24351646

Bank., W. (2019). Enabling the Business of Agriculture 2019. World Bank Group, Washington D.C.

Barratt, M., & Oke, A. (2007). Antecedents of supply chain visibility in retail supply chains: A resource-based theory perspective. *Journal of Operations Management, 25*(6), 1217–1233. DOI: 10.1016/j.jom.2007.01.003

Barriball, E., George, K., Marcos, I., & Radtke, P. (2020). Jump-starting resilient and reimagined operations: COVID-19 has created an imperative for companies to reconfigure their operations, and an opportunity to transform them. McKinsey & Company, May 2020. https://www.mckinsey.com/business-functions/operations/our-insights/jump-starting-resilientand-reimagined-operations

Baryannis, G., Validi, S., Dani, S., & Antoniou, G. (2018). Supply chain risk management and artificial intelligence: State of the art and future research directions. *International Journal of Production Research, 57*(7), 2179–2202. DOI: 10.1080/00207543.2018.1530476

Belanche, D., Casaló, L. V., Flavián, C., & Pérez-Rueda, A. (2021). The role of customers in the gig economy: How perceptions of working conditions and service quality influence the use and recommendation of food delivery services. *Service Business*, *15*(1), 45–75. DOI: 10.1007/s11628-020-00432-7

Belhadi, A., Kamble, S., Subramanian, N., Singh, R. K., & Venkatesh, M. (2024). Digital capabilities to manage agri-food supply chain uncertainties and build supply chain resilience during compounding geopolitical disruptions. *International Journal of Operations & Production Management*, *44*(11), 1914–1950. DOI: 10.1108/IJOPM-11-2022-0737

Bellad, A., & Belavadi, S. (2023). *Nutritional and Health Benefits of Millets*. AYUSHDHARA., DOI: 10.47070/ayushdhara.v10i5.1317

Bellany, K., Dhiba, Y., & Loulid, A. (2024). Blockchain and the new vendor-managed inventory: proposal of a conceptual model based on innovation in inter-organisational Supply Chain Management Practices. 2024 IEEE 15th International Colloquium on Logistics and Supply Chain Management (LOGISTIQUA), 1-8. https://doi.org/ DOI: 10.1109/LOGISTIQUA61063.2024.10571530

Ben-Daya, M., Hassini, E., & Bahroun, Z. (2019). Internet of things and supply chain management: A literature review. *International Journal of Production Research*, *57*(15-16), 4719–4742. DOI: 10.1080/00207543.2017.1402140

Bhalaji, R., Bathrinath, S., Ali, S. M., & Koppiahraj, K. (2024). Risk assessment in sustainable supply chain: Theoretical and managerial implications for circular economy in emerging economies. *International Journal of System Assurance Engineering and Management*, *15*(10), 1–16. DOI: 10.1007/s13198-024-02507-4

Bhargava, A., Bhargava, D., Kumar, P. N., Sajja, G. S., & Ray, S. (2022). Industrial IoT and AI implementation in vehicular logistics and supply chain management for vehicle mediated transportation systems. *International Journal of System Assurance Engineering and Management*, *13*(S1, Suppl 1), 673–680. DOI: 10.1007/s13198-021-01581-2

Bhawna, Kang, P. S., & Sharma, S. K. (2024). Bridging the gap: A systematic analysis of circular economy, supply chain management, and digitization for sustainability and resilience. *Operations Management Research*, 1–19.

Bian, W. L., Ju, S. D., Xu, J., & Ding, J. Z. (2011). An empirical research on online B2C customer perceptions of logistics services and related factors. *Guanli Gongcheng Xuebao*, *25*(2), 14–20.

Birkel, H., Hohenstein, N.-O., & Hähner, S. (2023). How have digital technologies facilitated supply chain resilience in the COVID-19 pandemic? An exploratory case study. *Computers & Industrial Engineering*, *183*, 109538. DOI: 10.1016/j.cie.2023.109538

Borgia, E. (2014). The Internet of Things Vision: Key Features, Applications, and Open Issues. Computer Communications.

Bosona, T., & Gebresenbet, G. (2013). Food traceability as an integral part of logistics management in food and agricultural supply chain. *Food Control*, *33*(1), 32–48. DOI: 10.1016/j.foodcont.2013.02.004

Bossert, T., Hsiao, W., Barrera, M., Alarcon, L., Leo, M., & Casares, C. (1998). Transformation of ministries of health in the era of health reform: The case of Colombia. *Health Policy and Planning*, *13*(1), 59–77. https://www.jstor.org/stable/45089471. DOI: 10.1093/heapol/13.1.59 PMID: 10178186

Boute, R., & Udenio, M. (2021). AI in Logistics and Supply Chain Management. PROD: Empirical (Supply) (Topic). https://doi.org/.DOI: 10.2139/ssrn.3862541

Brynjolfsson, E., & McAfee, A. (2017). The Business of Artificial Intelligence. *Harvard Business Review*.

Bumblauskas, D., Mann, A., Dugan, B., & Rittmer, J. (2020). A blockchain use case in food distribution: Do you know where your food has been. *International Journal of Information Management*, *52*, 102008. DOI: 10.1016/j.ijinfomgt.2019.09.004

Carter, C. R., & Rogers, D. S. (2008). A framework of sustainable supply chain management: Moving toward new theory. *International Journal of Physical Distribution & Logistics Management*, *38*(5), 360–387. DOI: 10.1108/09600030810882816

Carvalho, N., Chaim, O., Cazarini, E., & Gerolamo, M. (2018). Manufacturing in the fourth industrial revolution: A positive prospect in sustainable manufacturing. *Procedia Manufacturing*, *21*, 671–678. DOI: 10.1016/j.promfg.2018.02.170

Cetindamar, D., Shdifat, B., & Erfani, S. (2020). Assessing big data analytics capability and sustainability in supply chains.

Céu, M. S., & Gaspar, R. M. (2024). *A Review on Climate Change, Credit Risk, and Agriculture*. Rural Sustainability Research. [DOI:10.2478/plua-2024-0004]

Chang, C. W., & Chang, S. H. (2023). The Impact of Digital Disruption: Influences of Digital Media and Social Networks on Forming Digital Natives' Attitude. *SAGE Open*, *13*(3), 21582440231191741. DOI: 10.1177/21582440231191741

Chardine-Baumann, E., & Botta-Genoulaz, V. (2014). A framework for sustainable performance assessment of supply chain management practices. *Computers & Industrial Engineering*, *76*, 138–147. DOI: 10.1016/j.cie.2014.07.029

Charles, A. N., Akinyemi, O. V., & Blessing, C. (2023). Leveraging Artificial Intelligence and Communication Strategies to Optimize Supply Chains, Marketing Performance, and Customer-Centric Business Decision Making. *Communication In Physical Sciences*, *9*(4), 1101–1118.

Chatterjee, S., & Bose, A. (2021). Digital Transformation in Agriculture: The Impact of Blockchain and AI. *World Economic Forum.*

Chaudhary, J., Shelar, R., Thakur, K., & Singh, R. (2023). Millets in India: Production, Consumption and Impact on Food Security. Asian Journal of Agricultural Extension. *Economia e Sociologia*, *41*(8), 151–162.

Chen, H., Chiang, R. H., & Storey, V. C. (2012). Business intelligence and analytics: From big data to big impact. *Management Information Systems Quarterly*, *36*(4), 1165–1188. DOI: 10.2307/41703503

Chen, J., Guo, F., & Wang, W. (2018). Mobile health applications and their influence on healthy eating behaviour: A systematic review. *JMIR Health and Health*, *6*(10), e12379.

Chen, Q., & Zhang, N. (2015). Does e-commerce provide a sustained competitive advantage? An investigation of survival and sustainability in growth-oriented enterprises. *Sustainability (Basel)*, *7*(2), 1411–1428. DOI: 10.3390/su7021411

Choi, T. M., Wallace, S. W., & Wang, Y. (2017). Big data analytics in operations management. *Production and Operations Management*, *27*(10), 1868–1881. DOI: 10.1111/poms.12838 PMID: 26766385

Choi, T.-M., Dolgui, A., Li, G., Sethi, S. P., & Yue, X. (2023). Special issue: Advancing supply chain resilience for excellence in the post-pandemic era. *Frontiers of Engineering Management*, *10*(1), 1–4. DOI: 10.1007/s42524-022-0246-9

Chopra, S., & Meindl, P. (2021). Supply Chain Management STRATEGY, PLANNING, AND OPERATION (5th ed.). Pearson.

Chopra, S., Gupta, R., & Mehra, R. (2022). Role of personalized nutrition apps in promoting healthier food choices among digital natives. *Health Informatics Journal*, *28*(3), 1–14.

Chowdhury, M. M. H., & Quaddus, M. (2016). Supply chain readiness, response and recovery for resilience. *Supply Chain Management, 21*(6), 709–731. DOI: 10.1108/SCM-12-2015-0463

Christopher, M. (2016). Logistics & Supply Chain Management. Pearson Education.

Christopher, M. (2016). Logistics and Supply Chain Management: Logistics & Supply Chain Management. Pearson UK.

Churchill, C. (2006). *Protecting the Poor: A Microinsurance Compendium.* International Labour Organization.

Colehower, J. (2023). Using Technology to Improve Supply-Chain Resilience. *Harvard Business Review.*

Cole, R., Stevenson, M., & Aitken, J. (2019). Blockchain technology: Implications for operations and supply chain management. *Supply Chain Management, 24*(4), 469–483. Advance online publication. DOI: 10.1108/SCM-09-2018-0309

Cosma, S., & Rimo, G. (2024). Redefining insurance through technology: Achievements and perspectives in Insurtech. *Research in International Business and Finance, 70,* 102301. DOI: 10.1016/j.ribaf.2024.102301

Coulibaly, A., Kouakou, B., & Chen Jie, C. J. (2011). Phytic acid in cereal grains: structure, healthy or harmful ways to reduce phytic acid in cereal grains and their effects on nutritional quality.

Daios, A., Kladovasilakis, N., Kelemis, A., & Kostavelis, I. (2025). AI applications in supply chain management: A survey. *Applied Sciences (Basel, Switzerland), 15*(5), 2775. DOI: 10.3390/app15052775

Dash, R., McMurtrey, M., Rebman, C., & Kar, U. (2019). Application of Artificial Intelligence in Automation of Supply Chain Management. Journal of Strategic Innovation and Sustainability. https://doi.org/.DOI: 10.33423/jsis.v14i3.2105

Dash, R., McMurtrey, M., Rebman, C., & Kar, U. K. (2019). Application of artificial intelligence in automation of supply chain management. *Journal of strategic innovation and sustainability, 14*(3), 43-53.

Das, M. (2020). *Overcoming Financial Barriers in Sustainable Agriculture. Organisation for Economic Co-operation and Development.* OECD.

Dauvergne, P. (2022). Is artificial intelligence greening global supply chains? Exposing the political economy of environmental costs. *Review of International Political Economy, 29*(3), 696–718. DOI: 10.1080/09692290.2020.1814381

De Leeuw, J., Vrieling, A., Shee, A., Atzberger, C., Hadgu, K. M., Biradar, C. M., Keah, H., & Turvey, C. (2014). The potential and uptake of remote sensing in insurance: A review. *Remote Sensing (Basel)*, *6*(11), 10888–10912. DOI: 10.3390/rs61110888

Delfmann, W., Albers, S., & Gehring, M. (2002). The impact of electronic commerce on logistics service providers. *International Journal of Physical Distribution & Logistics Management*, *32*(3), 203–222. DOI: 10.1108/09600030210426539

Deloitte. (2020). *The Future of AI in Insurance: Transforming Underwriting and Claims Processing*. Deloitte Insights.

Devineni, S. K. (2024). AI in data privacy and security. [IJAIML]. *International Journal of Artificial Intelligence and Machine Learning*, *3*(01), 35–49.

Diabat, A., Govindan, K., & Panicker, V. V. (2012). Supply chain risk management and its mitigation in a food industry. *International Journal of Production Research*, *50*(11), 3039–3050. DOI: 10.1080/00207543.2011.588619

Donthu, N., Kumar, S., Pattnaik, D., & Lim, W. M. (2021). A Bibliometric Review of Research on Artificial Intelligence Applications in Business. *Journal of Business Research*, *123*, 389–404.

Donthu, N., Kumar, S., Pattnaik, D., & Lim, W. M. (2021). AI in Insurance: Reducing Fraud and Optimizing Supply Chains. *Journal of Financial Services Marketing*, *26*(3), 345–362.

Draycott, S. G., & Kline, P. (1994). Further investigation into the nature of the BIP: A factor analysis of the BIP with primary abilities. *Personality and Individual Differences*, *17*(2), 201–209. DOI: 10.1016/0191-8869(94)90026-4

Druehl, J. C., & Hsuan, J. (2018). *Technological Innovations: Impacts on Supply Chains. Burgess, The Executive Guide to Artificial Intelligence*. Springer International Publishing., DOI: 10.1007/978-3-319-63820-1

Dubey, R., Gunasekaran, A., Childe, S. J., Papadopoulos, T., Blome, C., & Luo, Z. (2017). Antecedents of resilient supply chains: An empirical study. *IEEE Transactions on Engineering Management*, *66*(1), 8–19. DOI: 10.1109/TEM.2017.2723042

Dubey, R., Gunasekaran, A., Papadopoulos, T., Childe, S. J., Shibin, K. T., & Wamba, S. F. (2017). Sustainable supply chain management: Framework and further research directions. *Journal of Cleaner Production*, *142*, 1119–1130. DOI: 10.1016/j.jclepro.2016.03.117

Dutta, P., Suryawanshi, P., Gujarathi, P., & Dutta, A. (2019). Managing risk for e-commerce supply chains: An empirical study. *IFAC-PapersOnLine*, *52*(13), 349–354. DOI: 10.1016/j.ifacol.2019.11.143

Elkington, J. (1997). *Cannibals with Forks: The Triple Bottom Line of 21st Century Business*. Capstone Publishing.

Ellaturu, V., & Rajalakshmi, L. (2024). Ai-Driven Solutions for Supply Chain Management. *Journal of Informatics Education and Research*. https://doi.org/.DOI: 10.52783/jier.v4i2.849

Enyejo, J. O., Adeyemi, A. F., Olola, T. M., Igba, E., & Obani, O. Q. (2024). Resilience in supply chains: How technology is helping USA companies navigate disruptions. *Magna Scientia Advanced Research and Reviews*, *11*(2), 261–277. DOI: 10.30574/msarr.2024.11.2.0129

Esan, O., Ajayi, F. A., & Olawale, O. (2024). Supply chain integrating sustainability and ethics: Strategies for modern supply chain management. *World Journal of Advanced Research and Reviews*, *22*(1), 1930–1953. DOI: 10.30574/wjarr.2024.22.1.1259

Esfahbodi, A., & Zhang, Y. (2020). Sustainable supply chain management in developed vs. Emerging economies: Evidence from the UK and China's manufacturing industry. In *Encyclopedia of Renewable and Sustainable Materials* (pp. 537–549). Elsevier. DOI: 10.1016/B978-0-12-803581-8.11506-1

Esfahbodi, A., Zhang, Y., & Watson, G. (2016). Sustainable supply chain management in emerging economies: Trade-offs between environmental and cost performance. *International Journal of Production Economics*, *181*, 350–366. DOI: 10.1016/j.ijpe.2016.02.013

Eshun, B. T. B., Chan, A. P., & Osei-Kyei, R. (2021). Conceptualizing a win–win scenario in public–private partnerships: Evidence from a systematic literature review. *Engineering, Construction, and Architectural Management*, *28*(9), 2712–2735. DOI: 10.1108/ECAM-07-2020-0533

Espiñeira, M., & Santaclara, F. J. (Eds.). (2016). *Advances in food traceability techniques and technologies: improving quality throughout the food chain*. Woodhead Publishing.

Faggioni, F., Rossi, M. V., & Sestino, A. (2024). Conceptualizing supply chain resilience in exogenous crisis times: Toward a holistic definition. *Journal of the Knowledge Economy*, *15*(4), 17308–17332. Advance online publication. DOI: 10.1007/s13132-024-01816-0

FAO. (2021). *Regenerative Agriculture for Climate Resilience*. Food and Agriculture Organization.

Farooq, M., & Yen, Y. Y. (2024). Artificial Intelligence in Supply Chain Management: A Comprehensive Review and Framework for Resilience and Sustainability.

Faugere, L., & Montreuil, B. (2016, June). Hyperconnected city logistics: smart lockers terminals & last mile delivery networks. In *Proceedings of the 3rd International Physical Internet Conference,* Atlanta, GA, USA (Vol. 29, p. 5).

Feyen, E., Lester, R., & Rocha, R. (2021). *The Digital Transformation of Microinsurance*. World Bank Publications.

Finkenstadt, D. J., & Handfield, R. (2021). Blurry vision: Supply chain visibility for personal protective equipment during COVID-19. *Journal of Purchasing and Supply Management*, *27*(3), 100689. DOI: 10.1016/j.pursup.2021.100689

Food and Agriculture Organization (FAO). (2020). [*Overcoming Water Challenges in Agriculture*. FAO, Rome. Retrieved from https://www.fao.org/publications]. *The State of Food and Agriculture, 2020,* •••.

Fosso Wamba, S., & Akter, S. (2015). Big data analytics for supply chain management: A literature review and research agenda. In Enterprise and Organizational Modeling and Simulation: 11th International Workshop, EOMAS 2015, Held at CAiSE 2015, Stockholm, Sweden, June 8-9, 2015, Selected Papers 11 (pp. 61-72). Springer International Publishing. DOI: 10.1007/978-3-319-24626-0_5

Gadanakis, Y. (2024). Advancing Farm Entrepreneurship and Agribusiness Management for Sustainable Agriculture. *Agriculture*, *14*(8), 1288. DOI: 10.3390/agriculture14081288

Gandomi, A., & Haider, M. (2015). Beyond the hype: Big data concepts, methods, and analytics. *International Journal of Information Management*, *35*(2), 137–144. DOI: 10.1016/j.ijinfomgt.2014.10.007

Ganeshkumar, C., Jena, S. K., Sivakumar, A., & Nambirajan, T. (2023). Artificial intelligence in agricultural value chain: Review and future directions. *Journal of Agribusiness in Developing and Emerging Economies*, *13*(3), 379–398. DOI: 10.1108/JADEE-07-2020-0140

Gebauer, H., & Reynoso, J. (2013). An agenda for service research at the base of the pyramid. *Journal of Service Management*, *24*(5), 482–502. DOI: 10.1108/JOSM-04-2013-0090

Gebrekidan, B. H., Agaba, M., & Dhehibi, B. Adoption of Climate-Smart Agricultural Technologies and Practices in Fragile and Conflict-Affected Settings: A Review and Meta-Analysis.

Geng, R., Mansouri, S. A., Aktas, E., & Yen, D. A. (2017). The role of Guanxi in green supply chain management in Asia's emerging economies: A conceptual framework. *Industrial Marketing Management, 63*, 1–17. DOI: 10.1016/j.indmarman.2017.01.002

George, A. S. (2025). Advancements in Artificial Intelligence for Industrial Robotics and Intelligent Drones: A Comprehensive Review. *Partners Universal Innovative Research Publication, 3*(1), 44–51.

Gereffi, G., Humphrey, J., & Sturgeon, T. (2022). The digital transformation of global value chains: Implications for food security and sustainability. *World Development, 154*, 105896.

Geron, Llanto, & Badiola. (2016). *Financial Inclusion in Agricultural Credit: A Demand and Supply Perspective*. Philippine Journal of Public Policy

Gharbaoui, O., Boukhari, H., & Mazouz, Y. (2024). Analyzing the evolution of artificial intelligence (AI) in supply chain management: a bibliometric analysis. *2024 International Conference on Circuit, Systems and Communication (ICCSC)*, 1-7. https://doi.org/DOI: 10.1109/ICCSC62074.2024.10617358

Giglio, F. (2020). Access to Credit and Women Entrepreneurs: A Systematic Literature Review. *European Research Studies Journal, 23*(4), 312–335

Giovanni, P. (2020). Blockchain and smart contracts in supply chain management: A game theoretic model. *International Journal of Production Economics, 228*, 107855. DOI: 10.1016/j.ijpe.2020.107855

Goul, M., Henderson, J. C., & Tonge, F. M. (1992). The emergence of artificial intelligence as a reference discipline for decision support systems research. *Decision Sciences, 23*(6), 1263–1276. DOI: 10.1111/j.1540-5915.1992.tb00448.x

Govindan, K., Soleimani, H., & Kannan, D. (2015). Reverse logistics and closed-loop supply chain: A comprehensive review to explore the future. *European Journal of Operational Research, 240*(3), 603–626. DOI: 10.1016/j.ejor.2014.07.012

Govindan, , Rajendran, S., Sarkis, J., & Murugesan, P. (2014). Multi criteria decision making approaches for green supplier evaluation and selection: A literature review. *Journal of Cleaner Production, 98*, 66–83. DOI: 10.1016/j.jclepro.2013.06.046

GSMA. (2021). *AI and Mobile-Based Insurance in Emerging Markets*. GSMA Research.

Gubbi, J., Buyya, R., Marusic, S., & Palaniswami, M. (2013). Internet of Things (IoT): A vision, architectural elements, and future directions. *Future Generation Computer Systems*, *29*(7), 1645–1660. DOI: 10.1016/j.future.2013.01.010

Hansen, T., Sørensen, M. I., & Eriksen, M. L. R. (2018). Understanding consumer values and behavior towards organic food through social media analytics. *Journal of Retailing and Consumer Services*, *42*, 110–120.

Hassan, A., Bhattacharya, P., Dutta, P. K., Verma, J. P., & Kundu, N. K. (Eds.). (2024). *Quantum computing and supply chain management: A new era of optimization: A new era of optimization*. IGI Global.

Hobbs, J. E. (2020). Food supply chains during the COVID-19 pandemic. *Canadian Journal of Agricultural Economics/Revue canadienne d'agroeconomie, 68*(2), 171-176.

Hua, W., & Jing, Z. (2015). An empirical study on e-commerce logistic service quality and customer satisfaction. *WHICEB Proceedings*, 269–275.

Hugos, M. H. (2018). *Essentials of Supply Chain Management*. Wiley. DOI: 10.1002/9781119464495

Ivanov, D., Dolgui, A., & Sokolov, B. (2019). The impact of digital technology and Industry 4.0 on the ripple effect and supply chain risk analytics. *International Journal of Production Research*, *57*(3), 829–846. DOI: 10.1080/00207543.2018.1488086

Iyer, S. (2019). *Policy Interventions for Sustainable Agricultural Development. Food and Agriculture Organization*. FAO.

Jacobs, R., & Chase, R. (2018). *Operations and Supply Chain Management* (15th ed.). The McGraw-Hill Education.

Jaiswal, A., Negi, P., & Singh, N. (2024). Emerging Paradigms in Sustainable Supply Chain Management: A Comparative Study of Pre–and Post–COVID-19 Research Trends. *Abhigyan*, *42*(1), 32–42. DOI: 10.1177/09702385241233077

Janjevic, M., & Winkenbach, M. (2020). Characterizing urban last-mile distribution strategies in mature and emerging e-commerce markets. *Transportation Research Part A, Policy and Practice*, *133*, 164–196. DOI: 10.1016/j.tra.2020.01.003

Jarvenpaa, S. L., & Todd, P. A. (1996). Consumer reactions to electronic shopping on the World Wide Web. *International Journal of Electronic Commerce*, *1*(2), 59–88. DOI: 10.1080/10864415.1996.11518283

Javed, M. K., & Wu, M. (2020). Effects of online retailer after delivery services on repurchase intention: An empirical analysis of customers' past experience and future confidence with the retailer. *Journal of Retailing and Consumer Services, 54*, 101942. DOI: 10.1016/j.jretconser.2019.101942

Jeble, A., et al. (2018). Big Data Analytics in Supply Chain Management. International Journal of Advanced Operations Management.

Joel, O. S., Oyewole, A. T., Odunaiya, O. G., & Soyombo, O. T. Leveraging artificial intelligence for enhanced supply chain optimization: A comprehensive review of current practices and future potentials, International Journal of Management & Entrepreneurship Research P-ISSN: 2664-3588, E-ISSN: 2664-3596 Volume 6, Issue 3, P.No.707-721, March 2024 DOI: DOI: 10.51594/ijmer.v6i3.882

Joong-Kun Cho, J., Ozment, J., & Sink, H. (2008). Logistics capability, logistics outsourcing and firm performance in an e-commerce market. *International Journal of Physical Distribution & Logistics Management, 38*(5), 336–359. DOI: 10.1108/09600030810882825

Joshi, S., & Sharma, M. (2023). Assessment of implementation barriers of blockchain technology in public healthcare: Evidences from developing countries. *Health Systems (Basingstoke, England), 12*(2), 223–242. DOI: 10.1080/20476965.2023.2206446 PMID: 37234469

Kalfin, S., Sukono, , Supian, S., & Mamat, M. (2022). Insurance as an alternative for sustainable economic recovery after natural disasters: A systematic literature review. *Sustainability (Basel), 14*(7), 4349. DOI: 10.3390/su14074349

Kamble, S. S., Gunasekaran, A., & Sharma, R. (2020). Modeling the blockchain enabled traceability in agriculture supply chain. *International Journal of Information Management, 52*, 101967. DOI: 10.1016/j.ijinfomgt.2019.05.023

Kannan, D.. (2014). Role of stakeholder pressure and knowledge management in sustainable supply chain management: Empirical evidence from the Indian cement industry. *International Journal of Production Economics, 171*, 160–172.

Kapoor, D. (2020). The Social Impact of Sustainable Agriculture on Rural Communities. *World Bank Report.*

Kapoor, K. K., & Dwivedi, Y. K. (2022). Consumer engagement in digital food marketing: A review and research agenda. *Journal of Business Research, 146*, 187–202.

Kar, A. K., & Navin, L. (2021). Diffusion of blockchain in insurance industry: An analysis through the review of academic and trade literature. *Telematics and Informatics, 58*, 101532. DOI: 10.1016/j.tele.2020.101532

Kareem, S., Fehrer, J. A., Shalpegin, T., & Stringer, C. (2025). Navigating tensions of sustainable supply chains in times of multiple crises: A systematic literature review. *Business Strategy and the Environment, 34*(1), 316–337. DOI: 10.1002/bse.3990

Karmaker, C. L., Bari, A. M., Anam, M. Z., Ahmed, T., Ali, S. M., de Jesus Pacheco, D. A., & Moktadir, M. A. (2023). Industry 5.0 challenges for post-pandemic supply chain sustainability in an emerging economy. *International Journal of Production Economics, 258*, 108806. DOI: 10.1016/j.ijpe.2023.108806

Kassa, A., Kitaw, D., Stache, U., Beshah, B., & Degefu, G. (2023). Artificial intelligence techniques for enhancing supply chain resilience: A systematic literature review, holistic framework, and future research. *Computers & Industrial Engineering, 186*, 109714. DOI: 10.1016/j.cie.2023.109714

Kaswengi, J., & Lambey-Checchin, C. (2020). How logistics service quality and product quality matter in the retailer–customer relationship of food drive-throughs: The role of perceived convenience. *International Journal of Physical Distribution & Logistics Management, 50*(5), 535–555. DOI: 10.1108/IJPDLM-01-2019-0036

Kawa, A. (2020). Out-of-Home Delivery as a Solution of the Last Mile Problem in E-commerce. *Smart and Sustainable Supply Chain and Logistics–Trends, Challenges. Methods and Best Practices, 1*, 25–40.

Kawa, A., & Światowiec-Szczepańska, J. (2021). Logistics as a value in e-commerce and its influence on satisfaction in industries: A multilevel analysis. *Journal of Business and Industrial Marketing, 36*(13), 220–235. DOI: 10.1108/JBIM-09-2020-0429

Kazancoglu, I., Ozbiltekin-Pala, M., Mangla, S. K., Kumar, A., & Kazancoglu, Y. (2023). Using emerging technologies to improve the sustainability and resilience of supply chains in a fuzzy environment in the context of COVID-19. *Annals of Operations Research, 322*(1), 217–240. DOI: 10.1007/s10479-022-04775-4 PMID: 35789688

Kim, D., Cavusgil, S. T., & Cavusgil, E. (2013). Does IT alignment between supply chain partners enhance customer value creation? An empirical investigation. *Industrial Marketing Management, 42*(6), 880–889. DOI: 10.1016/j.indmarman.2013.05.021

Korepin, V., Dzenzeliuk, N., Seryshev, R., & Rogulin, R. (2021). Improving supply chain reliability with blockchain technology. *Maritime Economics & Logistics*. Advance online publication. DOI: 10.1057/s41278-021-00197-4

Kosasih, E., Papadakis, E., Baryannis, G., & Brintrup, A. (2023). A review of explainable artificial intelligence in supply chain management using neurosymbolic approaches. *International Journal of Production Research*, *62*(4), 1510–1540. DOI: 10.1080/00207543.2023.2281663

Koufteros, X., Droge, C., Heim, G., Massad, N., & Vickery, S. K. (2014). Encounter satisfaction in e-tailing: Are the relationships of order fulfillment service quality with its antecedents and consequences moderated by historical satisfaction? *Decision Sciences*, *45*(1), 5–48. DOI: 10.1111/deci.12056

Kouhizadeh, M., & Sarkis, J. (2018). Blockchain practices, potentials, and perspectives in greening supply chains. *Sustainability (Basel)*, *10*(10), 3652. DOI: 10.3390/su10103652

Krishnan, R., Arshinder, K., & Agarwal, R. (2022). Robust optimization of sustainable food supply chain network considering food waste valorization and supply uncertainty. *Computers & Industrial Engineering*, *171*, 108499. DOI: 10.1016/j.cie.2022.108499

Kshetri, N. (2018). Blockchain's roles in meeting key supply chain management objectives. *International Journal of Information Management*, *39*, 80–89. DOI: 10.1016/j.ijinfomgt.2017.12.005

Kumar, R. (2020). Sustainable Agricultural Practices and Supply Chain Efficiency. *Food and Agriculture Organization (FAO).*

Kumar, A. (2019). Exploring young adults'e-waste recycling behaviour using an extended theory of planned behaviour model: A cross-cultural study. *Resources, Conservation and Recycling*, *141*, 378–389. DOI: 10.1016/j.resconrec.2018.10.013

Kumar, A., Singh, R. K., & Shankar, R. (2020). Value chain strategies for the sustainability of millets: A systematic review. *Agricultural Systems*, *178*, 102740.

Laaper, S. F. (2017). Using blockchain to drive supply chain innovation. London, UK: Deloitte.

Liu, W., He, Y., Dong, J., & Cao, Y. (2023). Disruptive technologies for advancing supply chain resilience. *Frontiers of Engineering Management*, *10*(2), 360–366. DOI: 10.1007/s42524-023-0257-1

Liu, X., He, M., Gao, F., & Xie, P. (2008). An empirical study of online shopping customer satisfaction in China: A holistic perspective. *International Journal of Retail & Distribution Management*, *36*(11), 919–940. DOI: 10.1108/09590550810911683

Liu, Z., Wang, S., Zhang, Y., Feng, Y., Liu, J., & Zhu, H. (2023). Artificial intelligence in food safety: A decade review and bibliometric analysis. *Foods*, *12*(6), 1242. DOI: 10.3390/foods12061242 PMID: 36981168

Lloyd's. (2018). Insuring the Frontier: The Role of Insurance in Emerging Markets. Lloyd's of London.

Luthra, S.. (2016). Barriers to industrial symbiosis in Indian firms: A TISM approach. *Journal of Cleaner Production*, *148*, 141–157.

Luthra, S., & Mangla, S. K. (2018). When strategies matter: Adoption of sustainable supply chain management practices in an emerging economy's context. *Resources, Conservation and Recycling*, *138*, 194–206. DOI: 10.1016/j.resconrec.2018.07.005

Mani, V., Gunasekaran, A., & Delgado, C. (2018). Enhancing supply chain performance through supplier social sustainability: An emerging economy perspective. *International Journal of Production Economics*, *195*, 259–272. DOI: 10.1016/j.ijpe.2017.10.025

Mathiyazhagan, K., Majumdar, A., & Appolloni, A. (2023). Guest editorial: Resilience in sustainable supply chain post-COVID-19: future pathways. *International Journal of Logistics Management*, *34*(4), 873–878. DOI: 10.1108/IJLM-07-2023-603

McAfee, A., & Brynjolfsson, E. (2012). Big data: The management revolution. *Harvard Business Review*, *90*(10), 60–68. PMID: 23074865

McKinsey. (2022). *The Role of AI in Fraud Detection and Claims Processing*. McKinsey Insights.

Mennella, C., Maniscalco, U., De Pietro, G., & Esposito, M. (2024). Ethical and regulatory challenges of AI technologies in healthcare: A narrative review. *Heliyon*, *10*(4), e26297. DOI: 10.1016/j.heliyon.2024.e26297

Menon, R. (2020). *The Need for Training and Capacity Building in Agri-Entrepreneurship. United Nations Environment Programme*. UNEP.

Mentzer, J. T., Flint, D. J., & Hult, G. T. M. (2001). Logistics service quality as a segment-customized process. *Journal of Marketing*, *65*(4), 82–104. DOI: 10.1509/jmkg.65.4.82.18390

Mentzer, J. T., Rutner, S. M., & Matsuno, K. (1997). Application of the means-end value hierarchy model to understanding logistics service value. *International Journal of Physical Distribution & Logistics Management*, *27*(9/10), 630–643. DOI: 10.1108/09600039710188693

Messina, D., Soares, A. L., Barros, A. C., & Zimmermann, R. (2023). How visible is your supply chain? A model for supply chain visibility assessment. In Supply Chain Forum [). Taylor & Francis.]. *International Journal (Toronto, Ont.), 24*(4), 462–474.

Mills, C. (2022). The Role of AI in Optimizing Insurance Supply Chains. *Insurance & Technology Journal, 18*(2), 45–62.

Mishra, D., Gunasekaran, A., Papadopoulos, T., & Childe, S. J. (2018). Big Data and supply chain management: A review and bibliometric analysis. *Annals of Operations Research, 270*(1-2), 313–336. DOI: 10.1007/s10479-016-2236-y

Moagar-Poladian, S., Dumitrescu, G. C., & Tanase, I. A. (2017). Retail e-Commerce (E-tail)-evolution, characteristics and perspectives in China, the USA and Europe. *Global Economic Observer, 5*(1), 167.

Moktadir, M. A., Rahman, T., Rahman, M. H., Ali, S. M., & Paul, S. K. (2018). Drivers to sustainable manufacturing practices and circular economy: A perspective of leather industries in Bangladesh. *Journal of Cleaner Production, 174*, 1366–180. DOI: 10.1016/j.jclepro.2017.11.063

Moosavi, J., Naeni, L., Fathollahi-Fard, A., & Fiore, U. (2021). Blockchain in supply chain management: a review, bibliometric, and network analysis. Environmental Science and Pollution Research, 1 - 15. https://doi.org/.DOI: 10.1007/s11356-021-13094-3

Mugoni, E., Kanyepe, J., & Tukuta, M. (2024). Sustainable Supply Chain Management Practices (SSCMPS) and environmental performance: A systematic review. *Sustainable Technology and Entrepreneurship, 3*(1), 100050. DOI: 10.1016/j.stae.2023.100050

Mun, J., Housel, T., Jones, R., Carlton, B., & Skots, V. (2020). Acquiring artificial intelligence systems: Development challenges, implementation risks, and cost/benefits opportunities. *Naval Engineers Journal, 132*(2), 79–94.

Nagurney, A., Zhang, D. and Zhang, D. (2021). Artificial intelligence and supply chain management: A comprehensive literature review and research agenda. Journal of Business Research. Journal of Business Research, 130, pp.392–402., pp. 392–402.

Nambela, N. (2020). *The impact of adopting sustainable supply chain management practices on the performance of public sector organisations in Zambia: A case study of Zambia Air force (ZAF).*

Nasaruddin, F., Gani, A., Karim, A., Hashem, I., Siddiqa, A., & Yaqoob, I. (2017). Big IoT Data Analytics: Architecture, Opportunities, and Open Research Challenges. *IEEE Access : Practical Innovations, Open Solutions*, *5*, 5247–5261. DOI: 10.1109/ACCESS.2017.2689040

Nasir, M. S., & Butt, S. A. (2025). The Role of Supplier Relationship Management in Reducing Operational Risks. *Economic Trends and Business Review*, *3*(1), 34–49.

Naz, F., Kumar, A., Majumdar, A., & Agrawal, R. (2022). Is artificial intelligence an enabler of supply chain resiliency post COVID-19? An exploratory state-of-the-art review for future research. *Operations Management Research : Advancing Practice Through Research*, *15*(1), 378–398. DOI: 10.1007/s12063-021-00208-w

Nsisong Louis Eyo-Udo. (2024). Leveraging artificial intelligence for enhanced supply chain optimization. *Open Access Research Journal of Multidisciplinary Studies*. https://doi.org/.DOI: 10.53022/oarjms.2024.7.2.0044

Nweje, U., & Taiwo, M. (2025). Leveraging Artificial Intelligence for predictive supply chain management, focus on how AI-driven tools are revolutionizing demand forecasting and inventory optimization. *International Journal of Science and Research Archive*, *14*(1), 230–250. DOI: 10.30574/ijsra.2025.14.1.0027

Odulaja, B. A., Oke, T. T., Eleogu, T., Abdul, A. A., & Daraojimba, H. O. (2023). Resilience in the face of uncertainty: A review on the impact of supply chain volatility amid ongoing Geopolitical Disruptions. *International Journal of Applied Research in Social Sciences*, *5*(10), 463–486. DOI: 10.51594/ijarss.v5i10.634

OECD. (2021). *Sustainable Agriculture and Market Access: Global Trends and Challenges*. Organization for Economic Co-operation and Development.

Pagell, M., & Wu, Z. (2009). Building a more complete theory of sustainable supply chain management using case studies of 10 exemplars. *The Journal of Supply Chain Management*, *45*(2), 37–56. DOI: 10.1111/j.1745-493X.2009.03162.x

Pakdeechoho, N., & Sukhotu, V. (2018). Sustainable supply chain collaboration: Incentives in emerging economies. *Journal of Manufacturing Technology Management*, *29*(2), 273–294. DOI: 10.1108/JMTM-05-2017-0081

Palazzo, M., & Vollero, A. (2022). A systematic literature review of food sustainable supply chain management (FSSCM): Building blocks and research trends. *The TQM Journal*, *34*(7), 54–72. DOI: 10.1108/TQM-10-2021-0300

Parkhi, S., Joshi, S., Gupta, S., & Sharma, M. (2015). A Study of Evolution and Future of Supply Chain Management. *AIMS International Journal of Management*, *9*(2), 95–106.

Patalas-Maliszewska, J., Szmołda, M., & Łosyk, H. (2024). Integrating Artificial Intelligence into the Supply Chain in Order to Enhance Sustainable Production—A Systematic Literature Review. *Sustainability (Basel)*, *16*(16), 7110. Advance online publication. DOI: 10.3390/su16167110

Patel, S., Kumar, N., & Sharma, P. (2022). Digital advisory services for smallholder farmers: Opportunities and challenges. *Agricultural Systems*, *198*, 103376.

Phan, V. D. V., Huang, Y. F., Hoang, T. T., & Do, M. H. (2023). Evaluating barriers to supply chain resilience in vietnamese SMEs: The fuzzy VIKOR approach. *Systems*, *11*(3), 121. DOI: 10.3390/systems11030121

Polo, L. (2025). A Supply Chain Approach Highlighting the Use of Artificial Intelligence and Computer Vision to Improve the Efficiency of Food Supply Chains in the United States. *International Journal for Multidisciplinary Research*, *7*(2), 1–24.

Porwal, A., Bhagwat, G., Sawarkar, J., & Kamble, P. (2023). An overview of millets-the nutri-cereals: Its nutritional profile, potential health benefits, and sustainable cultivation approach. *International Journal of Science and Research Archive*, *10*(1), 841–859. DOI: 10.30574/ijsra.2023.10.1.0828

Pournader, M., Shi, Y., Seuring, S., & Koh, S. (2019). Blockchain applications in supply chains, transport and logistics: A systematic review of the literature. *International Journal of Production Research*, *58*(7), 2063–2081. DOI: 10.1080/00207543.2019.1650976

Prasad, H. (2020). *Financial Strategies for Sustainable Agri-Startups. International Monetary Fund*. IMF.

Qader, G., Junaid, M., Abbas, Q., & Mubarik, M. S. (2022). Industry 4.0 enables supply chain resilience and supply chain performance. *Technological Forecasting and Social Change*, *185*, 122026. DOI: 10.1016/j.techfore.2022.122026

Radhakrishnan, G. V., Gabhane, M., Jha, S., Al Said, N., & Murthy, B. S. R.G V Radhakrishnan. (2025). AI and IOT in supply chains: Creating intelligent and autonomous business operations. *Journal of Information Systems Engineering & Management*, *10*(11s), 625–632. DOI: 10.52783/jisem.v10i11s.1664

Rajeev, A., Pati, R. K., Padhi, S. S., & Govindan, K. (2017). Evolution of sustainability in supply chain management: A literature review. *Journal of Cleaner Production*, *162*, 299–314. DOI: 10.1016/j.jclepro.2017.05.026

Rao, P., & Holt, D. (2005). Do green supply chains lead to competitiveness and economic performance? *International Journal of Operations & Production Management*, *25*(9), 898–916. DOI: 10.1108/01443570510613956

Rejeb, A., Rejeb, K., Abdollahi, A., Zailani, S., Iranmanesh, M., & Ghobakhloo, M. (2021). Digitalization in food supply chains: A bibliometric review and key-route main path analysis. *Sustainability (Basel)*, *14*(1), 83. DOI: 10.3390/su14010083

Rha, J. S. (2020). Trends of research on supply chain resilience: A systematic review using network analysis. *Sustainability (Basel)*, *12*(11), 4343. DOI: 10.3390/su12114343

Riad, M., Naimi, M., & Okar, C. (2024). Enhancing supply chain resilience through artificial intelligence: Developing a comprehensive conceptual framework for AI implementation and supply chain optimization. *Logistics (Basel)*, *8*(4), 111. DOI: 10.3390/logistics8040111

Rothgerber, H. (2020). A plant-based diet and health sustainability: The role of consumer attitudes. *Appetite*, *148*, 104617.

Saidi, D., Bassou, A. A., Alami, J. E. L., & Hlyal, M. (2024). Sustainability and resilience analysis in supply chain considering pricing policies and government economic measures. *International Journal of Advanced Computer Science and Applications*, *15*(1). Advance online publication. DOI: 10.14569/IJACSA.2024.0150127

Samuels, A. (2025). Digital transformation in supply chains: Improving resilience and sustainability through AI, Blockchain, and IoT. *Frontiers in Sustainability*, *6*(1584580), 1584580. Advance online publication. DOI: 10.3389/frsus.2025.1584580

Sánchez-Flores, R. B., Cruz-Sotelo, S. E., Ojeda-Benitez, S., & Ramírez-Barreto, M. E. (2020). Sustainable supply chain management—A literature review on emerging economies. *Sustainability (Basel)*, *12*(17), 6972. DOI: 10.3390/su12176972

Sandhu, N., & Hussain, Z. (2020). Labor Rights and Social Equity in Agricultural Supply Chains. *Journal of Agricultural Economics*.

Saridakis, G., Lai, Y., Mohammed, A. M., & Hansen, J. M. (2018). Industry characteristics, stages of E-commerce communications, and entrepreneurs and SMEs revenue growth. *Technological Forecasting and Social Change*, *128*, 56–66. DOI: 10.1016/j.techfore.2017.10.017

Sarkis, J., Zhu, Q., & Lai, K. (2011). An organizational theoretic review of green supply chain management literature. *International Journal of Production Economics*, *130*(1), 1–15. DOI: 10.1016/j.ijpe.2010.11.010

Sarma, M., & Pais, J. (2011). *Financial Inclusion and Agricultural Credit Access*. World Bank Reports.

Seow, R. (2023). Entrenching Supply Chain Resilience Beyond Boundaries: A Dynamic Framework in Post-Covid Landscape. [JTOM]. *Journal of Technology and Operations Management, 18*(2), 20–48. DOI: 10.32890/jtom2023.18.2.3

Seuring, S., & Müller, M. (2008). From a literature review to a conceptual framework for sustainable supply chain management. *Journal of Cleaner Production, 16*(15), 1699–1710. DOI: 10.1016/j.jclepro.2008.04.020

Seyedan, M., & Mafakheri, F. (2020). Predictive big data analytics for supply chain demand forecasting: Methods, applications, and research opportunities. *Journal of Big Data, 7*(1), 53. Advance online publication. DOI: 10.1186/s40537-020-00329-2

Shahzadi, G., Jia, F., Chen, L., & John, A. (2024). AI adoption in supply chain management: A systematic literature review. *Journal of Manufacturing Technology Management, 35*(6), 1125–1150. Advance online publication. DOI: 10.1108/JMTM-09-2023-0431

Shamsuzzoha, A., & Pelkonen, S. (2025). A robotic process automation model for order-handling optimization in supply chain management. *Supply Chain Analytics, 9*(100102), 100102. DOI: 10.1016/j.sca.2025.100102

Sharma, V., & Patel, A. (2021). *The Role of Fintech in Enhancing Agri-Entrepreneurship. United Nations Development Programme*. UNDP.

Shen, R., Zhou, F., Ye, X., Zhong, L., & Feng, S. (2024). Research on the application of artificial intelligence technology in supply chain management. *E3S Web of Conferences*. https://doi.org/.DOI: 10.1051/e3sconf/202456503017

Shil, S. K., Islam, M. R., & Pant, L. (2024). Optimizing US supply chains with AI: Reducing costs and improving efficiency. *International Journal of Advanced Engineering Technologies and Innovations, 2*(1), 223–247.

Shoomal, A., Jahanbakht, M., Componation, P. J., & Ozay, D. (2024). Enhancing supply chain resilience and efficiency through internet of things integration: Challenges and opportunities. *Internet of Things : Engineering Cyber Physical Human Systems, 27*, 101324. DOI: 10.1016/j.iot.2024.101324

Sikander, A. (2024). Artificial intelligence and the circular economy: How AI advances waste reduction. *Green Environmental Technology, 1*(2), 23–34.

Silvestre, B. S. (2015). Sustainable supply chain management in emerging economies: Environmental turbulence, institutional voids and sustainability trajectories. *International Journal of Production Economics, 167*, 156–169. DOI: 10.1016/j.ijpe.2015.05.025

Singh, C., Thakkar, R., & Warraich, J. (2022). Blockchain in Supply Chain Management. European Journal of Engineering and Technology Research. https://doi.org/.DOI: 10.24018/ejeng.2022.7.5.2888

Singh, P. (2019). Infrastructure Challenges in Rural Supply Chains. *World Bank Report.*

Singh, N., & Adhikari, D. (2023). Challenges and solutions in integrating AI with legacy inventory systems. *International Journal for Research in Applied Science and Engineering Technology*, *11*(12), 609–613. DOI: 10.22214/ijraset.2023.57376

Singh, P. K. K. (2024). Measuring the broader value proposition of digital transformation in supply chains. *International Journal of Supply Chain Management*, *13*(1), 16–24. DOI: 10.59160/ijscm.v13i1.6222

Singh, R. K.. (2021). Analysing the interaction of barriers in the adoption of sustainable supply chain management practices in MSMEs. *Journal of Cleaner Production*, ●●●, 281.

Singh, R., Modgil, S., & Shore, A. (2023). Building artificial intelligence enabled resilient supply chain: A multi-method approach. *Journal of Enterprise Information Management*, *37*(2), 414–436. DOI: 10.1108/JEIM-09-2022-0326

Singh, S., & Srivastava, S. (2019). Engaging consumers in multichannel online retail environment: A moderation study of platform type on interaction of e-commerce and m-commerce. *Journal of Modelling in Management*, *14*(1), 49–76. DOI: 10.1108/JM2-09-2017-0098

Sodiya, E. O., Umoga, U. J., Amoo, O. O., & Atadoga, A. (2024). AI-driven warehouse automation: A comprehensive review of systems. *GSC Advanced Research and Reviews*, *18*(2), 272–282. DOI: 10.30574/gscarr.2024.18.2.0063

Steegh, R., Van De Voorde, K., Paauwe, J., & Peeters, T. (2025). The agile way of working and team adaptive performance: A goal-setting perspective. *Journal of Business Research*, *189*, 115163.

Stevens, W. (2023). Robotic process automation in supply chain. *European Journal of Supply Chain Management*, *1*(1), 1–10.

Stiglitz, J., & Weiss, A. (1981). Credit Rationing in Markets with Imperfect Information. *The American Economic Review*.

Susatyono, J. D., Suasana, I. S., & Rozikin, K. (2024). Integrating Big Data and Edge Computing for Enhancing AI Efficiency in Real-Time Applications. *Journal of Technology Informatics and Engineering*, *3*(3), 337–349. DOI: 10.51903/jtie.v3i3.204

Tadesse, M., & Brans, J. P. (2012). Risk and Insurance in Developing Countries: A Study on Microinsurance. *The Journal of Risk and Insurance*, *79*(3), 811–835.

Talla, R. R. (2022). Integrating blockchain and ai to enhance supply chain transparency in energy sectors. *Asia Pacific Journal of Energy and Environment*, *9*(2), 109–118. DOI: 10.18034/apjee.v9i2.782

Taylor, P. (2023). Amount of data created, consumed, and stored 2010-2020, with forecasts to 2025. Statista. Available online: https://www. statista. com/statistics/871513/worldwide-data-created/(accessed on 24 October 2023).

Theeraworawit, M., Suriyankietkaew, S., & Hallinger, P. (2022). Sustainable supply chain management in a circular economy: A bibliometric review. *Sustainability (Basel)*, *14*(15), 9304. DOI: 10.3390/su14159304

Thomas, M. J., Veiga, M. M., Marshall, B. G., & Dunbar, W. S. (2019). Artisanal gold supply chain: Measures from the Ecuadorian Government. *Resources Policy*, *64*, 101505. DOI: 10.1016/j.resourpol.2019.101505

Toorajipour, R., Sohrabpour, V., Nazarpour, A., Oghazi, P., & Fischl, M. (2021). Artificial intelligence in supply chain management: A systematic literature review. *Journal of Business Research*, *122*, 502–517. Advance online publication. DOI: 10.1016/j.jbusres.2020.09.009

Touboulic, A., et al. (2015). Theories in sustainable supply chain management: A structured literature review. *International Journal of Physical Distribution & Logistics Management*, *45*(1\2), 16–42.

Tseng, Y. Y., Yue, W. L., & Taylor, M. A. (2005, January). The role of transportation in logistics chain. Eastern Asia Society for Transportation Studies.

Tsolakis, N. K., Keramydas, C. A., Toka, A. K., Aidonis, D. A., & Iakovou, E. T. (2014). Agrifood supply chain management: A comprehensive hierarchical decision-making framework and a critical taxonomy. *Biosystems Engineering*, *120*, 47–64. DOI: 10.1016/j.biosystemseng.2013.10.014

Ucar, A., Karakose, M., & Kırımça, N. (2024). Artificial intelligence for predictive maintenance applications: Key components, trustworthiness, and future trends. *Applied Sciences (Basel, Switzerland)*, *14*(2), 898. DOI: 10.3390/app14020898

Udeh, E. O., Amajuoyi, P., Adeusi, K. B., & Scott, A. O. (2024). The role of IoT in boosting supply chain transparency and efficiency. *Magna Scientia Adv. Res. Rev.*, *12*(1), 178–197. DOI: 10.30574/msarr.2024.11.1.0081

UNDP. (2021). *Sustainable Agriculture and Food Security: Empowering Rural Communities.*

Vadigicherla, M. S. (2024). Enhancing Supply Chain Resilience through Emerging Technologies: A Holistic Approach to Digital Transformation. *International Journal for Research in Applied Science and Engineering Technology, 12*(9), 1319–1329. DOI: 10.22214/ijraset.2024.64326

Vakulenko, Y., Shams, P., Hellström, D., & Hjort, K. (2019). Service innovation in e-commerce last mile delivery: Mapping the e-customer journey. *Journal of Business Research, 101*, 461–468. DOI: 10.1016/j.jbusres.2019.01.016

Van Hoek, R. (2001). The contribution of performance measurement to the expansion of third-party logistics alliances in the supply chain. *International Journal of Operations & Production Management, 21*(1), 15–29. DOI: 10.1108/01443570110358431

Villar, A., Paladini, S., & Buckley, O. (2023). Towards supply chain 5.0: Redesigning supply chains as resilient, sustainable, and human-centric systems in a post-pandemic world. *Operations Research Forum, 4*(3). https://doi.org/DOI: 10.1007/s43069-023-00234-3

Wakil, K., Alyari, F., Ghasvari, M., Lesani, Z., & Rajabion, L. (2020). A new model for assessing the role of customer behavior history, product classification, and prices on the success of the recommender systems in e-commerce. *Kybernetes, 49*(5), 1325–1346. DOI: 10.1108/K-03-2019-0199

Waldman, K. B., & Kerr, J. M. (2014). Limitations of Certification and Supply Chain Standards for Environmental Protection in Commodity Crop Production. *Annual Review of Resource Economics, 6*(1), 429–449. DOI: 10.1146/annurev-resource-100913-012432

Walker, H., & Jones, N. (2012). Sustainable supply chain management across the UK private sector. *Supply Chain Management, 17*(1), 15–28. DOI: 10.1108/13598541211212177

Waller, M. A., & Fawcett, S. E. (2013). Data science, predictive analytics, and big data: A revolution that will transform supply chain design and management. *Journal of Business Logistics, 34*(2), 77–84. DOI: 10.1111/jbl.12010

Wangsa, I. D., Vanany, I., & Siswanto, N. (2022). Issues in sustainable supply chain's futuristic technologies: A bibliometric and research trend analysis. *Environmental Science and Pollution Research International, 29*(16), 22885–22912. DOI: 10.1007/s11356-021-17805-8 PMID: 35064513

Weber, Y., & Tarba, S. Y. (2014). Strategic agility: A state-of-the-art introduction to the special section on strategic agility. *California Management Review*, *56*(3), 5–12. DOI: 10.1525/cmr.2014.56.3.5

Westland, J. C. (2010). Lower bounds on sample size in structural equation modeling. *Electronic Commerce Research and Applications*, *9*(6), 476–487. DOI: 10.1016/j.elerap.2010.07.003

Wilkin, C., Ferreira, A., Rotaru, K., & Gaerlan, L. R. (2020). Big data prioritization in SCM decision-making: Its role and performance implications. *International Journal of Accounting Information Systems*, *38*, 100470. DOI: 10.1016/j.accinf.2020.100470

Winardi, S., Wong, N. P., Halim, A., & Megawan, S. (2024). Enhancing Warehouse Inventory Management through IoT Tools for Monitoring Stock Items. In 2024 2nd International Conference on Technology Innovation and Its Applications (ICTIIA) (pp. 1-6). IEEE. DOI: 10.1109/ICTIIA61827.2024.10761815

Wodecki (2019). Influence of Artificial Intelligence on Activities and Competitiveness of an Organization, in Artificial Intelligence in Value Creation, Cham: Springer International Publishing, 2019, pp. 133–246. .DOI: 10.1007/978-3-319-91596-8_3

XiaoYan, Q., Yong, H., Qinli, D., & Stokes, P.XiaoYan. (2012). Reverse logistics network design model based on e-commerce. *The International Journal of Organizational Analysis*, *20*(2), 251–261. DOI: 10.1108/19348831211227864

Yadav, S., Singh, H. C., & Singh, D. R. (2021). Nutritional quality of millets and their value-added products with the potential health benefits: A review. *International Journal of Current Microbiology and Applied Sciences*, *10*(10), 163–175. DOI: 10.20546/ijcmas.2021.1010.019

Yang, C.-C. (2020). The effectiveness analysis of the practices in five quality management stages for SMEs. *Total Quality Management & Business Excellence*, *31*(9–10), 955–977. DOI: 10.1080/14783363.2018.1456010

Yang, Z., Guo, X., Sun, J., Zhang, Y., & Wang, Y. (2024). What Does Not Kill You Makes You Stronger: Supply Chain Resilience and Corporate Sustainability Through Emerging IT Capability. *IEEE Transactions on Engineering Management*, *71*, 10507–10521. DOI: 10.1109/TEM.2022.3209613

Yazdanparast, A., Manuj, I., & Swartz, S. M. (2010). Co-creating logistics value: A service-dominant logic perspective. *International Journal of Logistics Management*, *21*(3), 375–403. DOI: 10.1108/09574091011089808

Zamani, E. D., Smyth, C., Gupta, S., & Dennehy, D. (2023). Artificial intelligence and big data analytics for supply chain resilience: A systematic literature review. *Annals of Operations Research*, *327*(2), 605–632. DOI: 10.1007/s10479-022-04983-y PMID: 36212520

Zejjari, I., & Benhayoun, I. (2024). The use of artificial intelligence to advance sustainable supply chain: Retrospective and future avenues explored through bibliometric analysis. *Discover Sustainability*, *5*(1), 174. Advance online publication. DOI: 10.1007/s43621-024-00364-6

Zhang, X., Zhou, G., Cao, J., & Wu, A. (2020). Evolving strategies of e-commerce and express delivery enterprises with public supervision. *Research in Transportation Economics*, *80*, 100810. DOI: 10.1016/j.retrec.2019.100810

Zhang, Y., Ren, S., Liu, Y., & Si, S. (2017). A big data analytics architecture for cleaner manufacturing and maintenance processes of complex products. *Journal of Cleaner Production*, *142*, 626–641. DOI: 10.1016/j.jclepro.2016.07.123

Zhao, S., Wu, F., Jia, T., & Shu, L. (2018). The impact of product returns on price and delivery time competition in online retailing. *Computers & Industrial Engineering*, *125*, 658–667. DOI: 10.1016/j.cie.2018.01.007

Zhao, X., Xu, Y., Vasa, L., & Shahzad, U. (2023). Entrepreneurial ecosystem and urban innovation: Contextual findings in the lens of sustainable development from China. *Technological Forecasting and Social Change*, *191*, 122526. DOI: 10.1016/j.techfore.2023.122526

Zhu, S., Song, J., Hazen, B. T., Lee, K., & Cegielski, C. (2018). How supply chain analytics enables operational supply chain transparency: An organizational information processing theory perspective. *International Journal of Physical Distribution & Logistics Management*, *48*(1), 47–68. DOI: 10.1108/IJPDLM-11-2017-0341

Zikopoulos, P., Eaton, C., deRoos, D., Detusch, T., & Lapis, G. (2012). *Understanding Big Data: Analytics for Enterprise Class Hadoop and Streaming Data (IBM.)*. McGraw.

About the Contributors

Anupama Sethi is a Senior Lecturer at the Monash Business School, Monash University Australia. Her background lies in the area of development economics. She has a PhD, MPhil and MA in economics, along with a Bachelor of Education. She is passionate about creating a positive learning environment and making the learning experience intellectually engaging and enjoyable for students. Anupama has been a consistent and significant contributor to the development and delivery of economics teaching over several years. Anupama's efforts have been recognised with the Department teaching awards, including Dean's Citation for Outstanding Contribution to Student Learning, and appreciation by her students.

Sivakumar V is a distinguished academic with over 26 years of teaching experience, currently serving as the Dean of the College Development Council and Professor & Head of the Department of Logistics Management at Alagappa University, Karaikudi, India. He earned his Ph.D. from Alagappa University in 2013 and specializes in marketing management, agricultural marketing, international logistics, and consumer research. An accomplished researcher, Dr. Sivakumar has published 52 journal articles, presented 62 conference papers, and authored 17 books. He leads a significant RUSA project focused on e-logistics and supply chain management practices concerning Chennai Port Trust. As a convener, he organized an international conference on sustainable tourism and has guided six Ph.D. theses, contributing immensely to the academic community.

Iyappan A is an accomplished academic with a rich background in management, currently serving as an Associate Professor at the International Institute of Business Studies, Bangalore, India since April 2024. He holds a Post Doctoral Fellowship from ICSSR, focusing on sustainable management techniques in agripreneurship, and a Ph.D. in Management, awarded for his critical review of retail marketing in Thoothukudi District. With six years of teaching experience, Dr. Iyappan specializes in entrepreneurship, retailing, supply chain management, marketing management, and strategic management. His research contributions include 12 published journals and 11 conference articles, earning an H-index of 5 with 44 citations. He is actively involved in ongoing RUSA-funded projects at Alagappa University, aimed at revolutionizing retail laundry services and promoting hyper-local agro produce.

***

Morarji A is a distinguished Professor in the Department of Corporate Secretaryship, School of Management, Alagappa University, Karaikudi. With over 24 years of teaching and 18 years of research experience, he has made remarkable contributions to the fields of corporate governance, energy management, and CSR. Dr. Morarji earned his Ph.D. in Corporate Secretaryship from Alagappa University and has successfully supervised numerous Ph.D. and M.Phil. scholars, guiding groundbreaking research in his areas of expertise. He has an impressive portfolio of academic and administrative roles, including Coordinator of the University Placement Cell, Nodal Officer for PPMS, and a member of various academic committees such as the Board of Studies at Periyar University and the Doctoral Research Committee at VIT, Vellore. He has been a resource person at numerous national and international conferences, sharing insights on digital transformation, disaster management, and sustainability practices. His scholarly output includes over 30 research articles published in high-impact journals, several book chapters, and participation in funded projects. Notable among these are his projects on societal development through CSR and energy consumption practices, supported by ICSSR and RUSA 2.0. Dr. Morarji's research also focuses on areas like organizational citizenship behavior and gender diversity in corporate governance, further cementing his reputation as a thought leader in the field.Dr. Morarji has been recognized for his contributions to academia with awards such as the Best Teacher Award from the Global Management Council, Ahmedabad. His international exposure includes presenting papers in countries like Malaysia, highlighting his global academic influence.An inspiring educator and researcher, Dr. Morarji continues to shape the future of corporate education and research with his dedication and visionary outlook.

Arun Kumar Asaithambi has over 11 years of experience spanning teaching, research, and industry. His expertise lies in behavioral science, with a focus on marketing, human resources, and behavioral finance. Holding a Ph.D. in Behavioral Finance, his research delves into the psychological factors shaping consumer behavior, employee interactions, and financial decision-making. By adopting a multidisciplinary approach, he offers valuable insights into the critical role of human behavior across these interconnected fields. He has an extensive publication record, with numerous articles in the areas of behavioral finance, consumer behavior, and human resource management. Additionally, he has co-authored the book HRM Strategy and Planning, which reflects his depth of knowledge in the field. Beyond academia, he has actively contributed to organizing international conferences, HR conclaves, workshops, and various professional events, demonstrating his commitment to fostering knowledge exchange and advancing industry practices.

Pathiettampadiyan B is a dedicated full-time research scholar at the Department of Rural Industries and Management, Gandhigram Rural Institute (GRI), Tamil Nadu. His research focuses on rural industrial development, entrepreneurship, sustainable business practices, and supply chain management. He actively contributes to academic research, aiming to enhance rural economies through innovative management and industrial strategies.

Elamurugan Balasundaram received the B.C.A. Degree in St Joseph's arts and science college from University of Madras, in 2004, the M.B.A. degree in Bishop Heber College from Bharathidasan University, Tiruchirappalli, in 2006, and the Ph.D. Degree in Management from Annamalai University, Chidambaram, India, in 2015. His research and teaching interests include theory and application of Human resource Practices, Marketing Management, Economics and Econometrics. Dr. Elamurugan currently serves as an Associate Professor of Management Studies, SRM Valliammai Engineering College, Puducherry. He has published over 13 papers in peer reviewed journals and international conferences and also with four book chapters.

Kruthika Devi C is a dedicated research scholar pursuing her Doctoral degree in Management Studies at Marudhupandiyar College, affiliated with Bharathidasan University. She holds a B.Tech. in Civil Engineering and an MBA with specializations in Finance and Operations Management. Ms. Kiruthika has demonstrated her academic excellence by qualifying for the National Eligibility Test (NET) conducted by UGC. Her interdisciplinary background, combining engineering, finance, and operations management, enables her to bring a unique perspective to her research. With a strong foundation in both technical and management fields, she is committed to advancing knowledge in the area of management studies.

Ramkumar Dhanasekaran is an Associate Professor in the Department of Business Administration, Sri Meenakshi Government Arts College for Women (A), Madurai. He is a post-graduate in Business Administration and has completed Ph. D., in Relationship Marketing area. He has 29 years of teaching experience. He has published more than 25 research papers in various journals and teaches courses like Marketing Management, Operations Research and Organisational Behaviour.

Sridhar G is a full-time research scholar in the Department of Rural Industries and Management at The Gandhigram Rural Institute – Deemed to be University, Gandhigram, Tamil Nadu, India. TIJER In September 2024, he co-authored a research paper titled "Impact of EI on Analytical Behaviour of Children in Tamil Nadu," published in TIJER – International Research Journal. TIJER This study examines how emotional intelligence influences the analytical behavior of children in Tamil Nadu.

Samuel H is an academic and professional associated with the Industries and Management department at the Gandhigram Rural Institute (GRI) in Tamil Nadu, India. GRI is a prominent institution focusing on rural development, and it offers a range of programs emphasizing sustainable development, rural industries, and community empowerment. Dr. Samuel Thavaraj specializes in industries and management, with a particular interest in rural industry development, entrepreneurship, and sustainable business practices. His work is centered around enhancing the economic potential of rural communities by promoting effective management techniques, supporting small and medium enterprises, and fostering sustainable industry practices. As a faculty member, Dr. Thavaraj is involved in research, teaching, and guiding students on topics such as rural economy, industrial management, sustainable development strategies, and rural entrepreneurship. ORCID ID: 0000-0002-6294-976X

Mary Isabella T is an academic professional affiliated with Sakthi College of Arts and Science for Women, India. She is dedicated to the advancement of higher education, student empowerment, and scholarly research. Her academic interests include management studies, social development, women's education, and interdisciplinary research that addresses contemporary societal and organizational challenges. As an educator, Mary Josephine Isabella is known for her student-cantered teaching approach and commitment to creating an engaging learning environment. She encourages students to develop professional competence, leadership qualities, and research-oriented thinking. Her teaching philosophy emphasizes practical learning, academic integrity, and holistic development. She has actively participated in academic conferences, seminars, faculty development programmes, and research initiatives that support continuous professional growth. Her scholarly contributions reflect an interest in exploring innovative ideas and applying research insights to educational and societal contexts. Through collaborative academic activities, she aims to strengthen institutional research culture and promote meaningful knowledge exchange. Mary Josephine Isabella also believes in the importance of women's education and empowerment through skill development and quality learning opportunities. Her association with Sakthi College of Arts and Science for Women aligns with her commitment to fostering inclusive and progressive education. Through her dedication to teaching, mentoring, and academic research, she continues to contribute positively to the growth of students and the broader academic community.

Rosanth Ivan is an Assistant Professor in the Faculty of Management Studies with expertise in finance, accounting, and management education. Contributed to academic research and authored study materials for undergraduate and postgraduate programmes, focusing on areas such as financial modelling, behavioural finance, and risk management. Academic interests include empirical research, innovative teaching methodologies, and applications of financial analytics in decision-making.

Rincy James is a researcher and academic associated with Mother Theresa Women's University, India. She is committed to academic excellence, research innovation, and the promotion of quality higher education. Her scholarly interests focus on interdisciplinary research, educational development, and emerging trends in management and social science studies. She actively engages in academic activities that contribute to knowledge creation and professional growth. With a keen interest in research methodology and contemporary academic issues, Rincy James has participated in conferences, seminars, workshops, and collaborative learning initiatives. Her academic work demonstrates a thoughtful approach toward addressing real-world challenges through systematic research and critical analysis. She believes in integrating theoretical knowledge with practical insights to create meaningful academic outcomes. Rincy James is passionate about student development and strives to encourage learners to cultivate creativity, critical thinking, and research aptitude. Her academic involvement reflects a strong dedication to continuous learning and scholarly contribution. She also values ethical research practices and promotes inclusive and learner-centered educational environments. As an emerging scholar, she aims to contribute significantly to academia through publications, collaborative projects, and innovative research perspectives. Her association with Mother Theresa Women's University has provided a strong platform for academic exploration and professional advancement. Through her commitment to education and research, Rincy James continues to build a promising academic profile that contributes positively to the educational and research community in India.

Aarthi Dhakshana JD is a dedicated academic professional currently serving as the Deputy Controller of Examinations at Dhanalakshmi Srinivasan University, where she oversees examination processes and ensures academic integrity. She holds a Ph.D. in agricultural product management, demonstrating a strong commitment to research and innovation. With over 8 years of teaching and research experience,

Dr. Aarthi has been instrumental in shaping curricula that bridge theoretical knowledge with practical application. Her tenure as an Assistant Professor at several esteemed institutions highlights her dedication to student development and academic excellence. Her research interests include finance, systems management, and agricultural marketing, and she has contributed numerous publications to reputable academic journals. Additionally, Dr. Aarthi has authored book chapters and books. She is an active participant in national and international conferences, where she has presented numerous papers, promoting collaborative learning and interdisciplinary approaches. Currently, she is guiding several Ph.D. scholars, nurturing their research capabilities and helping them make meaningful contributions to their respective fields

Gurupandi M is a distinguished academician and an exceptional leader in the field of commerce. As an Associate Professor of Commerce at Alagappa University, Dr. Gurupandi has consistently demonstrated a remarkable commitment to research, innovation, and academic excellence.

Kathiravan M is currently serving as a Professor at The Oxford College of Engineering, Bangalore. He holds a Ph.D. in HR from Anna University, Chennai. He earned his MBA in HR and Marketing (2004) and B.Com. in Commerce (2002) from Bharathidasan University, Tiruchirappalli. With over 20 years of teaching experience in reputed educational institutions, he has contributed extensively to academia through research and publications. He has authored 20 research articles in renowned journals.

Vijay M is an Assistant Professor in the Department of Management Studies at Periyar Maniammai Institute of Science & Technology (Deemed to be University), where he teaches Human Resource Management (HR) and Finance. He is dedicated to creating an engaging and student-centered learning environment, blending core management theory with practical business applications. Dr. M. Vijay's teaching approach emphasizes critical thinking, real-world problem solving, and professional development, helping students gain the knowledge and skills needed for successful careers in HR, finance, and organizational leadership.

S. Poorani Mithila, M.Com., Ph.D., PGDCA, MBA is a distinguished academic and researcher currently pursuing an ICSSR Post-Doctorate at Alagappa University. With a strong foundation in Commerce, Accounting, Human Resource Management, and Entrepreneurship Development, she has made significant contributions to the fields of Artificial Intelligence, Blockchain, and Fintech, particularly in the insurance industry. Her doctoral research focused on the Professional Competence of Agents and the Attitude of Policyholders on Products and Services of the Life Insurance

Corporation of India in Sivaganga District. Expanding on this, her postdoctoral work explores the intersection of AI and Blockchain in Fintech to democratize the insurance market. Dr. Mithila has published extensively in Scopus and UGC CARE-listed journals, with research covering topics such as business intelligence in insurance, digital financial inclusion, and AI-driven financial planning. She has also presented numerous papers at national and international conferences and actively participates in faculty development programs and workshops on research methodology, data analytics, and digital transformation. Beyond research, she has served as an Adjunct Faculty at Alagappa University and has been actively involved in organizing academic programs, guest lectures, and professional development workshops. Her expertise and dedication to transforming the insurance sector through technology-driven solutions continue to shape the future of financial services and digital innovation.

Domnic Nachathiram is a passionate academician and researcher specializing in management studies, Assistant Professor at PMIST, Thanjavur. She has been Research Advisor to 4 scholars who are pursuing under her Guideship. She has been honoured with Best Academician Award recently in March 2026.Expertise in organizational behaviour, strategic management, Marketing, Economics, compensation management and human resource management. She employs innovative teaching methods to foster student growth, earning widespread acclaim. Her holistic approach to education and research reflects her commitment to empowering individuals positively and organizations to achieve excellence.

Sugali Naik has 14 years of teaching experience in both undergraduate and postgraduate programs. He has actively participated in over 25 national and international conferences, contributing to academic discussions in his field. With more than 14 research publications in reputed journals, including UGC Care and Scopus, Dr. Naik has established himself as a dedicated researcher. He is the author of two books, Advanced Financial Management and Derivatives Management. His research interests span Accounts, Finance, Banking, and Insurance. Currently, he serves as a co-guide for a Ph.D. scholar at Annamalai University and is a Life Member of the Indian Accounting Association.

Aranganathan P holds a Bachelor of Engineering (B.E.) in Mechanical and Production Engineering and a Master of Business Administration (MBA) with a specialization in Human Resource Management. He earned his Ph.D. in Management (HR) from Bharathiar University, India. A prolific author, he has written five books, including Principles of Management, Operations Management, Logistics and Supply Management, Management Skill Development, and Total Quality Management.

Additionally, he has over 30 publications in esteemed international and national peer-reviewed, high-indexed journals, conference proceedings, and edited books. Dr. Aranganathan has successfully guided four scholars to complete their Ph.D. degrees in the fields of management and commerce. His primary research interests lie in Strategic Human Resource Management and Sustainable Business Practices.

Monica Pushpabai V served as assistant professor and head of the department of Journalism and Mass Communication, Thiru. Vi. Ka. Government College of arts Thiruvarur and Rani Anna Government College for Women, Tirunelveli. ORCID ID: 0009-0007-5493-8378

Sivarethinamohan R is an Associate Professor at Symbiosis Centre for Management Studies, Bengaluru campus, Symbiosis International Deemed University, Pune, India. Previously, He held dean, director, principal, and vice chancellor positions in prestigious institutions and universities. He is a sustainability Leader with 30+ years of experience in corporate finance, climate finance, Data science, Air pollutants, Digital Twin, Biochar, climate change, Blockchain Technology in Environment Sustainability, IoT enabled Smart Cities, Nanotechnology in agriculture and food production health robots, Accounting Fraud Detection. He has participated in and presented research papers at national and international conferences and holds nearly 75 article publications in leading journals indexed in Scopus (40), and Web of Science (18) to his credit. He is on the Editorial Board of over 7 peer-reviewed journals, including some prestigious ones. He has edited a couple of books and published textbooks with Tata McGraw Hill and Prentice Hall of India. His research and academic experience have helped him bring innovations in the teaching methodology and effectively convey the practical application of the course. He published five Patents and three copyrights.

Suresh R.V., Associate Professor in Marketing, Gnanam School of Business has comprehensive experience across academia, research and corporate spreading over two decades in various institutes of repute. Apart from Patent Publications and Grants of both national and international, he has published articles in peer reviewed journals, contributed chapters in four books, and authored three books. He has been the editorial board member for national and international Book Publishers. His knowledge has been disseminated as Resource Person in various institutions. He was recipient of "Faculty of Academic Excellence Award" in ICSSR sponsored International Conference in 2022. He had exhibited sound administrative skill by holding various positions Viz. President - IIC, Coordinator - IPR Cell, Advisor - Planning & Evaluation committee, Centre for Research and Member in Board of Studies.

Manikandan S is an Assistant Professor of Systems and Operations in GSB. He received his Post Graduation in Management from Anna University, Chennai, M.Tech from PRIST University, Thanjavur and his Under Graduation in B. Tech from SASTRA University, Thanjavur. He is a certified Lean Six Sigma Green Belt holder from AU TVS center for Quality Management, Anna University, Chennai and also an ISO 9001:2008 certified Internal auditor from TATA Projects Quality Service. He has immense experience of 5 years in the area of academics, and 7.5 years in the area of IT. He is the overall in charge of IT facility in GSB.

Jolly Silva holds a Ph.D. in Corporate Infrastructure Management Practices from Alagappa University, Karaikudi, awarded in 2018. She is currently an Associate Professor at Nanjil Catholic College of Arts and Science, Kanyakumari District, Tamilnadu. With 20 years of teaching experience, Dr. Silva has contributed significantly to academia through her roles as Staff Council Secretary, Academic Counselor at IGNOU, and Chief Superintendent for University Examinations. Her research expertise lies in corporate infrastructure management, digital learning infrastructure, and green HR practices, with numerous publications in national and international journals, including UGC Care-listed ones. Dr. Silva has participated in over 20 webinars and workshops and has presented papers at various national and international conferences. She has also authored multiple textbooks, such as Auditing Principles & Practices and Principles of Management. As a former university rank holder and gold medalist, she continues to inspire her students and colleagues with her commitment to excellence in education and research.

S. Vijayanand is currently working as Assistant Professor in Government Arts and Science College, Idappadi in Tamilnadu. He has 23 years of industrial experience and 7 years of academic experience. He is being a reviewer in National and International Journals and published many articles in leading National and International Journal. His area of interest are Marketing, Human Resources and Logistics and Supply Chain Management.

Seema Vinod is an accomplished academician and researcher associated with Gandhigram Rural Institute, Assistant Professor in the field of Rural Industries and Management. With a strong academic background and dedication to higher education. Dr. Seema has contributed significantly to teaching, research, and student development. She completed her Ph.D. from Madurai Kamaraj University and has gained rich teaching experience by serving in various colleges and management institutions in Tamil Nadu. Her areas of specialization include management studies, human resource management, organizational behavior, and entrepreneurship development. Dr. Seema has published several research papers and actively participates in academic conferences, seminars, and workshops. She is also recognized for her contribution to innovation and academic excellence, receiving awards such as the Best Teacher Award and Education Excellence Award. In addition to academics, she has shown interest in institutional development and student mentoring activities. Her involvement in professional bodies and research initiatives reflects her commitment to improving the quality of education and management practices. Dr. Seema's academic journey demonstrates dedication, leadership, and continuous learning. Through her teaching and research contributions, she continues to inspire students and contribute to the advancement of management education and rural development studies in India.

Index

A

B

C

D

E

F

T

www.ingramcontent.com/pod-product-compliance
Lightning Source LLC
LaVergne TN
LVHW081524300926
849161LV00006B/1284
9798260018552